THE CRIMINAL LAW OF ISLAM

PROF. DR. ANWARULLAH

KITAB BHAVAN
New Delhi-110002 (India)

Kitab Bhavan
Publishers, Distributors, Exporters & Importers
1784, Kalan Mahal, Darya Ganj
New Delhi - 1100 02 (India)

Phone : (91-11) 23277392/93, 23274686, 30906494
website : www.kitabbhavan.com
Email : nasri@vsnl.com
Fax : (91-11) 23263383

First Edition 2006

ISBN : 81-7151-372-7

Published in India by :
Nusrat Ali Nasri for Kitab Bhavan
1784, Kalan Mahal, Darya Ganj
New Delhi - 1100 02 [India]

Printed in India at :
Nice Printing Press
Khureji Khas, Delhi-110051

Contents

Preface

In this book I have attempted to write and explain the Islamic Criminal Law in the method which is generally adopted in the modern law books. Islam has presented a comprehensive criminal law but unfortunately this part of Islamic law has been abandoned for a long time. The earlier Muslim jurists have done an intensive work on the Islamic Criminal Law but their books do not contain a proper list of contents which makes it extremely difficult to trace in them provisions relating to a particular problem. However, the valuable work of the earlier Muslim jurists gives us sufficient guidance and vigour to compile and implement Islamic Criminal Law in this modern time. On the other hand, due to their ignorance, most of the modern lawyers consider Islamic Criminal Law impracticable in the present day circumstances. It is thus imperative to write proper books on Islamic Criminal Law in the modern legal perspective. Proper books on Islamic Criminal Law are also required in view of the fact that some Islamic states of the modern world have implemented Islamic Criminal Law in twentieth century. This book is an initial step towards the noble objective of writing comprehensive books on Islamic Criminal Law in order to meet the modern requirements.

I have tried my best throughout this book to contact the original and authentic books on Islamic jurisprudence *(Fiqh)* on every problem of Islamic Criminal Law. I have discussed the arguments on which the jurists have based their opinions. While describing different problems of Islamic Criminal Law, I have produced the opinions of all schools of thought so that the reader may understand the whole background and form his own opinion therefrom. I have also utilized the work of the later and contemporary Muslim jurists and lawyers who have developed Islamic Criminal Law in their respective surroundings. I hope this book will be useful for the judges, lawyers, teachers and students of Islamic Law and those interested to know Islamic Law.

Prof Dr Anwarullah
Islamic Legal Specialist,
Ministry of Religious Affairs,
Brunei, Darussalam.

In the Name of Allah, the Most Compassionate,
the Most Merciful

Introduction

Criminal law in a broad sense is the body of law that defines criminal offences, regulates the apprehension, charging and trial of suspected persons and fixes punishments and modes of treatment applicable to the offenders. The object of criminal law is to control the commission of the crimes so as to protect the rights and interests of the public and ensure peace in the society. A law is an obligatory rule of conduct imposed and enforced by the state. Islamic criminal law has indicated various crimes and has provided deterrent, reformative, retaliative and other kinds of punishments for them in order to maintain peace in the society and reform the offenders. In the absence of a proper criminal law, the entire social structure of a society stands on a very weak footing. Merely prohibiting the commission of an offence by the Government does not guarantee its compliance by the public but it is the sanction that guarantees the effectiveness of such prohibition, and if there had been no punishments, all prohibitions and restrictions would have been ineffective and of no use. [1] The Qur'ān states, "Whoever works evil, will be requited accordingly." (4:123) The jurists, therefore, unanimously agree that the enforcement of Islamic criminal law is the foremost duty of an Islamic State so as to protect the society from the evil effects of the crimes and reform the offenders and evil-doers.

Social values vary from society to society and culture to culture, but some values have been universally recognised and all

[1] Shāh Walī Allāh, *Ḥujjat Allah al-Bālighah,* Lahore: 1975, vol. 1, p.468

the ancient and sensate as well as the modern and idealist societies have given them due regard in their respective circumstances. These universally recognised values include the protection of life and the protection of property. Islamic criminal law being a universal law revolves around the following five fundamental points:

(i) protection of religion,
(ii) protection of life,
(iii) protection of the sanctity of family,
(iv) protection of property and
(v) protection of reason/or intellect.[2]

Islamic criminal law contains fixed and variable punishments. Punishments are for offences that are universally recognized, and the variation of time and place have no impact on them. These fixed punishments are called *ḥudūd*. Punishments for other crimes are variable according to the heinousness of the offence. Such a punishment is called *ta'zīr*.

The principles on which the Islamic theory of criminality focuses include the following:

(i) human beings are potentially capable of being driven to the right as well as the wrong path,
(ii) crimes are committed by people of their own free will and
(iii) everyone is liable for his wrong doings.

According to Islamic criminal law the benefit of the doubt goes to the accused. It is supported by the saying of the Prophet (p.b.u.h): "Avoid punishing whenever you find scope for it."[3] The Prophet (p.b.u.h.) also said, "Try to avoid punishing Muslims whenever possible and if there is a way for an accused to escape punishment, let him off. An error of the judge in letting off an accused is better than one in punishing him."[4] Besides providing deterrent punishments, Islamic criminal law has provided escape valves such as benefit of doubt, non-availability of the prescribed

---

2. Abū Ḥamid al-Ghazālī, *al-Mustaṣfā min 'Ilm al-Uṣūl,* vol. 2, p.66.
3. *Ibn Majah,* p.162
4 Ibn Asir, *Jāmi' al-Uṣūl,* vol.2, p.224

quantum and standard of evidence. However, the deterrent aspect of these fixed punishments plays its role and the criminal has the idea in his mind that these valves may not necessarily operate in his case.

One of the prominent aspects of Islamic criminal law is that it is so comprehensive and flexible that it is applicable to all the acts and omissions arising in every age, in every phase of social development, in the ever-changing circumstances of the society and fulfils the multifarious social needs at all times. The Islamic criminal law contains provisions which are so sublime and developed that they never fall below the social standard at any time.

There are seven sources of Islamic criminal law. These are as under:

1. The Holy Qur'ān
2. The *Sunnah* of the Holy Prophet Muhammad (p.b.u.h)
3. *Ijmā'* (consensus of opinion)
4. *Qiyas* (analogy)
5. *Ijtihād* (interpretation)
6. *Maṣlaḥah* (Public interest)
7. *'urf* (custom)

The vital difference between the Qur'ān and the *Sunnah*, and the remaining five sources has to be taken into consideration. The Qur'ān and the *Sunnah* constitute the bases of Islamic criminal law whereas the remaining five sources neither constitute the bases of Islamic criminal law, nor do they lend legitimacy to any new principles thereof. In fact, these sources are instrumental in drawing, from the Qur'ān and the *Sunnah,* corollaries that are compatible with their injunctions.

A considerable part of Islamic criminal law consists of crimes for which punishments have not been prescribed by the Holy Qur'ān or *Sunnah* of the Holy Prophet, and it has been left to the discretion of the legislators to prescribe punishments for them keeping in view the requirements of the circumstances relating to the time, place, convict and the state. It is for this reason that legislators and the jurists have developed Islamic Criminal Law in different times and places according to the relevant requirements and have established certain principles and rules which govern various aspects of the Islamic criminal law. Punishments prescribed by legislators change with the change in the requirements of the time, place and other circumstances. Further, with the passage of time new offences appear for which punishments have to be prescribed accordingly.

Chapter One

Meaning, Elements and Classification of Crimes

The words *jurm* (جرم), *jarimah*(جريمه) and *jināyah* (جنايه) are used for crime and offence in Islamic Criminal law. The root word *jurm* literally means to cut off. It is said "جرمه" (He cut it off), (جرم صوف الشـاة). (He sheared or cut off the wool of the sheep)[1]. The Holy Qur`ān says,

وَلاَ يَجْرِمَنَّكُمْ شَنَآنُ قَوْمٍ عَلَى أَلاَّ تَعْدِلُوا

> And let not a nation's hatred by any means occasion you or incite you to wrong and depart from justice. (5:8)

Thus the word *jurm* means a sin, a crime, a fault, an offence or an act of disobedience, a transgression, whether intentional or committed through inadvertence.[2] It is for this reason that this word has been used for unfair earning and unfair action. It has been used in verses 5:8, 11:89, 77:46 and 83:29 of the Holy Qur'ān in the same sense. The meaning derived from these verses is that all that is against justice and the right path is called *jurm* and the person who commits an unfair and unjust act is called *mujrim* (مجرم). All the orders of the *Sharī'ah* are fair being the

---

[1]Jamāl al-Dīn Muḥammad ibn Mukārram al-Anṣārī Ibn al-Manzūr, *Lisān i-Arab*, vol.10, pp.375-80

[2] Edward William Lane, *Arabic English Lexicon (Madd al-Qāmūs)* Bk.1 pt.2, p.368

orders of Allah and His Prophet (p.b.u.h) and their disobedience amounts to *jurm.*

Therefore the word *jurm* signifies to do what has been prohibited in the *Sharī'ah* or not to do what has been ordered by the *Sharī'ah* to be done for which punishment of *ḥadd* or *ta'zīr* has been prescribed.[3]

Explaining the meaning of the word *jinayah,* William Lane writes, "The word *jinayah* primarily means,

- act of gathering, plucking or taking a fruit from a tree;
- an evil thing or action;
- The doing a forbidden action;
- specially used in this last sense.

It generally signifies a crime, an offence or an injurious action, for which one should be punished".[4]

According to the majority of the jurists *jināyah* signifies all kinds of prohibited and injurious actions whether they relate to the human body, to property or to other violations. But according to some jurists it signifies a prohibited act which is committed upon a person like murder and hurt while according to others it signifies the offences liable to *ḥudūd* and *qiṣāṣ* penalties. Generally the jurists do not differentiate between *jurm* and *jināyah* and consider them synonymous.[5]

However, as jurists are concerned with proving the crimes in a court and execution of their punishments, they have defined *jurm* and *jināyah* in that context. According to al-Mawardi: crimes are wrongful acts in *Sharī'ah* for which punishments have been prescribed by God whether *ḥadd* (fixed punishment) or *ta'zīr* (discretionary punishments).[6] Wrongful act means an act the doing or omission of which is declared prohibited by the *Sharī'ah.* It is an act that adversely affects the rights of individuals or the society or interferes with peace and tranquility. In short, crime is an act or omission in which any provision of divine law is violated and is declared punishable.

---

[3] Abū Zahrah, *Al-Jarimah*, pp.23-24

[4] Lane, Edward William, op.cit, Bk1, pt.2, p.472

[5] Abd al-Qādir 'Awdah, *al-Tashrī' al Jina'ī al-Islāmī*, vol.1, p.65

[6] Al-Mawardī, *al-Aḥkām al-Sulṭāniyyah*, p.192

The Islamic law, in principle, declares the right to life and property as inviolable. Hence, any act of a person that may prove harmful to another person's life or property when the person committing the act has no claim against them, is a crime and would necessitate imposition of penalty on the offender.

The definition of crime/offence in the *Sharī'ah* is in conformity with its definition in modern law. According to modern law, crime is an act prohibited or omission required by law. A contemporary author, Sardar Muhammad Iqbal Mokal, writes, "A crime is an act of commission or omission, contrary to municipal law, tending to the prejudice of the community for which punishment can be inflicted as the result of judicial proceeding taken in the name of state. The definite meaning attached to the word crime is "an act or omission punishable by law".[7]

In Islamic law as well as in the modern law, the commission or omission of an act is not considered crime until punishment has been prescribed for such commission or omission.[8]

Moreover, according to Islamic law a crime has two characteristics, (i) Public wrong, and (ii) Moral wrong.

The first characteristic of a crime is that it is generally an act which infringes a private right, and at the same time has a harmful effect on the public. A crime usually threatens the security of the society and its effects cannot be removed by compensating the injured party. In such cases, a crime becomes a state crime. Any individual can initiate a criminal prosecution, whether or not he has suffered any special harm over and above other members of the public. Under Islamic criminal procedure, a complaint from the victim or his representative is not necessary in matters of crimes that have harmful effects on the public. Such crimes violate the rights of Allah, because they concern the public as a whole and not only the individual. Every human being is the vicegerent of Allah and it is his first and foremost duty to safeguard the rights of Allah. All the crimes liable to *ḥudūd* relate to public rights. Many of the crimes liable to *ta'zīr* also relate to public rights. It is for this reason that in all *ḥudūd* crimes and in many of *ta'zīr* crimes,

---

[7] Sardar Muḥammad Iqbal Mokal, *Law terms and Phrases,* p.273
[8] 'Awdah, , *al-Tashrī' al Jina'ī al-Islāmī* vol.1, p.67

the vast majority of persecutions are carried out by the police or other public officers who have no personal interest therein. An individual who starts a prosecution may not discontinue it at will, for it is not only his concern but that of every citizen. Crimes contrast with civil wrongs such as torts and breaches of contracts wherein the person injured may sue, and may freely discontinue the proceedings at any time and may forgive the defendant terminating his liability. In crimes, even if a victim or his heirs pardon the criminal he may be punished to secure the public interests, if required in the circumstances of the case.

Islamic criminal law provides punishments, to achieve the collective good and to safeguard it. Crimes are usually acts which lead to breach of peace. There are very few acts, which are either purely beneficial or purely harmful. The majority of human acts are both beneficial as well as harmful at the same time. Every person has a natural inclination towards his benefits rather than towards harm and losses. Thus everyone acts for his own benefit even if it is against the interest of the community. He avoids acts that incurs a loss even if it is beneficial for the public. Similarly when a person considers the hardship involved in the discharge of his duty, he naturally feels inclined to evade it. But when he takes into account the punishment of neglecting his duty he prefers to bear the hardship involved. The Islamic criminal law has thus identified certain acts as crimes with a view to safeguard collective interests and the system on which the entire social edifice rests and to enable the community to survive with peace and harmony.

The second characteristic of a crime is that it is an act, which is morally wrong. Islamic criminal law lays great stress on moral virtues and preserves public morality in the society. Any act, which is detrimental to morality is considered a crime and entails punishment. The springs of the Islamic criminal law lie in religion, which enjoins inculcation of moral virtues and induces man to do good. The Islamic religion aims at the creation of a righteous and pious society. It prohibits all kinds of indecent and obscene acts and speech. If morals are acted upon, life, property, honour, peace and tranquility will remain safeguarded. For example, adulterous acts such as sexual kissing, lying of a man and a woman on one bed, though committed with the consent of the parties, is a crime and must be punished because of it being detrimental to public morality. Public morality is an essential part of Muslim society. Islamic criminal law has a long list of acts that constitute offences of a moral nature and prevention of these offences leads to moral improvement and promotion of spiritual values. Islamic law emphasizes the vital importance of morality and deals severely with every immoral individual.[9]

Elements of Crime

According to Islamic criminal law, an accused is convicted when three fundamental elements of the crime exist. These three elements must be proved, as their absence renders the accused innocent. These three elements are simplified in the following three categories:-

1. A clear provision which prohibits an act declining it a crime and specifies its punishment. This is known as the legal element of crime.
2. An action which amounts to the commission or omission of the particular act that is defined as a crime. This is known as the substantial element of crime.
3. Maturity, responsibility and accountability of the offender. This is known as the cultural element of crime.

Legal Element of a Crime

In order to treat an act as a crime, there must be an explicit provision in *Sharī'ah* sources declaring that the act is unlawful and prescribing punishment for that. Such provision must be obligatory. For example the Holy Qur'ān states:

وَالسَّارِقُ وَالسَّارِقَةُ فَاقْطَعُوا أَيْدِيَهُمَا

> As for the thief, both male and female, cut off their hands. (5:38)

الزَّانِيَةُ وَالزَّانِي فَاجْلِدُوا كُلَّ وَاحِدٍ مِّنْهُمَا مِئَةَ جَلْدَةٍ

> The adulterer and the adulteress, scourge each one of them with hundred stripes. (24:2)

---

[9] Ibid., vol. 2, pp. 67-70.

يَا أَيُّهَا الَّذِينَ آمَنُواْ كُتِبَ عَلَيْكُمُ الْقِصَاصُ فِي الْقَتْلَى

O you who believe! Retaliation is prescribed for you in cases of murder. (2:178)

Moreover, it is a fundamental rule of the *Sharī'ah* that unless a relevant provision exists, a person shall not be punished for any act. The Holy Qur'ān states:

وَمَا كُنَّا مُعَذِّبِينَ حَتَّى نَبْعَثَ رَسُولاً

We never punish until we have sent a messenger. (17:15)

وَمَا كَانَ رَبُّكَ مُهْلِكَ الْقُرَى حَتَّى يَبْعَثَ فِي أُمِّهَا رَسُولًا يَتْلُو عَلَيْهِمْ آيَاتِنَا

And never did your Lord destroy the population till he had raised in their mother (town) a messenger reciting unto them our revelations. (28:59)

It is important to mention that punishment in *Sharī'ah* sources is either prescribed expressly as in the cases of crimes liable to *ḥudūd, qiṣāṣ* and *diyat* or it is left to the discretion of a ruler or a judge to prescribe it in the relevant circumstances as in the cases of crimes liable to *ta'zīr*. Thus the provisions regarding crimes liable to *ta'zīr* must also exist before a criminal is punished for any such act whether in the form of a codified law or in the form of a compiled collection like books, magazines or publications. However, the details of the punishments in such cases need not be provided but that these acts are punishable must be known to the person who commits any such act. It is only in the cases of the crimes of *ḥudūd* and *qiṣāṣ* for which punishments have been prescribed by the Holy Qur'ān or the *Sunnah* of the Holy Prophet that the criminal must know the kind and quantum of the punishment for the relevant crime. It is under this principle that Ḥaḍrat 'Umar compiled the criminal laws and sent copies to various parts of the empire in the time of Caliph Abū Bakr. The later jurists have suggested that all the criminal laws of an Islamic state must be publicised throughout the state so that everyone is aware of them. This is necessary because most of the crimes relate to *ta'zīr* for which punishments have not been prescribed by the

Holy Qur'ān and the *Sunnah* of the Holy Prophet and have been left to the discretion of the rulers to prescribe in their respective circumstances. The jurists opine that basically every act is permissible except the act which is prohibited by a *Sharī'ah* source.[10]

Further the mere existence of a *Sharī'ah* provision is not sufficient to incriminate a person and punish him on its violation; it is necessary that the relevant provision be legislated and enforced before the commission of the crime and must be in force at the time and place of the commission of the crime. The provisions of the Islamic Criminal law do not operate retrospectively and punishments for crimes are awarded on the basis of the provisions existing at the time of their commission. Moreover, the criminal must have the capability of understanding the provisions relating to the crimes as well as the capability to commit the crime he charged for. The act constituting the crime must be possible with respect to the criminal; a lunatic or a minor cannot be bound by any obligation and none of their acts can be declared as crimes. Since commands and prohibitions give rise to legal obligations, they are addressed to a mature and rational person.

It is relevant to point out that the laws enacted by an Islamic state for the larger interest of the public are binding on the Muslims only if they are not contrary to the injunctions of the Holy Qur'ān and the *Sunnah* of the Holy Prophet. The Holy Qur'ān states,

يَا أَيُّهَا الَّذِينَ آمَنُواْ أَطِيعُواْ اللّهَ وَأَطِيعُواْ الرَّسُولَ وَأُوْلِي الأَمْرِ مِنكُمْ

O you who believe! Obey God and obey the Prophet,
and those who are in power among you. (4:59)

The above verse obligates Muslims to obey the laws of an Islamic state, provided such laws are not contrary to the Holy Qur'ān and the *Sunnah* of the Holy Prophet. Thus, all the enacted laws of an Islamic state come under the provisions of the Islamic criminal law if they are not contrary to the injunctions laid down in the Holy Qur'ān and the *Sunnah* of the Holy Prophet.

---

[10] *Ibid.*, vol. 1, pp 113-19

The following are the sources of Islamic criminal law:

(a) The Holy Qur'ān

The Holy Qur'ān is the first and basic source of Islamic law. The Holy Qur'ān is the book of Allah revealed to Prophet Muhammad (p.b.u.h) for the guidance of mankind within a period of twenty three years. The words of the Holy Qur'ān have a spiritual value and significance apart from what they lay down as law. No doubt can be entertained as to the authenticity of any verse of the Holy Qur'ān, the whole of which is proved by universally accepted testimony. The texts of the Holy Qur'ān were collected by the authority of the State soon after the death of the Holy Prophet. The Holy Qur'ān contains 114 surahs (chapters) and about 6342 verses. Some 500 verses of the Holy Qur'ān deal with legal matters. Each of these legal verses bears an injunction, either an order or a prevention, from which a decision arises in the form of a specific legal rule.

The Holy Qur'ān is a code that governs religious and social life. Some laws have been expressly mentioned in the text of the Holy Qur'ān while others are implied by the texts. The numerous and multifarious Qur'ānic injunctions are designed to promote man's welfare in this world and improve his prospects in the Hereafter. Most of the verses of the Holy Qur'ān which embody rules of law, were revealed to settle questions that actually arose for decision; some in order to repeal objectionable customs like infanticide, gambling, usury and unlimited polygamy; some for effecting social reforms such as raising the legal status of women, settling the question of succession and inheritance on an equitable basis, providing protection for the rights of minors and the disabled; and some for laying down the principles of punishment for the purpose of securing peace and order. The Holy Qur'ān also contains general injunctions which have formed the basis of important juristic references. The Holy Qur'ān aims at prohibiting all acts detrimental to society. However, the Holy Qur'ān has not mentioned all the laws and has left it to the rulers and legislators to enact new laws under the principles laid down in the Holy Qur'ān and *Sunnah* of the Holy Prophet as and when the circumstances require.

Qur'ānic prescriptions are distinguished by their formulation in a general form, which allows new cases to be adequately integrated into Islamic law.[11]

(b) The *Sunnah* of the Holy Prophet Muḥammad (p.b.u.h)

The *Sunnah* of the Holy Prophet is the second source of Islamic law. *Sunnah*, means any saying or action of the Holy Prophet or any saying or action of another person approved by the Holy Prophet. Thus, there are three kinds of *Sunnah*; namely, (i) the sayings of the Holy Prophet, (ii) the practices of the Holy Prophet, and (iii) the approbations of the Holy Prophet.

There are three legal aspects of the *Sunnah*:-

(1) *It supports or stresses a Qur'ānic injunction*. In this case, the injunction concerned is found both in the Holy Qur'ān and the *Sunnah*, for instance, prohibition of killing without justification, giving false evidence and stealing. All the assertive and prohibitive injunctions found in the Holy Qur'ān as well as the *Sunnah* fall under this head.

(2) *The Sunnah elucidates, interprets, qualifies and specifies Qur'ānic injunctions*. The Holy Qur'ān states, "And We have revealed to you the Book so that you may explain to mankind that which have been revealed for them". (27:44) For instance, the *Sunnah* lays down the details of prayers, *zakāt* and *ḥajj* as these have been mentioned in the Holy Qur'ān without specifying the procedure of prayer, the quantity of *zakāt* and the ways of performing *ḥajj*.

On most occasions the *Sunnah* qualifies the Qur'ānic injunctions and delimits their scope. For instance, the Holy Qur'ān allows trade and disallows usury. The *Sunnah* goes a step forward and specifies the forms of trade under this injunction. The Holy Qur'ān forbids eating of a dead animal and drinking of blood. But the *Sunnah* qualifies the application of this injunction and identifies the kind of dead animal and blood exempted from this prohibition. Again, the Holy Qur'ān specifies the offspring who are entitled to

---

[11] Abdur Rahīm *The Principles of Islamic Jurisprudence*, pp. 66-67; see also Abū Zahrah, *Uṣūl al-Fiqh*, pp. 22-28.

inheritance, but the *Sunnah* annuls the title of an heir guilty of murdering the person from whom he is inheriting. The Holy Qur'ān enjoins the amputation of a thief's hand, but the *Sunnah* qualifies this injunction by laying down that the value of the stolen property must be equal to one fourth of a dinar and that it should have been kept in a safe place, and it is then and only then that the punishment of amputation of the hand will operate.

(3) *The Sunnah provides an injunction not to be found in the Holy Qur'ān.* Hence any provision of Islamic law that has not emanated from the Holy Qur'ān must be taken to have originated in the *Sunnah*. For instance, the Holy Prophet said, "Marriage of a man with his wife's paternal aunt or wife of her paternal uncle is unlawful."[12]

According to the Holy Qur'ān, the provisions of *Sunnah* are imperative and binding. All the Muslim jurists unanimously agreed on their being obligatory. They treat what the Holy Prophet allowed as lawful and what he disallowed as unlawful. The Holy Qur'ān states, "Whatever the Prophet enjoins on you, accept and whatever he forbids for you, avoid." (59:7) The Holy Qur'ān further states, "O you who believe: Obey Allah and His Apostle." (8:20) The *Sunnah* of the Holy Prophet is, therefore, next to the Holy Qur'ān, the second source of Islamic law.

(c) *Ijmā'* (Consensus of opinion)

Ijmā' (consensus of opinion) means the agreement of all the jurists of Islam on any question of Islamic law at any time after the demise of the Prophet. Imām Shāfi'ī supports the authenticity of *Ijmā'* from the Holy Qur'ān in the verse of al-Nisā' (4:115):

وَمَن يُشَاقِقِ الرَّسُولَ مِن بَعْدِ مَا تَبَيَّنَ لَهُ الْهُدَى وَيَتَّبِعْ غَيْـرَ سَـبِيلِ الْمُؤْمِنِينَ نُوَلِّهِ مَا تَوَلَّى

(If anyone contends with the Messenger even after guidance has been plainly conveyed to him, and follows

---

[12] 'Abd al Qādir 'Awdah, *al-Tashrī' al-Jinā'ī al-Islāmī*, vol.1, pp.205-13 (English translation)

a path other than that of the believers, we shall leave him in the path he has chosen)

It is further supported by the *Sunnah* of the Holy Prophet who says, "My followers will never unite on what is wrong".[13] The jurists are of the view that *Ijmā'* is a sign and indication of the existence of authority from the Holy Qur'ān and the *Sunnah* of the Holy Prophet. Since it is not permissible to legislate with reference to some authority in Islam, the majority of jurists hold that *Ijmā'* must be based on the authority from the Holy Qur'ān and the *Sunnah* of the Holy Prophet. Thus, this is the first significance of *Ijmā'*. The second significance is that the rule-making powers are delegated to the implementing bodies in order to meet the problems in a society, which requires the formulation of rules and regulations for the implementation of law. This power is given by way of *Ijmā'* and such a delegated power must be within the principles of Islamic law.

Ijmā' will be considered on any question of law when there is no provision about such a question in the Holy Qur'ān and in the *Sunnah* of the Holy Prophet. The law laid down by consensus of opinion is authoritative and binding. Any *Ijmā'* may be reversed and abrogated by a subsequent *Ijmā'* except the *Ijmā'* of the Companions of the Holy Prophet. *Ijmā'* must not contradict the Holy Qur'ān and the *Sunnah* of the Holy Prophet.

(d) *Ijtihād* (Interpretation)

Ijtihād literally means to exert. Technically, it means to exert with a view to form an independent judgment on a legal question. The jurists exert with the purpose to interpret the law from the Holy Qur'ān and the *Sunnah* of the Holy Prophet and to apply it to the prevalent conditions of the society. *Ijtihād* has been approved by the *Sunnah* of the Holy Prophet. Mu'ādh ibn Jabal reported that when the Holy Prophet sent him as the governor of Yemen, the Prophet asked Mu'ādh how he would judge when the occasion arose, and he replied that he would judge in accordance with the Book of Allah. He asked what he would do if he could not find guidance on any question of law in the Bock of Allah, and he

[13] *Tirmizi,* p.38

replied that he would decide in accordance with the *Sunnah* of the Holy Prophet. He then asked what he would do if he could find no guidance in the Book of Allah and the *Sunnah* of the Holy Prophet, and he replied that he would do his best to form his own opinion to decide the matter. The Prophet tapped him on the chest and said, "Praise be to Allah who has disposed His Messenger's messenger towards something with which Allah's messenger is pleased."[14] The Prophet was satisfied with Mu'ādh's reply.

According to this *ḥadīth, Ijtihād* operates when there is no explicit text in the Holy Qur'ān and the *Sunnah* of the Holy Prophet for the problem at hand and the rule stated does not contravene the injunctions laid down in the Holy Qur'ān and the *Sunnah* of the Prophet. *Ijtihād* is an important source of Islamic law to make new laws for the Islamic society to keep up with the progress and advancement of human culture and civilization.

(e) *Qiyās* (analogy)

Qiyās or analogy is covered under *Ijtihād.* This is because *Ijtihād* is not the result of one's own opinion or reason but is based on analogy. *Qiyās* means measuring or judging things on the basis of equality and analogy. It is constituted by four elements. The first element is the original case. This is in the form of a specific precedent or a decided case, which acts as an authority to decide the new case. The second element is new set of facts or situation, which has common characteristics with the original case. The third is the legal effect of the original. The final element is the basis of analogy where the characteristic of the original case becomes a subject matter of the legal effect. For instance, the consumption of wine is prohibited. The basis of prohibition of wine is its characteristic of causing intoxication. Therefore, every intoxicant will be prohibited.

(f) *Maṣāliḥ al-Mursalah* (Public interest)

The doctrine of *maṣlaḥah mursalah* owes its origin to the conception that Islamic law is for social utility and its function is to promote benefit and prevent evil. Imām Mālik approves public interest as one of the sources of Islamic law and allows a

---

[14] Abū Dāwūd, p.118

deduction of law based on general considerations of the public interest. Islamic law provides law in three forms: in the form of clear texts, analogous precedents and indication to the right solutions in the form of guiding principles. If there is no legal text or analogous precedent, the legislation must be supported by some argument from the Holy Qur'ān and the *Sunnah* of the Holy Prophet. Thus, the third form of Islamic law falls within the scope of *Maṣāliḥ*.[15] In the case of *Maṣāliḥ Mursalah,* the jurists must establish rules on the basis of objective arguments, which are within the purview of a particular objective of Islamic law. There are five objectives in Islamic law i.e. protection of religion, protection of life, protection of reason, protection of lineage and protection of property. *Maṣāliḥ Mursalah* are in the nature of delegated legislation within definite guiding principles and defined objective. This means it eradicates the element of personal bias of the legislator.

(g) *'Urf* (Custom)

'Urf or custom is the norm or rule of action recognised by society. A custom is subject to the situations of a particular society. This means that customs of various groups differ. The elements of custom are a consistent way of behaviour, social in character, and of normative value. Thus, it is different from a mere habit. Custom is an important instrument of interpretation of law. The significance of custom for interpreting law is due to the phenomenon that every law is commonly carried into practice through a number of customs.

Custom has no binding force but it operates as a principle of subsidiary value. For instance, the dower payable in a marriage contract is either payable promptly or is deferred. In the absence of a stipulation in the contract, the allotment is presumed on the basis of custom. Thus, custom ranks as a stipulation.[16] Custom which is recognized as having the force of law must be generally prevalent among the people of the country in which the question of validity has arisen and must not contradict the injunctions of the Holy

---

[15] Riaz ul-Hasan Gilani, *Reconstruction of Legal thought in Islam*, pp.169-85

[16] Ibid., p. 187

Qur'ān and the *Sunnah*. The practice of a few individuals or of a limited class of men will not, however, be recognised as custom. Moreover, custom has authority only so long as it prevails, thus, the custom of one age has no force in another age.

Substantial Element of a Crime

The substantial element of a crime refers to an act or omission of the accused. It must be proved that there is an act or omission on the part of the accused, which constitutes a crime. The substantial element not only covers the conduct of the accused but such conduct must be accompanied with a particular result. For example, in case of a murder it must be proved that the conduct of the accused caused the death of the victim.

The offender passes through various stages before he commits an offence. First of all he thinks of the offence and then resolves to commit it. This stage is followed by preparation for the offence and procurement of instruments and necessary means of committing it; for instance buying a weapon for committing the offence of murder, getting hold of an instrument for breaking the wall of the house wherein theft is to be committed or buying a key which may open the locks of the door. When the offender acquires all these accessories, he moves ahead into the third stage of putting his plan into operation and thus attempts the commission of the offence. He does as he thinks fit and translates his plan into action thus, finalising the commission of the offence.

These are the stages through which an offender passes in the commission of an offence. The stages are described as under:

a. Intention

Thinking and intending is not a punishable offence. According to the *Sharī'ah,* no man is accountable for whatever ideas come into his mind, whatever acts he thinks of doing or whatever he intends to say or do. The Holy Prophet has said, "Allah has forgiven the people belonging to my *Ummah* for the notions coming into their minds unless they utter them or put them into practice." In short, one is accountable for one's words and deeds and not for one's thoughts and resolutions. This is one of the fundamental principles of the *Sharī'ah*, which it embodies right from the day of its revelation. This principle is found in all the modern laws, but was introduced at the end of the eighteenth century after the French Revolution and that too with exemptions while the *Sharī'ah* admits of no exemption.

b. Preparation

Muslim jurists have classified offences as complete and incomplete and have not divided them into the modern segments of preparation, attempt and completion. However, as in the ordinary law, the stage of preparation by acquiring accessories for committing an offence, is not a punishable act. The *Sharī'ah* provides no punishment for preparing for an offence by procuring the means necessary to commit it, unless of course, the procurement or production of such means in itself is a crime. For example, if a person intends to commit larceny by drugging somebody or getting him drunk, his procurement of an intoxicant and keeping such a prohibited thing in itself would be a punishable offence. Punishment for such an offence does not hinge upon the realization of the basic objective, viz. the commission of the intended larceny. The reason for excluding the procurement of the means required to commit an offence from punishable offences is that only an act constituting a crime entails punishment. An act assumes the character of a crime only when it results in the violation of the right of God or the right of the people. There is apparently nothing in the acquisition of accessories in preparation for the commission of a crime that may tantamount to a violation of such rights. The stage of preparation ends when the first step is taken towards the commission of the intended offence.

c. Attempt

This is the stage at which the act of an offender turns into an offence. An act is treated as an offence when it constitutes a crime i.e. it transgresses the right of an individual or that of the community. It is not necessary that such an act be the commencement of the material element of the crime in question. It is enough that the act in question is an offence in itself and the object thereof is to translate the material element of a crime into action, even if there still remain many steps between the commission of the material element and the actual act, as for example breaking the wall of a house in larceny or stealing into the house by breaking the door or opening the lock thereof with a false key. Each one of these acts is both attempted larceny and an offence in itself although many steps remain to be taken in order that the act may culminate in the crime of complete larceny. In short, if the offender breaks the wall, opens the door and enters the house he will be liable to punishment for committing an offence although the real object of the offence is not achieved. The criterion of punishment in the case of an attempted offence is that the act committed by the offender constitutes an offence, as for example, the act of breaking the wall.[17] Any act showing progress towards the actual commission of the offence constitutes attempt liable to punishment and all that goes before is known as the intention to commit, the resolution to do it and mere preparation. It is also called an incomplete crime. If a person, having instruments of theft, was arrested just in the front or on side of the house intended to be burgled or if a person with a gun was arrested while sitting in ambush on the way on which a specific person was expected to come, both acts may be punished with *ta'zīr*. In this connection Mawardi writes, "According to a famous Shāfi'ī jurist, Abū 'Abd Allāh al-Zubayrī, a person who is arrested near a house having instruments of theft with him and having intention of theft is liable to be punished with *ta'zīr*."[18]

When a person intends to commit a crime and takes all possible steps to consummate it, the offence may either be finally completed or may remain incomplete for some reason. If the offence is completed, the offender is liable for full punishment prescribed for the offence. However, if his intention to complete the offence is frustrated by something beyond his control, he will be liable for *ta'zīr* for commencing the offence. But if the non-completion of the offence is based on the volition of the offender, irrespective of the retraction being for repentance or for any other consideration, the offender shall not be liable for punishment unless one of the acts done is an independent offence. Attempt is therefore an intentional act which a person does towards the

---

[17] 'Abd al-Qādir, 'Awdah, *al-Tashrī' al-Jinā'ī al-islāmī,* vol.1 pp. 345-50
[18] Ibid.

commission of an offence but which fails in its object through circumstances independent of the volition of that person.[19]

Sometimes the offender passes through these stages separately and one after another in different times and places whereas sometimes he passes through these stages simultaneously and at the same time and place. The existence of these stages vary for different offences and the court shall determine them according to the circumstances of a particular case.

It is pertinent to mention here that *ḥadd* punishment shall not be given for an attempt to commit an offence liable to *ḥadd* and the offence of attempt shall be liable for *ta'zīr* in all cases.

Complicity

Sometimes a crime is committed by one person individually and sometimes many persons participate in the commission of a crime or cooperate with one another to commit it. Further, sometimes all the accomplices participate in the direct commission of the material part of the crime while sometimes an accomplice only agrees in the commission thereof with his accomplices and does not participate in the direct commission of the crime. But sometimes an accomplice instigates or abets another accomplice in the commission of the crime by various means without taking active part in the direct commission of the material part thereof. Thus, complicity is either direct or indirect. In any kind of complicity an accomplice shall be deemed to have been involved in the offence whether or not he has a tangible and active share in the commission of the material part of the offence. Direct complicity means that an accomplice participates in the commission of the material part of a crime. This sort of complicity consists in the commission of the essential part of a crime by several individuals. Such complicity is called plurality of accomplices. It is necessary for any kind of complicity that there must be agreement among the accomplices before the commission of the crime. Thus, if two or more persons commit an offence without prior agreement, they will not be treated as accomplices, but will be treated as direct offenders and each will be liable for the part he plays in the commission of the crime.

[19] Ibid., p. 436.

The Muslim jurists have taken great care in explaining the injunctions relating the direct complicity and have focused full attention over the conditions of the direct commission of crimes for which punishments have been fixed by the Holy Qur'ān or the *Sunnah* of the Holy Prophet like *ḥudūd, qiṣāṣ* and *diyat* because these punishments are applicable to the criminals who directly commit any of these offences. But as far as crimes liable to *ta'zīr* are concerned, the jurists have not described in detail the matters relating to the direct or indirect complicity in such crimes. The reason for this is that these crimes are not fixed and are likely to vary considerably with time, space and standpoint. Moreover, their punishments being variable are amendable to diminution or enhancement.

A general rule of the Islamic criminal law is that the punishment of *ḥadd* is applied to a criminal who directly commits any such crime and not to the one who simply has a share in the cause of the commission thereof. An accomplice in the cause of any such crimes shall be liable for *ta'zīr* and not for *ḥadd.* Imām Abū Ḥanīfah applies this rule in a very subtle manner whereas other jurists exempt them from the crimes of murder and bodily injuries.

A person may commit a crime along with some other persons. For instance, a person murders a man and two or three other persons join him in committing that murder by firing simultaneously at the victim, all of them shall be liable for the punishment of death as *qiṣāṣ*. However, in case of a crime liable to *ḥadd,* any accomplice who has fulfilled all the conditions of such crime shall be liable for *ḥadd,* and the one who has not fulfilled such conditions individually shall not be liable for *ḥadd* but shall be liable for *ta'zīr.*

According to the majority of the jurists there is difference between the accountability for crimes committed in agreement or union and that of crimes committed with concurrence.

Concurrence in this particular context means that several accomplices are inclined towards the commission of the same offence, but no plan is prepared beforehand. For instance, a brawl starts all of a sudden and the accomplices rush to the spot and attack their common enemy. One of them chops off his hand and the second beheads him. The former in this case shall be liable to the extent of cutting the victim's hand, while the latter for decapitation. In such a case it may be said of the accomplices to be in concurrence, but they will not be responsible for one another's act.

As distinct from the concurrence mentioned above, agreement or union signifies that the accomplices work out a plan beforehand for the commission of the same offence. When the time for the real event comes, they move ahead to cooperate with each other. For instance, two persons agree to kill somebody and arrive at the spot to translate their plan into action. One of them cuts off a finger of the victim's hand and the other butchers him. In such a case both the accomplices will be liable for intentional murder.[20] Imām Abū Ḥanīfah, however does not differentiate between agreement and concurrence and opines that each accomplice in both cases shall be liable for his own part in the crime.

When an offender commits an act which amounts to the initiation of a crime, he will be treated as a direct accomplice. He will also be treated as such when he does a criminal act with the intention of committing an offence. In a crime liable to *ta'zīr* the punishment of a direct accomplice is identical to that to which the culprit committing it all alone is liable, although the offender with a complicity in offence may not do all the acts he may have done when committing it single handedly. Similarly if an indirect accomplice is the real cause of the crime, he will be treated as a direct accomplice.

If a person committing the actual offence directly serves as a tool in the hands of the accomplice and the latter uses him as he wishes, the accomplice having a direct share in the cause of the crime will also be regarded as being guilty of the crime except in an offence liable to *ḥadd* wherein he will be liable for *ta'zīr*. For instance, a person orders another obedient person to kill somebody and he kills him accordingly. According to Imām Mālik, Imām Shāfi'ī and Imām Aḥmad the man ordering the homicide will be treated as direct accomplice, although he does not play any direct role in the essential part of the offence. They argue that the person ordered to commit murder serves as a mere tool in the hands of the

[20] Ibid., vol.1, pp. 360-61

former having no choice in the matter and the person ordering it is the real cause of the murder.[21] But Imām Abū Ḥanīfah does not regard the person ordering the commission of the crime as a direct accomplice except when such an order involves coercion.[22]

It is important to note that common intention of the accomplices is also necessary for a common punishment. Thus if many persons cause the death of a person and they had no common intention, they shall not be liable for the same punishment. For instance, two persons murder another person, one murders him intentionally being his enemy and the second murders him in self-defence or one is sane and the other is insane. In such a case the one who murders him intentionally and is sane shall be liable for *qiṣāṣ* while the other shall not be liable for any punishment. Therefore the punishment of an accomplice is subject to his qualifications and intention. Further the intention or qualification of one accomplice shall not affect the intention and qualification of another accomplice.

In the absence of common intention and plan every accomplice shall be liable for his own act. However, every accomplice shall be liable for punishment if he has any role in the commission of the offence or its cause.

Indirect Complicity

Indirect complicity means an accomplice who does not participate in the commission of the material part of a crime but has a share in the cause of the crime incidentally or through incitation, abetment, cooperation or facilitation.

Incitation and abetment

Incitation means to induce the offender to commit an offence to the extent that it motivates the commission of the offence. Incitation itself is an offence punishable with *ta'zīr.* However, incitation does not make an accomplice liable for death punishment like that of the other accomplice who actually killed the victim unless it involves coercion.

---

[21] Ibn Qudāmah, *al-Mughnī,* vol. 9, p. 331

[22] Al-Kāsānī, *Badā'i' al-Ṣanā'i'*, p. 180

It is relevant to mention that to order a person to kill another person or to compel a person to kill another person also constitutes incitation. The difference between order and compulsion is that the former does not affect the choice of the offender and allows him the freedom to carry it out or not while coercion does not leave choice for the person under coercion, and the only choice of such person is to commit the offence or face the consequences with which he is threatened. Incitation varies in various crimes. According to Imām Mālik, if the inciter is present on the spot while the offence is being committed, he shall be treated as the main culprit whether or not he cooperates with the real offender provided he is in a position to commit the offence, if the real offender does not.

A person who abets the offender is an indirect accomplice of the offender though he may not have agreed with him to the commission of the offence in advance. For instance, a person who keeps an eye on the way for a killer or gives him his gun to help him in the commission of the offence of murder is the abettor and indirect accomplice of the offender. The jurists differentiate between the actual offender and the abettor. They unanimously maintain that the actual offender is the one who commits or attempts to commit an offence whereas an abettor is the one who does not himself commit or attempt to commit the offence, but helps or co-operates with the real offender in the commission of the offence. The jurists use the term direct accomplice (*sharik mubashir)* and indirect accomplice *(sharik mutasabbib)* and have not used the term abettor independently.

The jurists differ on the question of a person who seizes the victim but the victim is killed by another person. According to some jurists the person seizing the victim is the abettor of the killer and does not have a direct share in the commission of the actual offence. This is the opinion of Imām Abū Ḥanīfah and Imām Shāfi'ī. They argue that the person seizing the victim does have a share in the cause of the actual offence but the offence has actually been committed by the other person, and that direct commission of act dominates participation in the cause thereof, provided that the actual offender does not act under duress. But according to Imām Mālik and Imām Aḥmad, both the persons seizing the victim and the killer are the direct accomplices and the real offenders. They maintain that the killer commits murder directly while the seizer becomes the cause of the offence and that the result of contribution towards the cause of the offence and the actual commission thereof is identical. Such a result could not have ensued if either of the two acts had not been committed.[23] The difference arises out of the question of the application of rules as to the method resorted to in the commission of an offence, whether the mode of commission is direct complicity or indirect complicity. It varies according to the kinds of crimes committed by many persons.

Imām Mālik opines that in the case of prior agreement for the commission of an offence, the abettor would be treated as a direct accomplice of the real offender if he is found on the spot during the commission of the offence in such a position that if the main offender seeks his help in committing the offence, he is able to help him immediately. In this case both the real offender and the abettor shall be liable for the same punishment of *qiṣāṣ*. But if the abettor is found in such a position that he is unable to be helpful in the commission of the offence, then he would be treated as an indirect accomplice. But according to other jurists the abettor is an indirect accomplice unless he is directly guilty of the offence.[24]

It is one of the fundamental principles of the Islamic criminal law that the punishments of *ḥudūd* are not meant for the indirect accomplice. It enjoins that anyone who shares the commission of an offence by any means of complicity shall not be liable to *ḥadd*, whether he participates in it by agreement, incitation or abetment. The indirect accomplice will, however, be liable to *ta'zīr*. It is because the punishments of *ḥudūd* are severe whereas the offence of an indirect accomplice is lighter and less dangerous than that of the real culprit. Therefore, the punishment to which the two are liable respectively cannot be equal. However, a person who agrees to the commission of an offence, instigates another to commit an offence or abets in the commission thereof is liable for *ta'zīr* even if such agreement, incitation or abetment does not produce the desired result. Sometimes the part played by an indirect accomplice amounts to the commission of the material part of the

---

[23] Ibn Qudāmah, *al-Mughnī*, vol. 9, p. 333
[24] *Mawahib al-Jalil,* vol.6, p.242

offence and is thus treated as a direct accomplice. The punishment of direct accomplices is equal. However, in the case of an offence liable to *ḥadd,* each direct accomplice must have completed the commission of the offence individually. The qualification and intention of the accomplices must be identical failing which it will affect their punishment and everyone will be punished according to his own qualifications and intention. The punishment of a direct accomplice and indirect accomplice is identical in an offence liable to *ta'zīr*.

Complicity in suicide

Suicide has been declared prohibited in Islam like killing another person. The Holy Qur'ān says,

وَلاَ تَقْتُلُواْ النَّفْسَ الَّتِي حَرَّمَ اللّهُ إِلاَّ بِالحَقِّ

> And slay not life, which Allah hath forbidden save with right. (17:33)

وَلاَ تَقْتُلُواْ أَنفُسَكُمْ إِنَّ اللّهَ كَانَ بِكُمْ رَحِيمًا

> Kill not yourselves. For Allah is ever merciful to you. (4:29)

The Holy Prophet said, "The person who kills himself with a piece of iron will reappear in Hell with the same piece of iron, beating his stomach therewith; the person who kills' himself by taking poison, will have the same poison in his hand committing suicide with it perpetually and the person who falls from the mountain by rolling himself to death, will be perpetually committing the same act of suicide in Hell".

If a person commits suicide and he dies, such an act is not punishable as death invalidates punishment. Imām Shāfi'ī, however, holds that in the case of both willful and inadvertent suicide, expiation must be imposed on the property of the deceased. But if the act of suicide turns out to be abortive and the delinquent escapes death, then the offender shall be liable for *ta'zīr* for attempted suicide.

However, prohibition of suicide demands that the person having complicity in such an offence shall be liable for punishment whether his complicity consists of incitation, agreement or abetment.

Negative complicity

According to the majority of the jurists complicity by a negative act is not punishable offence. For instance, a man sees some people committing theft from a house and keeps quiet; or he sees a man killing a third person but does not stop him; or he witnesses a man throwing into the river a child who cannot swim but does not ask him to desist from such a brutal act nor does anything to save the child either. In all these cases the silent spectator is not the abettor of the offender in as much as his silence cannot be treated as complicity in the offence and as such he shall not be liable for any punishment. They argue that the silent spectator in such cases is not in agreement with the offender and has no concern with the offender and the offence. Moreover, the silence of the spectator is not designed to let the offence occur, nor is there any casual relationship between his silence and the commission of the offence. Some jurists, however, differentiate between the person who is able to prevent the offence in such cases and one who is unable to do so. If a person is in a position to stop the offender from the commission of the offence and save the aggrieved party from harm, he shall be held accountable for his silence. But the person who is unable to prevent the offence and save the life or property of the victim shall not be held accountable for his silence in such cases.

Cultural Element of Crime

Cultural element or mental element of crime means that a person should have requisite legal capacity and should bear the consequences of the crime which he commits intentionally with full awareness of the consequences and significance thereof. Islamic criminal law holds only those living persons responsible who are under obligation and understand the reason for such an obligation. Children are not held accountable for wrongful acts till they reach the age of puberty. The Holy Qur'ān states:

وَإِذَا بَلَغَ الْأَطْفَالُ مِنكُمُ الْحُلُمَ فَلْيَسْتَأْذِنُوا كَمَا اسْتَأْذَنَ الَّذِينَ مِن قَبْلِهِمْ

And when the children among you come to puberty, let them ask for permission (to enter the house) as do those senior to them (in age). (24:59)

The Holy Prophet said, "Three persons are not accountable: a child until he reaches the age of puberty, a sleeping person until he awakes and an insane person until he becomes sane."[25]

A child becomes an adult either on attaining a certain limit of age or puberty. Regarding age Imām Mālik, Imām Shāfi'ī and Imām Aḥmad opine that a child becomes an adult on attaining the age of 15 years whether male or female. But according to Imām Abū Ḥanīfah a female child becomes adult by attaining the age of 17 years while a male child becomes adult on attaining the age of 18 years. Puberty is attained by a child when his or her sex glands become functional and the secondary sexual characteristics emerge. The sign of puberty in a male adolescent is known by his potency to impregnate a woman and the discharge of semen, and a girl's puberty is known by her menstruation, nocturnal pollution and pregnancy.

"Sane" means a person who understands what he says and gives rational answers to the questions put to him. The Holy Qur'ān states:

يَا أَيُّهَا الَّذِينَ آمَنُواْ لاَ تَقْرَبُواْ الصَّلاَةَ وَأَنتُمْ سُكَارَى حَتَّى تَعْلَمُواْ مَا تَقُولُونَ وَلاَ جُنُبًا إِلاَّ عَابِرِي سَبِيلٍ حَتَّى تَغْتَسِلُواْ

Oh you who believe! Approach not prayers with a mind befogged until you can understand all that you say. (4:43)

The Islamic law does not hold a person who commits an offence under duress accountable nor a person who is incapable of deliberate choice. The Holy Qur'ān states:

[25] Imām Aḥmad ibn Ḥanbal, *Musnad,* vol.9, p.278

فَمَنِ اضْطُرَّ غَيْرَ بَاغٍ وَلَا عَادٍ فَلَا إِثْمَ عَلَيْهِ

But he who is driven by necessity neither craving nor transgressing, it is no sin for him. (1-173)

The Holy Prophet said, "My Ummah is exempted from mistake, forgetfulness and the act done under coercion."[26]

Thus the commission of crime in the following circumstances will be considered an exception to criminal responsibility:

i. Minority
ii. Insanity
iii. Intoxication and
iv. Coercion

Intoxication

Intoxication means to be out of one's senses because of the use of liquor or any other intoxicant. An intoxicated person is one who is out of his senses is incapable of understanding anything and distinguishing between right and wrong. This is the view of Ímām Abū Ḥanīfah. But according to the other three Imāms, an intoxicated person is one who is in a state of delirium. Thus, a person who does not know what he utters is intoxicated.

According to the predominant opinion of all schools of thought in jurisprudence, if a person who is out of his senses is forced to drink an intoxicating liquor or if he drinks it of his own accord without knowing that it is a strong drink or drinks it as a medicine, he will not be liable to punishment for he commits the offence when he is stupefied and is thus like an insane person. However, any person who uses an intoxicant intentionally without any excuse or takes an intoxicating drug unnecessarily and who is, consequently, out of his senses, will have to account for every offence he commits intentionally or by mistake. He will be punished for it; for he lost his senses of his own accord and that too by doing something which in itself constitutes an offence. He will be punished so that he may be reformed and also that it is necessary to do so, as annulment of punishment in such a case would encourage every criminal to drink.

---

[26] Tirmizi. pp. 2-4

Some jurists, however, opine that the intoxicated person is not accountable at all for whatever he does. As understanding is the basis of accountability, he cannot be held responsible in the absence of understanding.[27]

Insanity and Diminished Responsibility

Insanity means loss of understanding, mental disorder or enervation of understanding. The lack of mental faculties takes various forms. Sometimes it consists in the total loss of mental faculties which the jurists term as total insanity. At other times it is intermittent or partial, and is known as lunacy. In such cases the mind ceases to perform its normal function in one particular matter, while in all other matters the faculty of understanding remains intact. Sometimes the mental faculties are not totally lost but are just enervated. In such a case understanding is not completely absent. It is subnormal. Such a state is known as idiocy.

There are other cases of the loss of mental faculties and each case is given a separate name but all of them are due to the loss of understanding. The law relating to various manifestations of insanity is that whenever the faculty of understanding ceases to function, criminal accountability comes to an end and the other way round. In other words a person devoid of understanding is exempted from punishment, whether he is an idiot or a mad man. In certain nervous diseases also the patients lose consciousness and understanding. In such conditions they act and utter words without having the least consciousness of what they do and say and they do not know the significance thereof. These patients are not accountable for their wrongful acts provided their understanding is suspended or reduced to the degree of idiocy at the time of committing unwarrantable acts. Idiocy is the condition of a person who is deficient in intelligence, whose speech is incoherent and whose action is indiscreet, whether such condition is innate or is the result of some disease developed at a later stage. In other words idiocy is a lesser degree of madness and therefore, it may be said that in the case of insanity intelligence is lost altogether, whereas in idiocy intelligence is deficient. There are

---

[27] 'Awdah, *al-Tashrī' al-Jinā'i' al-Islāmī,* vol. 1, pp.215-16

various degrees of such deficiency but the understanding of an idiot is not equal to a man with average intelligence, whatever the degree of his idiocy. But an idiot is not accountable for his wrongful acts.

However, if a person has any degree of sense and understanding he will be liable for punishment if he commits a crime in such a condition, though his punishment will be reduced. Diminished responsibility is an abnormal state of mind that does not constitute complete insanity but is a special defence. The abnormality of mind must substantially impair the mental responsibility of the accused for his acts i.e. reduce his powers of control, judgement or reasoning to a condition that would be considered abnormal by the ordinary man. It may be caused by disease, injury or mental sub-normality, and is liberally interpreted to cover such conditions as depression or irresistible impulse.[28]

According to Islamic criminal law everyone is responsible for his own acts and not for the act of any other person. The Holy Qur'ān states:

وَلَا تَكْسِبُ كُلُّ نَفْسٍ إِلَّا عَلَيْهَا وَلَا تَزِرُ وَازِرَةٌ وِزْرَ أُخْرَىٰ

Every soul draws the need of its act on none but itself: no bearer of burden shall bear the burden of another. (6:164)

In Islamic criminal law the criminal responsibility and accountability rests on three bases, namely;

(i) The person commits a prohibited act.
(ii) The person commits an offence with his free consent.
(iii) The person who commits an offence is an adult and sane and can differentiate between right and wrong.

In the absence of the first basis there is no criminal responsibility and thus the question of penalty does not arise. In the absence of the second and the third bases, criminal responsibility is there but there is no punishment.

The purpose of criminal accountability is to safeguard the public interest and peace in the society because the commission of

---

[28] Ibid.

crimes is detrimental to the collective order and system of beliefs as well as to the life, property, honour and sentiments of the individual interest. Acts that appear prejudicial to the interests of the individual adversely affect collective interests in the ultimate analysis.

There are a number of mental attitudes which a man may have possessed at the time of commission of the offence. These include intention, negligence, mistake, forgetfulness, ignorance of law, omission, strict liability.[29]

(a) Intention

The majority of crimes are so defined as to require proof of intention to bring about various consequences. It is thus of great importance to know what is meant by 'intention'. It is also called 'criminal intent'. Criminal intent means the willingness or determination of a person to do a forbidden act or refrain from a mandatory act knowing that the act he is going to commit or omit is forbidden and constitutes a crime liable for punishment. Intention is the purpose or design with which an act is done. In other words criminal intent is to make up one's mind to commit or omit an act which one knows is forbidden or enjoined, as the case may be, or to commit an offence with the intention of defying the law. For instance, someone throws a stone out of the window and it hits a passerby in the street and he dies. Now the person concerned committed an act which constitutes an offence but if he has no criminal intent regarding the death of the passerby he shall not be responsible for his death but if he has criminal intent to kill the passerby he shall be responsible for that.

The difference between the material commission of an offence and its criminal intent is the same as the difference between intention and purpose. Criminal intent implies willingness for the commission of a prohibited act. Purpose means the intended outcome of such an act. Both of them may signify the intention of the forbidden act as well as the proposed result thereof. The criminal intent or the purpose of offence usually exists in the mind of the offender before he commits the crime. For instance, he makes up his mind to kill someone and kills him

---

[29] Ibid.

after sometime. But sometimes the idea of committing the offence enters his mind just when he commits it. This generally happens in a riot or brawl when the offender commits the offence all of a sudden. However, it makes no difference in Islamic criminal law whether the criminal intent precedes the offence or coincides with it, in either case the punishment is identical. Actually the punishment of an offence is based on the combination of the intention and commission of the offence. Mere intention without commission of the offence entails no punishment.[30] Intention is a state of mind existing at the time a person commits an offence and may be determined by act or circumstances deducible therefrom. Sometimes the intention of the offender is determined by the manner with which he commits the offence or the weapon he uses in the commission of the offence. A person who contemplates any result, as not unlikely to follow from a deliberate act of his own, may be said to intend that result, whether he desires it or not. If a person foresees that death or serious bodily harm is a highly probable consequence of his act, intends that consequence.

Common and specific intents

In the case of the common intent the offender decides to commit an offence being conscious of the fact that what he is about to do is an unlawful act. Common intent is sufficient for punishing a person for a crime in general offences. For instance, in a criminal act of causing hurt it is sufficient to prove that the offender has the intention of committing an unlawful act in a concrete form. But in the case of certain offences common intent does not suffice. In such offence the offender must have intended specific result by the forbidden act which he proposes to commit. This is the case with crime like intentional murder or theft. Thus in the case of murder it is sufficient that the offender should strike the victim or deal out a blow to him knowing that infliction of hurt is a prohibited act. In such a case, it is necessary that the criminal intent includes the offender's will to kill the victim by causing hurt. In other words the offender should not only have common intention, but also the specific intent or the element of will to produce a result in the case of intentional murder. Similarly in the case of theft it is not only

---

[30] 'Awdah, *al-Tashrī' al-Jinā'i al-Islāmī*, vol.1, pp.409-11

sufficient that the thief takes away some property belonging to another person knowingly that he is committing an unlawful act but also that he should deliberately want to own that property. If he takes it away without intending to own it, he is not guilty of theft.

In certain cases involving the condition of specific intent, the criminal intent coincides with the motive of crime. For instance, if a person kills another person standing in his way in order to get rid of him, his specific intent would coincide with his motive; but the motive has no effect on the offence or the punishment. But as it is congruent with the specific intent it affects the offence or the punishment as the specific intent and not as the motive. The motive of crime has nothing to do with the criminal intent; nor does it affect the pattern of crime or its punishment in so far as the offences of *ḥadd* and *qiṣāṣ* are concerned but it is not so in the case of *ta'zīr* wherein the court may take into account the motive of the crime in the determination of the quantum of the punishment. However, Imām Mālik does not attach the string of specific intent in the case of homicide and opines that common intent is sufficient for conviction in the case of murder. It is based on the argument that Imām Malik does not recognise any such thing as quasi-intentioned murder. According to him there are only two kinds of murder, namely:

(i) intentional murder and
(ii) murder by mistake.

The other jurists believe in a third kind as well which is quasi-intentional murder.[31]

If a person intends to do a definite wrong to a definite person or persons, his intent will be definite. The act intended by him would be treated as definite even if the pattern thereof entails limited results, for example, a person butchers another person or persons with a knife or throws a bomb conscious of the fact that it will kill several people - an act with indefinite possibilities. In this latter case the offender cannot possibly determine the results of his act as he can in butchering the victim with a knife.

---

[31] Ibid., pp.450-52

If the offender is conscious of the potential results of his act and intends to produce all or some of those results his offence would in spite of its indefinite results, be treated as a definite act, whatever the results produced by it.

The victim will also be treated as determined if he is amenable to determination in any respect. If his name, personality or quality cannot be identified, but can nevertheless be determined somehow or other, he will be regarded as definite. For instance, a person intends to murder one of the members of a particular organization to achieve his end and shoots at all the members thereof whether they are known to him or not and one of them is killed. In such a case he will be deemed to have killed a definite person because the organisation in question is definite both individually or collectively.

The intention of an offender to do a definite wrong to an indefinite person will be regarded as definite intent. If the identity of a person intended to be wronged cannot be determined before the wrong is done, such a person would be deemed indefinite.

In determining the accountability of the offender and the sort of offence he is guilty thereof, the jurists generally place both definite and indefinite intent on equal footing and regard them as subject to the same injunction except when the offence consists of murder and the criminal intent is indefinite. Some jurists of the Shāfi'ī School hold that if the offender intends to kill an indefinite person, he shall be guilty of quasi-intentional murder and not intentional murder. But Mālikīs, some Ḥanafīs, some Shāfi'īs and some Ḥanbalīs do not differentiate between definite and indefinite intents in criminal cases including murder. Hence, according to them if the act of the offender results in causing death to a person he is liable to intentional murder whether or not his intention of murder involves a definite victim.[32]

Direct and Indirect Intent

If an offender commits an offence conscious of its results and with intention to produce those results, his intention will be direct intent, whether or not the intended victim is a definite person. For example, a person sets fire to a house and another person who is in

[32] Ibid., pp. 415-16.

the house is burned to death. If the offender had intended the death of the victim, his intention is direct intent. On the other hand if an offender intends to commit a definite act which, when committed, produces an effect he may not have intended nor does he exercise any control over the emergence of such an effect, his intention will be treated as indirect intent. This is known as probable intent. For instance, if a person intends to cause a minor hurt to another person to chastize or discipline him, or he intends to torture him. In such a case the offender is not only accountable for the intended and expected results of his act but is also held responsible for the consequences which he cannot foresee. If the hurt causes the death of the victim in this case, the offender shall be liable for quasi-intentional murder.

According to Imām Abū Ḥanīfah, Imām Shāfi'ī and Imām Aḥmad the offence of intentional murder does not involve probable intent, whereas Imām Mālik recognizes the presence of probable intent in it and holds the offender responsible on account of such intent in every case. The basis of the difference is that Imām Mālik divides the murder into two kinds, namely;

(i) intentional murder and
(ii) committed by mistake.

According to him every murder not committed by mistake is intentional murder liable to death punishment. The intention to transgress in a murder case is sufficient to hold the offender responsible. The other Imāms on the other hand, classify murder into three kinds, namely:

(i) intentional murder,
(ii) quasi-intentional murder and
(iii) murder committed by mistake

They qualify intentional murder with the offender's intention to take the life of the victim in addition to his intention to commit the act which may cause the death. If the offender intends to commit the offence but has no intention to kill the victim, he shall be guilty of quasi-intentional and not intentional murder and shall be liable to a lesser punishment than that of intentional murder.

Thus the condition of the intention to take the life of the victim excludes probable intent from intentional murder. In case of probable intent the offender cannot foresee the death of the victim. All the jurists recognize the presence of probable intent in the offences lesser than murder, for instance, causing hurt to a person by beating etc. Imām Abū Ḥanīfah and Imām Mālik agree that if the offender is intentionally guilty of such a crime he may in all cases be taken to account because of probable intent. Some of the Ḥanbalies also subscribe to this opinion. But Imām Shāfi'ī endorses the view held by a majority of the Ḥanbalies to the effect that the offender is accountable only for those consequences which he may have intended; that he is to be taken to account because of probable intent as one willfully guilty and that the consequences of the offence committed by him will be treated as subject to the provision relating to the intended consequences. Such consequences are deemed to be the results that generally ensue from a given offence. However, if the consequences are neither intended nor consist of such results as generally manifest themselves in the wake of a given offence are unintended consequences or are results subject to the provision pertaining to unintended consequences. But the offender will not be held responsible in respect of such consequences as an errant because he does not mean to commit the offence giving rise to those consequences. He will rather be held responsible as one quasi-willfully guilty and will thus be liable to a penalty ranging between punishments entailed by willful offence and criminal error.

In the case of unintended consequences the right criterion of the offender's accountability is to consider whether or not such unintended consequences normally manifest themselves or are to be seen occasionally. If they generally manifest themselves then the offender must be mindful of them and must be conscious of their inevitable relationship with the original offence he intends to commit. Hence, if he intends to commit the offence he necessarily intends those consequences as well. The criterion is based on the emergence of normal consequences and does not rest on relative basis which varies with individuals and with the difference in their modes of thinking and their varying capacities to comprehend the consequences.[33]

Probable intent

Even though Muslim jurists do not mention the theory of probable intent, their collective views would establish one of the most modern theories dealing with this problem. Thus, for example, Ibn Qudamah states;

> "If someone deliberately creates a hole in a ship loaded with people—an act which usually sinks a ship—and if those aboard the ship die in it because they are in a deep sea or because they cannot swim, retribution is due on that person if someone for whom retribution is due has been killed. He is also liable for the ship as well as what it carries in terms of property and people."[34]

Ibn 'Ābidīn has further suggested that the intent to kill is not a precondition of the murder to be considered premeditated. If the offender sought to injure only a man's hand (i.e had not intended to kill) and injures his neck (i.e the man dies), then the murder is premeditated; but if he injures another person's neck (i.e someone else dies), then it is a case of accidental homicide. 'Allamah al-Dardīr writes;

> "A crowd not conspiring against one person would be sentenced to death if they beat him deliberately and unjustly and he dies immediately or is carried away being unconscious and remains so until he dies. A group conspiring to kill or beat someone is also sentenced to death on the basis that they all intended the beating even though only one of them dealt the fatal blow, since if it were the case that the particular perpetrator had not dealt the blow surely one of the other non-perpetrators would have dealt it."[35]

---

33 Ibid., pp.424-26

34 Ibn Qudāmah, *al-Mughnī,* vol. 7, p. 114

35 'Awdah, *al-Tashrī' al-Jinā'ī al-Islāmī*, vol. 2, p.221

Thus even though one had not dealt the blow, he had intended the death of the victim, and, therefore it must have been part of his probable intent that another's aggression with his consent would lead to the death. He would, therefore, be responsible for premeditation for the murder committed by another. It is a fiction that allows the court to reach the result of imposing criminal responsibility. This is analogous to the concept of being an accessory to a crime in western jurisprudence.

Criminal intent as to degree of premeditation

Jurists speak in terms which almost assume premeditation or deliberation even though it was never indicated. A Muslim shall not be killed for a slave or a non-Muslim *(al-dhimmī)* except in the case of assassination *(al-ghīla)*. This is murder in order to take the victim's money whether the murder was committed by stealth as, for example, if the perpetrator lures the victim to some place and kills him there to take his money, or if the murder is committed in the open in such a way that help could not have been sought. The latter, however, may be called *ḥirabah*. Thus, Imām Mālik has said, "In these cases there is no pardon and no reconciliation. The reconciliation of a subject is rejected and judgement concerning the case is left up to the ruler".

(b) Negligence

Negligence means the failure to use such care which a prudent and careful person would use under similar circumstances. It is the doing of some act which a person of ordinary prudence would have foreseen and avoided. The term negligence refers to that legal delinquency which results whenever a man fails to exhibit the care which he ought to exhibit, whether it be slight, ordinary or great. The doctrine of negligence rests on the duty of every person to exercise due care in his conduct towards others from which harm may result. According to some jurists negligence is the conduct which falls below the standard established by law for the protection of others against reasonable risk of harm. It is a departure from the conduct expected of a reasonably prudent person under like circumstances. Negligence itself is a punishable offence such as careless driving. Negligence is sometimes advertent negligence and amounts to recklessness. Recklessness is the deliberate taking of an unjustifiable risk in which such risk is involved. A man is reckless with respect to the consequence of his act, when he foresees that it may occur, but does not desire it nor foresees it as virtually certain. It is the realisation that the circumstances may exist, without either knowing or hoping that they do. For example, a person points a gun at another person and pulls the trigger. If he does not know it is loaded, but realises that it may be, he is reckless with respect to the circumstance whether he hopes it is unloaded or just does not care whether it is loaded or not. If he is reckless with respect to this circumstance, it follows that he is also reckless with respect to the consequence of the death of that person; that is, he foresees it as certain. The person who acts recklessly should have known of the risk involved in his act, or deliberately closes his mind to its existence when he acts.

(c) Mistake

Mistake means the commission of a crime without being intended by the offender. Criminal errors are committed unintentionally or even against the intention. In many cases it so happens that the offender proposes to do a definite act which is not an offence in itself, but this legitimate act gives rise to an act which is regarded as an offence. For instance, a person shoots an arrow aiming at a bird but it hits a man.

The commission of an offence by mistake is not accountable and the offender shall not be liable for punishment on such offence. The Holy Qur'ān states:

لَيْسَ عَلَيْكُمْ جُنَاحٌ فِيمَا أَخْطَأْتُم بِهِ وَلَكِن مَّا تَعَمَّدَتْ قُلُوبُكُمْ

> And there is no sin for you in the acts you commit by mistake but that will be a sin for you which your hearts intend. (33:5)

The Holy Prophet said," The people of my community are exempted from the accountability of the acts done by mistake or obliviously or under duress."

Sometimes the mistake is the result of the negligence of the offender and in such a case the offender shall be accountable for his negligence and shall be punished for that such as negligent driving which causes injury to or death of another person.

However, punishment in case of mistake through negligence shall be less than the punishment in case of intentional commission of the said offence.

The jurists, however, differ in case of homicide where the victim is killed by mistake. Mistaking a person means that the offender intends to kill a definite person but kills someone else instead. For example, a person intends to kill Zaid and kills a person thinking that he is Zaid but later it is revealed that the victim was not Zaid but Bakar. According to Imām Mālik and some Ḥanbalīs the offender in this case shall be liable for intentional murder because he intended to kill a person and he actually killed a person irrespective of whom he killed as all human beings are equal in blood. But according to Imām Abū Ḥanīfah and Imām Shāfi'ī as well as some Ḥanbalīs if a person intends to kill a definite person but errs doing so and kills or hurts someone else or commits a conjectural error and realises afterwards that the victim was not the person he actually wanted to murder then the offender will be accountable for erroneous homicide or erroneous infliction of hurt, for the victim is not the person whom he actually intended to kill or hurt, and had he known that he was mistaken, he would never have committed this criminal act.[36]

1. Forgetfulness

Forgetfulness means not to be able to remember a thing when required. Under Islamic law forgetfulness equates to mistake. The Holy Qur'ān states:

رَبَّنَا لاَ تُؤَاخِذْنَا إِن نَّسِينَا أَوْ أَخْطَأْنَا

> Our Lord! Do not punish us if we forget or mistake. (2:286)

The Holy Prophet said, "My *Ummah* has been forgiven for mistake, and forgetfulness and the acts done under coercion".

Jurists differ on the question of the effect of forgetfulness on accountability. Some of them hold that forgetfulness is a common excuse for exemption from punishment. The general principle of

---

[36] Ibid., p. 438

Islamic law in this regard is that if anyone does an act unmindfully, he is not accountable for that and therefore, deserves no punishment. But if the unmindful person is exempted from criminal accountability, his civil accountability is not nullified; for Islamic law treats the life and property of human beings as protected and the excuse as admitted for criminal liability does not affect civil liability in the case of life and property. What this view comes to is that if the offender forgets that the act he is going to commit is unlawful and commits it notwithstanding, he will not be liable to punishment but unmindfulness does not invalidate the obligations, when he realizes his transgression; or else he would be awarded the prescribed punishment. There are other jurists who think that forgetting is not an excuse for application of injunctions to mundane affairs, save those pertaining to the rights of Allah. In the event of a violation of divine rights, forgetting is to be treated as an excuse only when a natural motive of the commission of crime exists, while there is nothing to remind the transgressor of the unlawfulness of the act he is about to commit. For instance, in eating and drinking unmindfully when one is fasting, a natural tendency is at work, but there is at the same time, nothing to remind the transgressor of the unlawfulness of his act. But in the case of violation of the right of an individual, forgetfulness can on no account be acceptable as an excuse.

Doubtless, there do exist such crimes which relate to the rights of Allah such as adultery and drinking, but it may be said of them that such cases are rare wherein forgetfulness is accepted as a lawful excuse; for a prohibited act is seldom forgotten. Moreover, there is the condition that a natural motive should be at work behind the criminal act the unmindful offender is going to commit, while there is nothing to remind him of its unlawfulness. For example, a person who has recently converted to Islam feels thirsty and drinks wine unlawfully. Or take another example, a man divorces his wife but unmindfully enters into sexual intercourse with her.

In the light of both the views discussed above, a mere contention of unmindfulness or forgetfulness is not enough for the exculpation of the offender. The first and foremost requirement which is absolutely essential is that the offender proves to have committed the offence unmindfully. Obviously, production of such a proof is extremely difficult. That is why the question of forgetfulness is of little consequence in a discussion of crimes. No person can prove on cogent grounds that he has been unmindfully guilty of an offence. According to the second view forgetfulness does not nullify obligations. These remain unaffected. If a person unmindfully guilty is necessarily liable to punishment, then forgetfulness will be treated as a case of doubt invalidating the *ḥadd*. He will be liable to *ta'zīr* punishment instead. Thus in accordance with the second view the effect of forgetfulness on crimes is confined to certain limits. Under some circumstances the punishment of an unmindful offender is remitted, while under other circumstances the punishment of *ḥadd* will be invalidated.[37]

2. Ignorance of law

One of the principles of Islamic law is that the offender is accountable for the commission of a forbidden act when he knows fully that the act is unlawful. If he is not aware of the unlawfulness thereof his accountability will not be valid.

Possibility of knowledge is sufficient for the knowledge of prohibition. If a man is sensible and can easily find out whether an act is prohibited or not; if he studies the prohibitory provisions of the Islamic law or enquires about it from the religious scholars then such a person will be deemed aware of forbidden acts and his plea of ignorance will not be admissible. The jurists concur on this point. "Excuse of ignorance of Islamic injunctions is not acceptable in an Islamic state". Hence every obligated person will be treated as having the knowledge of the Islamic injunctions on the basis of the possibility of knowing and the presence of knowledge is not necessary. For this reason, a prohibitory provision will be treated as if everyone knows it, provided that the possibility of acquiring its knowledge exists although most people may not actually be aware of it or may not be having a full knowledge thereof, provided that it is possible for all of them to acquire the knowledge of that prohibitory provision. In short Islamic law does not impose the condition of the knowledge thereof in practice. The reason for this is that such a condition would give rise to a very difficult situation. All the people when

---

[37] Ibid, p.430

called to account would come out with the excuse that they were ignorant of the unlawfulness of the act committed by them and thus all the provisions of law would be suspended.[38]

3. Omission

Sometimes a failure to take action constitutes a crime where such an action is required by the Islamic law or custom. For instance, if a person watches another person being drowned in a shallow pool or being burnt in a fire and whom he can save but does not and he dies thereof, he is responsible for his death as if he had intended to kill the victim. Similarly if a mother does not feed her baby, and he dies thereof, she shall be treated as a wilful killer of her baby, though she commits no positive crime. In the same way if a person imprisons another person and deprives him of food and water and he dies thereof, the person holding the victim prisoner is a wilful murderer of the victim as if he intended to kill him. The jurists differ on the point whether the person who causes omission is responsible for the crime committed in consequence thereof. Imām Mālik is of the view that he is responsible for that while Imām Abū Ḥanīfah and some Ḥanbalīs opine that he is not responsible for that. However, in every case of omission the person who fails to take action will not be held responsible for the crime resulting from this omission. He is amenable to accountability only in cases wherein it is binding upon him according to Islamic law or custom, or it is a condition of a valid contract not to omit that act.

4. Strict Liability

Crimes which do not require intention or even negligence are known as 'offences of strict liability'. These are the crimes that have obvious effects or at least a single element of such a crime is of an apparent significance. The Muslim jurists have not discussed the crimes of strict liability independently because they include them in *ta'zīr* which is determined by the legislature or court in accordance with the prevailing circumstances. However, there are certain examples in the works of the jurists that they consider crimes of strict liability and believe that the intention of the offender is not required for their proof. For instance, if a person

---

[38] Ibid., p. 441

commits contempt of the Holy Prophet in express contemptous words, he shall be punished for that and shall not be asked about his intention. Similarly, if a person sells or serves a famous dangerous drug he shall be punished and shall not be asked about his intention. In offences of strict liability, in which intention is not required, neither criminal intent nor culphable negligence is recognised as a necessary condition of responsibility, thus, defences like mistake are of no avail.

The greater the degree of social, moral and religious danger, the more likely is the offence to be interpreted as one of strict liability. Corruption, drugs, road accidents, pollution, obscene physical demonstrations and outraging religious feelings may be included in the offences of strict liability when they so qualify. However, it is up to the legislature to declare an offence as that of strict liability keeping in view its effects on the society. The need for the mental element is not ruled out in the proof of the offences of strict liability though a reasonable mistake as to the particular fact of such offence is not a defence. There may be other defences available in the case of an offence of strict liability such as compulsion. The Muslim jurists have been very cautious in declaring an offence as that of strict liability and exempting it from the proof of mental element because this is a deviation from the fundamental principle that the prosecution must prove the whole case.[39]

In modern law also the extensive use of offences of strict liability, even when so qualified, is to be deplored.

Accountability for dwelling

A single combat between two persons is called a duel whether mutually agreed or incidental. In a duel both the rivals are determined to kill or hurt each other. Any weapon can be used for a duel. Such a duel is allowed in war time with an opponent. But a duel in peace time which aims at killing or hurting the opponent is not allowed in Islam. However, a duel which aims at the demonstration of one's skill or superiority rather than torturing the rival, is a sport and is allowed in Islam such as wrestling.

---

[39] Ibid., p.446

If a person kills his rival in a duel aimed at killing and hurting each other, he shall be liable for the punishment of *qiṣāṣ* if he has killed him with the intention of killing. But if he wounded him and he died later on, the offender shall be liable for the punishment of quasi-intentional murder. Similarly in case of causing hurt to the rival, the offender shall be liable to the punishment of hurt.

Accountability in sports

Islam has stressed the importance of such sports which strengthen the body and cultivate the mind such as athletics and competitions of various kinds. The position of Islam regarding horsemanship and other valorous sports is absolutely clear. It has not only allowed them but also encouraged them. Thus the Holy Qur'ān says,

وَأَعِدُّواْ لَهُم مَّا اسْتَطَعْتُم مِّن قُوَّةٍ وَمِن رِّبَاطِ الْخَيْلِ

> Make ready for them all you can have of armed force and of horses tethered. (8:60)

The Holy Prophet said, 'A strong Muslim is better than a weaker Muslim." It is an established fact that the Holy Prophet won an event of race and took part in a camel race. Once when the Holy Prophet participated in a shooting competition with one of the archers, the rival archers withdrew and said, "In case of your joining the rival team, we cannot compete." The Holy Prophet replied that they should carry on as he was with all of them. The Holy Prophet threw down a wrestler named Rukhanah in a bout. It has also been related that the Holy Prophet threw a spear skillfully and rode a horse with and without a saddle.

The jurists therefore, unanimously opine that learning, establishing and developing any science, art or industry which is useful for the *Ummah* is compulsory on the Muslims as a whole. It is an imperative duty of the Muslims to practise and develop sports specially that which constitutes demonstration of courage, valour and force. Islam further allows compensations and prizes to those who compete in games.

In martial arts and sports the players and spectators are likely to receive injuries and sometimes one of them may be killed. The principle of Islamic law in this regard is that if sports do not involve violence and force, then the cases of death and injuries will be decided according to the general cases of death and hurts in Islamic criminal law because injuries and blows in such cases are not a part of the games. But if a sport involves use of force against the antagonist such as in wrestling, boxing, football, hockey, racing, and polo. If a player causes hurt or even death to another player or spectator during one of these games, the player concerned shall not be punished for that provided that he does not infringe the prescribed rules of the game. It is based on the reasoning that these injuries naturally result from such sports and there is no accountability for such injuries. But, if a player causes hurt or death to any other player or spectator in contravention of the prescribed rules of sports or commits it intentionally, he shall be liable for the punishment prescribed for such offence in Islamic criminal law. However, general death and hurts caused in sports are exempted from criminal accountability.

Equality

Another principle of the Islamic criminal law is equality before law and equal protection to all the members of the society. The Holy Qur'ān states:

يَا أَيُّهَا النَّاسُ إِنَّا خَلَقْنَاكُم مِّن ذَكَرٍ وَأُنثَى وَجَعَلْنَاكُمْ شُعُوبًا وَقَبَائِلَ لِتَعَارَفُوا إِنَّ أَكْرَمَكُمْ عِندَ اللَّهِ أَتْقَاكُمْ

> O Mankind! We have created you from a man and a woman, and have made you nations and tribes that you may know one another. The noblest among you, in the sight of Allah, is the one who is the best in conduct. (49:13)

The Holy Prophet said, "People are like the teeth of a comb".[40] The Holy Prophet said, "No Arab has superiority over a non-Arab nor any non-Arab over an Arab, nor any white man over a black man, nor a black man over a white man, save in respect of piety."[41]

---

[40] *Ṣaḥīḥ Muslim*, p.194

[41] Ibid.

The best example of equality before law has been furnished by the reaction of the Holy Prophet to a recommendation made by a Companion to him in favour of a woman thief against the imposition of the punishment of *ḥadd.* The Holy Prophet said, "By Allah if Fāṭimah the daughter of Muḥammad (p.b.u.h.) had committed theft, I would have certainly cut off her hand." The Holy Prophet then stood and addressed the congregation and said,

> "No doubt the earlier people were ruined as they left unpunished those among them who committed theft but were influential and imposed *ḥadd* on those among them who committed theft but were weak".[42]

The equality enjoined by the *Sharī'ah* is unconditional and unqualified that admits of no justification to discriminate in favour of one individual against another individual, one group against another group, one sex against another sex, one race or colour against another race or colour, a powerful person against a poor person and the ruler against the ruled. All the Islamic criminal laws are equally applicable to all the inhabitants of an Islamic state irrespective of cast, colour, region, position or religion. The Islamic criminal law is international in its nature but is territorial in its application and is applicable in an Islamic state only unless a non-Muslim state makes it applicable to its Muslims or all inhabitants.

Purpose of punishment

Since prohibition of acts is governed by consideration of common good, punishment is laid down for them. Punishment is an effective way to safeguard society against crimes and is thus a social necessity. The Holy Qur'ān states:

مَن يَعْمَلْ سُوءًا يُجْزَ بِه

Whoever works evil, will be requited accordingly. (4:123)

As punishment is a collective need it should remain within the limits of need. It will be wrong to let punishment exceed the quantum needed for collective security and prevention of harm to

---

[42] Muḥammad ibn Sulaymān al-Maghribī, *Jam' al-Fawā'id*, vol.1 p.499

social life resulting from the incident of crime, just as it will be wrong to let punishment fall short of the quantum needed to safeguard society against crimes.

The punishments must contain the following considerations:

(i) The punishment other than *ḥadd* or *qiṣāṣ* should be such as may serve to admonish and reform the offender and prevent him from committing the crime again. It should be flexible enough to enable the court to choose the kind of punishment suited to the circumstances of the case and to determine such quantity thereof as would serve the purpose. It requires diversity of punishment i.e. different kinds of punishments for the same offence and punishments with maximum and minimum limits enabling the court to choose the kind of punishment to be awarded and to determine its quantum between the two extremes.

(ii) The punishment should serve as a deterrent specially in a grievous offence to one who is not an offender so much so that if he thinks over the offence and the punishment thereof, he realizes that the potential damage resulting from the punishment is far greater than the benefits that are likely to accrue from the offence.

The punishment being commensurate with the crime, must be applicable to every offender committing the said offence without any discrimination.

Classification of Crimes

The Jurists have discussed three classifications of crimes on different aspects, namely:

1. classification according to punishment;
2. classification according to intention; and
3. classification according to violation of rights.

1. Classification according to punishment

Crimes in Islamic criminal law have been classified into three kinds on the basis of the quantum of punishment.

(i) *Qiṣāṣ* and *diyat* (crimes of retaliation and blood money);
(ii) *Ḥudūd* (crimes of fixed punishments) and
(iii) *Ta'zīrāt* (crimes of discretionary punishment)

(i) *Qiṣāṣ* and *Diyāt* (crimes of retaliation and blood money)

In Islamic criminal law punishments for some crimes have been provided by way of retaliation or blood money which are called *Qiṣāṣ* and *Diyāt*. These punishments have been prescribed as rights of the individuals which can be remitted or altered by the victim or his legal heirs. These are as follow:

a) Intentional murder;
b) Quasi-intentional murder;
c) Murder as a result of mistake; and
d) Hurts.[43]

(ii) *Ḥudūd* (crimes of fixed punishments)

These are the crimes for which the kind and the quantum of punishment has been fixed by the Qur'ān or *Sunnah* of the Prophet (S.A.W) as a right of God. These punishments can neither be increased nor decreased nor altered.[44] The following are some of these crimes:

(a) Adultery
(b) False accusation of adultery
(c) Theft
(d) Dacoity and robbery
(e) Drinking wine
(f) Apostasy

(iii) *Ta'zīrāt* (crimes of discretionary punishments)

Crimes other than those liable to *Ḥudūd, Qiṣāṣ* and *Diyat* are the crimes for which punishments have not been fixed by the Qur'ān or *Sunnah* of the Prophet (S.A.W) and their punishments have been left to the discretion of the legislator or judge to prescribe them in accordance with the circumstances. These crimes are innumerable and are called *Ta'zīrāt*.

---

[43] 'Abd al-'Azīz 'Āmir, *al-Ta'zīr fī al-Sharī'ah al-Islāmiyyah*, pp.38-40
[44] Al-Kasānī, *Badā'i' al-Ṣanā'i'*, vol.7, p.33

1. Classification according to intention

Regarding intention the crimes have been divided into two kinds:

(i) Intentional crimes, and
(ii) Un-intentional crimes

(i) Intentional crimes

These are the crimes wherein the criminal commits a crime knowing that he is committing an illegal act and understands the result of his act like intentional homicide, intentional hurt, etc. Any criminal who commits a crime with intention and knows that he is committing an illegal act shall be liable for the full punishment prescribed for the crime.[45] The willful commission of a crime liable to *ḥadd* or *qiṣāṣ* has no concern with the motive of the offender. However, motive helps in determining the intention of the offender.

(ii) Un-intentional crimes

In these crimes the criminal does not intend to commit a crime but the crime is committed by him through negligence or mistake, for example;

(a) The criminal drives a car and does not follow the traffic rules and all of a sudden meets with an accident and kills another person therein.

(b) The criminal does not even intend the act. For instance, overcoming of a heavy person who is sleeping on a weak person lying nearby and killing him.[46]

1. Classification according to violation of rights

The crimes on the basis of violation of rights have been divided into two kinds:

(i) crimes against the public and
(ii) crimes against individuals.

---

[45] 'Awdah, *al-Tashrī' al-Jinā'ī*, vol.1, pp.343-49
[46] Ibid., pp.83-84

(i) Crimes against public

These are the crimes which are preponderantly injurious to the society at large. Such crimes may be committed against individuals as well as against the public. According to the jurists they are called rights of Allah. A right is ascribed to Allah when it is purely in the interests of the community or wherein collective interest is predominant. Such crimes are punished to safeguard the interest of the society. Their punishments cannot be pardoned, diminished or extinguished by anyone. These crimes are called crimes liable to *ḥudūd* such as *zina,* theft, dacoity.

(ii) Crimes against individuals

These crimes directly affect the individuals though they are injurious to the public as well. According to the jurists they are called rights of individuals because they directly affect the interest of the individual and an individual can give up his right and can remit or compound the punishment. The crimes of *qiṣāṣ* (retaliation) and *diyāt* (blood money) are the instances of these crimes.[47]

It is pertinent to mention here that the distinction between the rights of God and the rights of the individual is made on the basis of the respective interests of the community and the individual. Assigning a particular interest or right to one or the other of these categories is purely a matter of juristic opinion. The specific definitions of *ḥudūd* by relating them to the rights of God and the rights of individuals and the consequences that have ensued from these formulations may be regarded as instances of juristic interpretation which might have served a good purpose but it is a fact that they have no origin in the Qur'ān and *Sunnah.* Basically all rights in Islam have been granted by Allah Almighty which are exercised and represented by the community of believers and their lawful government. Thus the rights of God and the rights of the individual are not totally separate from one another and violating the one often means automatic violation of the other. It may be concluded that all crimes consist of the violation of the limits of God and His Prophet, and the community and its leadership are

---

[47] Ibid., vol.2, p.99

within their rights to take all necessary measures to defend their common interests against criminality and violence without the need to draw hard and fast divisions between public and private interests.[48]

Difference of opinion among the jurists

The Muslim jurists of different schools of thought, according to their research, have adopted different views in many of the points relating to the Islamic criminal law.

However, the jurists agree that in matters relating to the Islamic criminal law, the court may not confine itself to the opinions of one sect or Imām (jurist) but may adopt any view among the views of different jurists, on the fact in issue, which is more suitable in the circumstances of a particular case or may adopt a different view compatible with the principles described therein. Islamic criminal law is a public law and is equally applicable to all the inhabitants of an Islamic state including non-Muslims and as such any particular sect or jurist should not be followed strictly. The differences of the jurists elaborate different aspects of any point of the Islamic criminal law and help in the conclusion of any such matter disputed in a court. The Muslim jurists have conducted considerable research on all aspects of the Islamic criminal law which is really a guide and model for the modern world in general and the Muslim world in particular. The scholarly discussions of the Muslim jurists in their innumerable books on Islamic criminal law denote that the Islamic criminal law has the capability of application in all times and places.

Applicability to Muslims and non-Muslims

Islamic criminal law is equally applicable to both Muslims and non-Muslims. For example, the punishment of *qiṣāṣ* in case of intentional murder is equal both for Muslims and non-Muslims residing in an Islamic state. If a Muslim murders a non-Muslim he shall be liable for *qiṣāṣ*. Similarly if a non-Muslim murders another non-Muslim he shall be liable for *qiṣāṣ* so also if he murders a Muslim. The blood and property of a non-Muslim are as sacred in Islam as that of a Muslim. The Holy Prophet said about

[48] Shahāb al-Dīn al-Qarāfī, *Kitāb al-Furūq*, p.141

non-Muslims, "For them what is for us and on them what is on us". In the same way the offences liable to *ḥudūd* are also equally applicable to both Muslims and non-Muslims because all these are common offences and are meant for the maintenance of peace in society. There is no discrimination between Muslims and non-Muslims with respect to the punishments of *ḥudūd*, *qiṣāṣ* and *diyat*. The discrimination between Muslims and non-Muslims arises only in an offence which is based on the violation of any religious command relating to personal laws, worship or rites. For example if non-Muslims believe that their religion has not prohibited them from drinking wine or any other intoxicating liquor, they will not be punished for drinking, but they will only be prohibited to drink publicly before the Muslims. As far as the offences liable to *ta'zīr* are concerned, they are equally applicable to Muslims and non-Muslims.

Chapter Two

Offence of Murder

The most atrocious act in Islam is murder, which means an act of a person causes the death of another person. The blood of a human being is sacred in Islam. The Holy Qur'ān says:

مَن قَتَلَ نَفْسًا بِغَيْرِ نَفْسٍ أَوْ فَسَادٍ فِي الأَرْضِ فَكَأَنَّمَا قَتَلَ النَّاسَ جَمِيعًا

Whoever kills a person for other than manslaughter or corruption in the land, it shall be as if he had killed all mankind and whoever saves the life of one person, it shall be as if he had saved the life of all mankind.(5:32)

وَمَن يَقْتُلْ مُؤْمِنًا مُّتَعَمِّدًا فَجَزَآؤُهُ جَهَنَّمُ خَالِدًا فِيهَا وَغَضِبَ اللَّهُ عَلَيْهِ وَلَعَنَهُ وَأَعَدَّ لَهُ عَذَابًا عَظِيمًا

If a person kills a believer intentionally, his recompense is Hell, to abide therein (forever), and the wrath and the curse of God are upon him'. (4:93)

وَلاَ تَقْتُلُواْ النَّفْسَ الَّتِي حَرَّمَ اللَّهُ إِلاَّ بِالْحَقِّ ذَلِكُمْ وَصَّاكُمْ بِهِ لَعَلَّكُمْ تَعْقِلُونَ

And slay not the life which Allah has made sacred, save in the course of justice. This He has commanded you, in order that you may discern. (6:151)

وَمَا كَانَ لِمُؤْمِنٍ أَن يَقْتُلَ مُؤْمِنًا إِلاَّ خَطَئًا وَمَن قَتَلَ مُؤْمِنًا خَطَئًا فَتَحْرِيرُ رَقَبَةٍ مُّؤْمِنَةٍ وَدِيَةٌ مُّسَلَّمَةٌ إِلَى أَهْلِهِ إِلاَّ أَن يَصَّدَّقُواْ فَإِن كَانَ

مِن قَوْمٍ عَدُوٍّ لَّكُمْ وَهُوَ مُؤْمِنٌ فَتَحْرِيرُ رَقَبَةٍ مُّؤْمِنَةٍ وَإِن كَانَ مِن قَوْمٍ بَيْنَكُمْ وَبَيْنَهُمْ مِّيثَاقٌ فَدِيَةٌ مُّسَلَّمَةٌ إِلَى أَهْلِهِ وَتَحْرِيرُ رَقَبَةٍ مُّؤْمِنَةً فَمَن لَّمْ يَجِدْ فَصِيَامُ شَهْرَيْنِ مُتَتَابِعَيْنِ

It is not for a believer to kill a believer unless it be by mistake. He who kills a believer by mistake must set free a believing slave and pay compensation to the family of the deceased unless they remit it freely. If the deceased belongs to a people at war with you and he is a believer, the freeing of a believing slave (is enough). And if he belongs to a people with whom you have a treaty of mutual alliance, compensation should be paid to his family and a believing slave be freed. For those who find this beyond their means, a fast for two consecutive months. (4:92)

وَلاَ تَقْتُلُواْ النَّفْسَ الَّتِي حَرَّمَ اللّهُ إِلاَّ بِالحَقِّ

And slay not the life which Allah has forbidden save with right. (17:33)

The Prophet (p.b.u.h.) said;

اول ما يحاسب به يوم القيامة الدماء

The first thing about which Allah will ask for on the Day of judgement is murders.[1]

The Prophet (p.b.u.h) on his last pilgrimage declared;

ان دماءكم واموالكم واعراضكم حرامكم عليكم كحرمة يومكم هذا و بلدكم

Your blood, your property and your prestige are as sacred as this city (Haram of Makkah) and this day (day of Arafah).[2]

---

[1] Muslim, *Sahīḥ Muslim,* p.248

[2] Imām Aḥmad ibn Ḥanbal, *Al-Musnad,* vol.3, p.138

According to the majority of the jurists, murder in Islamic criminal law is of three kinds, namely:

(i) Intentional murder (*Qatl-al-'amd)*
(ii) Quasi-intentional murder (*Qatl-Shibh-al-'amd*) and
(iii) Murder by mistake (*Qatl-al-Khatā'*)

Imām Mālik is of the view that murder is only of two kinds, namely:

(i) Intentional murder and
(ii) Murder by mistake

Imām Abū Ḥanīfah opines that murder is of five kinds:

(i) Intentional murder;
(ii) Quasi-intentional murder;
(iii) Murder by mistake;
(iv) Murder equivalent to mistake; and
(v) Indirect murder.[3]

1. Intentional murder (*Qatl al-amd*)

Intentional murder is a murder when an adult and sane person willfully and with the intention of causing death makes another person the direct object of his action which in general is fatal and that person dies as a result of that action. The jurists have stated that there are three basic conditions for incriminating an adult and sane person for committing intentional murder:

(i) The victim must be a living human being,
(ii) The victim must have died as a result of the action of the accused and
(iii) The offender has willful intention of causing death of the victim.

(i) The victim must be a living and protected human being

The first condition for intentional murder is that the victim must be a living human being at the time of death. His caste, colour, territory, religion, sex, status, health and age are not relevant. Thus, if a person, with the intention of causing death, attacks a

[3] 'Awdah, *al-Tashrī' al-Jinā'ī al-Islāmī*,. vol.2, p.7-9

dead person with a deadly weapon, he is not liable to intentional murder. In the same way if a person causes death of a child in the womb of the mother, he will not be liable to intentional murder. Similarly if a person causes death of an animal with the intention of causing death by doing an act which in the ordinary course of nature is likely to cause death, is not liable to intentional murder. If a person, with the intention of causing death, wounds another person grievously, which may or may not cause his death; but meanwhile another person by using a deadly weapon causes his death, then, according to the majority of jurists the second person is liable to intentional murder and not the first one. The first one is liable to the hurt he causes.[4]

Further the victim being a human being must be a protected person. All Muslims, non-Muslims who permanently reside in an Islamic state, non-Muslims who are either in a treaty or not at war with the Muslims and non-Muslims who enter an Islamic state with permission - all are protected persons in Islamic criminal law and their blood and property are inviolable and if anyone of them is murdered by a person, he will be liable to *qiṣāṣ*. The non-Muslims who are at war with the Muslims are not protected in Islamic criminal law. Thus, if a Muslim causes the death of any of such non-Muslims whether in the battle-field or otherwise he will not be liable to *qiṣāṣ*. Imām Abū Ḥanīfah is, however, of the view that a Muslim who resides in a non-Muslim country, which is at war with the Muslims, is not protected and if any person causes his death, he will not be liable to *qiṣāṣ* i.e. death. He argues that the basis of protection is an Islamic state which possesses the force of the implementation of the Islamic law.[5] But according to Imām Mālik, Imām Shafi'ī and Imām Aḥmad a Muslim is protected everywhere even in a country which is at war with the Islamic state because the basis of his protection is Islam.[6]

Similarly if a person causes the death of another protected person, he does not remain protected for the heirs of the murdered person and if any of his heirs causes the death of the murderer, he shall not be liable to intentional murder and shall be liable to

---

[4] Ibn Nujaym, *al-Baḥr al-Rā'iq,* vol.3, p.295

[5] Ibn Qudāmah, *al-Mughnī,* vol.9, p.327

[6]-Kasānī, *Bada'i al-Sana'i,* vol. 3, p.252

ta'zīr to be fixed in accordance with the circumstances. Moreover the rebels who start war against an Islamic state are not protected during war and if a Muslim causes death of any one of them during the war, he shall not be liable to *qiṣāṣ*. In the same way if a person commits a crime liable to death as *ḥadd* like dacoity and robbery, he does not remain protected and if any person causes his death, he shall not be liable to intentional murder, but shall be liable to *ta'zīr*.[7]

(ii) Murder must be the result of the act of the accused

The second condition for intentional murder is that the murder must be the result of a fatal act of the accused. Thus, if the act of the accused is not of the nature which in the ordinary course is likely to cause death, he will not be liable to intentional murder. Moreover the act must have been done by the accused and not suspected to have been done by someone else. The victim must have died of the act of the offender without any gap sufficient for recovery or for a fatal attack by another person.

According to the majority of the jurists, the use of a deadly weapon, like a heavy stone, club or hammer, or strangulation, or administering poison are included in the acts which are likely to cause death. However, it has been left to the court to determine as to which is likely to cause death and which is not in the circumstances of a particular case. In all such cases the offender shall be liable to intentional murder.[8] It has been related that a Jewish woman offered a poisonous piece of mutton to the Prophet and he ate some of it but threw it after a while. One of his Companions named Bishar, who was with him at that time, also ate from it. Later on Bishar died because of it. On the death of Bishar, Prophet ordered that the Jewish woman be put to death. Similarly, death caused by fire or throwing into deep water shall amount to intentional murder, if under ordinary circumstances it is not possible for the victim to survive.[9]

In order to determine whether an act by which death is caused is likely to cause death or not, the means by which death is caused,

---

[7] 'Awdah, *al-Tashrī' al-Jinā'ī al-Islāmī*, vol. 2, pp. 15-16
[8] Ibid., pp.25-26
[9] Syed Sabiq, *Fiqh al-Sunnah,* vol.2, p.437

environment, weather, custom and usage, the opinion of an expert and the physical condition of the accused and the victim shall be taken into consideration.[10]

According to Imām Mālik, if a person causes the death of another person with the intention of causing death, it will be considered intentional murder whether he has used a deadly weapon, heavy stone, wood or any other thing, or has used any other method for causing his death such as strangulation and whether his act is generally fatal or not.[11]

According to Imām Shāfi'ī and Imām Aḥmad murder will be considered intentional murder if the accused has used such a weapon or such a method which in general is likely to cause death. But if the accused has used such a thing or such a method which in general does not cause death like beating with a stick, he will not be liable to intentional murder. They rely on a *ḥadīth* related on the authority of 'Abd Allāh bin 'Abbās that the Prophet said,"If a person kills another person by throwing a stone, by whip or by a staff, he will be liable to *diyat* like that of the murder by mistake". However, they opine that in order to determine whether a weapon or any other thing used in the commission of the offence, is fatal or not, other circumstances with respect to the accused and his act may also be taken into consideration.[12]

Imām Abū Ḥanīfah limits intentional murder to the use of a weapon or of a thing which can be used like a weapon which cuts off limbs like a gun, razor, or knife. Thus if a person causes death of another person with a large unsharpened stone or a big stick, he will not be liable to intentional murder. But Imām Abū Yūsuf and Imām Muḥammad do not agree with the opinion of Imām Abū Ḥanīfah and they have adopted the view of Imām Shāfi'ī and Imām Aḥmad that a murder with anything which is generally fatal will be considered intentional murder. This is the preferred opinion among Hanafites.[13]

Sometimes the act of the offender directly causes the death of the victim, for example, shooting him with a gun, or slaughtering

---

[10] Ibid., p.28

[11] Mālik bin Anas, *Al-Mudawwanah,* vol. 3, p.108

[12] Ibn Qudāmah, *al-Mughnī*, vol.9, pp.321-22

[13] Al-Kāsānī, *Badā'i' al-Ṣanā'i,* vol.7, p.233

him with a razor and sometimes it indirectly causes the death of another person, for example, to compel someone to murder him, to give false evidence against him in a murder case with which he is punished with *qiṣāṣ* (retaliation) or offering him poisonous food that causes his death. In all such cases the offender will be liable to intentional murder if he acts with the intention of causing the death of the victim. This is the opinion of the majority of the jurists. But Imām Abū Ḥanīfah differentiates between the punishment of murder caused by a direct act of the offender and the punishment of murder caused by an indirect act of the offender. He considers the first to be punished with *qiṣāṣ* (i.e. death) and the second with *diyat.*[14]

Death caused by two or more persons jointly

If two or more persons jointly cause the death of any other person by taking practical part in it, all of them shall be liable to intentional murder. This is based on the decision of Ḥaḍrat 'Umar. In the period of Ḥaḍrat 'Umar a husband of a woman in the city of San'a went missing and he had one son from his previous wife. Meanwhile, this woman developed illicit relations with another man. This woman told her new friend to kill this young son of her missing husband. He refused at first, but when the woman insisted, he agreed to kill the young boy. Thus, one day the friend of that woman, another person, she herself and one of her servants jointly killed the young son of her missing husband, cut off his limbs and threw him in a well. But when the matter leaked out and news spread among the people, the governor of Yemen arrested the friend of that woman and he disclosed the whole story of the case and confessed to the commission of the offence. All of them were arrested and they all confessed to the offence. The governor informed Caliph 'Umar of the case. Ḥaḍrat 'Umar ordered him to execute all of them and said, "If all the inhabitants of San'a had joined in it, I would have executed all of them".[15]

---

[14] 'Awdah, *al-Tashrī' al-Jinā'ī al-Islāmī,* vol.2, p.36

[15] Ibn Ḥajar al-Asqalānī, *Bulūgh al-Marām*, Tradition No. 1203

It has been related from Ḥaḍrat 'Alī that he ordered the killing of three persons who had jointly killed another person.[16]

Thus according to the jurists, if two or more persons cause the death of another person jointly and the act of each of them is individually sufficient to cause death, all of them shall be liable to intentional murder. Similarly, all of them shall be liable to intentional murder if their acts cannot be identified or distinguished as to whose act is sufficient to cause death and whose act is not. This is the opinion of Imām Mālik, some Ḥanafites and some Shāfi'īs. But according to Imām Abū Ḥanīfah, Imām Shāfi'ī and Imām Aḥmad, all of them shall not be liable to intentional murder in the second case but shall be liable to the hurts caused. And if their acts can be distinguished or identified then the offender whose act is individually sufficient to cause death shall be liable to intentional murder. The offender whose act is individually not sufficient to cause death shall be liable according to the nature of his act. If the act of none of them is individually sufficient to cause death and death is caused as a result of the cumulative effect of the acts of all of them in furtherance of a plan, then all those offenders who are directly involved in the commission of the offence shall be liable to intentional murder. The offenders who are not directly involved in the commission of offence shall be liable according to the nature of their acts, but if the death is caused without a plan, they all shall be liable to quasi-intentional murder. Moreover if two or more offenders cause hurts one after the other without a plan and such hurts result in the death of the victim, the offender causing the hurt, which in the ordinary course of nature is likely to cause death, shall be liable to intentional murder and the other offenders shall be liable according to the nature of the hurt caused by each of them. If their hurts cannot be identified as to whose hurt is fatal and whose hurt is not fatal, then there is a difference of opinion among the jurists. According to some jurists, all of them shall be liable to intentional murder while others opine that all of them shall be liable for hurts alone.[17]

---

[16] Ibn Qudāmah, *al-Mughnī*, vol.9, pp.365-66

[17] 'Awdah, *al-Tashrī' al-Jinā'ī al-Islāmī*, vol.2, pp.41-45

(i) The offender must have the intention to cause death of the victim

The third condition, and the main ingredient of intentional murder, is that the offender must have intended to cause death of the victim. Criminal intention means willingness of a person to do a prohibited act or refrain from a mandatory act knowing that the act he is going to commit or omit is forbidden. The Holy Qur'ān states:

وَلَيْسَ عَلَيْكُمْ جُنَاحٌ فِيمَا أَخْطَأْتُم بِهِ وَلَكِن مَّا تَعَمَّدَتْ قُلُوبُكُمْ

> There is no blame on you if you make a mistake; What counts is the intention of your hearts. (33:5)

The Prophet said, "Actions are rewarded according to intentions."[18] The Holy Qur'ān, while condemning murder, states:

وَمَن يَقْتُلْ مُؤْمِنًا مُّتَعَمِّدًا فَجَزَآؤُهُ جَهَنَّمُ خَالِدًا فِيهَا وَغَضِبَ اللَّهُ عَلَيْهِ وَلَعَنَهُ وَأَعَدَّ لَهُ عَذَابًا عَظِيمًا

> If a person kills a believer intentionally, his recompense is Hell, to abide therein forever (long time), and the wrath and the curse of God are upon him. (4:93)

In this verse the Qur'ān has expressly used the word 'intention' which shows that the intention of the offender to cause death of the victim by his act which actually causes his death is necessary for his liability to intentional murder. In the absence of the intention to cause death of the victim, the offender shall not be liable to intentional murder. Thus if a person beats or attacks another person without having the intention of causing him death and he dies as a result of that beating or attack, he shall not be liable to intentional murder. However, as the intention is a secret thing and cannot be determined precisely, except by the confession of the offender, the jurists have not discussed it independently in detail but they, in case of the absence of the confession of the offender, usually take into consideration the weapon used, the evidence produced and the relevant circumstances which help in

---

[18] Al-Bukhārī, *Saḥīḥ*, p.2

determining the intention of the accused. The jurists concur that if an offender uses a deadly weapon and the victim dies as a result of that the offender will be considered to have committed intentional murder because the use of a deadly weapon denotes his intention to cause the death of the victim. Likewise, if a person throws another person from a high place into deep water from where he cannot escape and dies therein, the offender will be liable to intentional murder, because his intention is obvious from his act. Sometimes previous enmity between the accused and the victim or any obvious ignoble motive of the accused establishes that the offender might have intended to cause the death of the victim. However, all these sources are not certain and require to be looked into thoroughly by searching for other corroborations so as to reach a degree of certainty so that guilt is proved beyond any reasonable doubt.

> It is relevant to mention that to Islamic criminal law it matters little whether the motive of the offender in an offence of intentional murder, is noble or is ignoble, motive has nothing to do with the criminal intent, nor does it affect the pattern of crime or its punishment. Motive, however, helps in determining the intention of the offender. Moreover, the testimony of two credible witnesses on the commission of his offence also establishes the intention of the accused.[19]

Causing death under compulsion

Compulsion (اکراہ) means to cause a person by force to do an act without his consent and choice by threatening him with death, grievous hurt or heavy financial loss and the person being put under compulsion is reasonably apprehensive that such will be the consequence if he does not obey the person causing compulsion. Some jurists have divided compulsion into two kinds, namely;

(i) Complete compulsion (اکراہ تام)

(ii) Incomplete compulsion (اکراہ ناقص)

---

[19] 'Awdah, *al-Tashrī' al-Jinā'ī al-Islāmī*,, pp.79-83

Complete compulsion means compulsion wherein the person compelled is threatened with instant loss of life or lives and incomplete compulsion means compulsion wherein the compelled person is threatened with less than instant loss of life.[20] According to the majority of the jurists, only complete compulsion is effective in grievous offences like murder and hurt and not the imperfect compulsion. But some jurists, however, opine that any compulsion is effective in offences of murder and hurt wherein a powerful person forces another person to do an act without consent by threatening him of loss of life, grievous hurt or heavy financial loss and the person being put under compulsion is reasonably under the apprehension that such act will otherwise be the consequence if he does not obey the person causing compulsion. Incomplete compulsion is however, effective in other than grievous offences.[21] Compulsion is sometimes practical wherein threat and intimidation has been translated into action and sometimes it is inherent wherein threat and intimidation is apprehended. The Holy Qur'ān states, "save him who is forced thereto and whose heart is still content with faith."[22] The Holy Prophet said, "My Ummah has been exempted from the liability of any act done by mistake, forgetfulness or under compulsion".[23]

Conditions of compulsion

Jurists have laid down the following four conditions for the validity of compulsion:

1. The threat should be serious and of great harm so as to neutralize the consent of the person under compulsion, for example, death, grievous injury or long confinement. The seriousness of the threat is determined according to the position of the person under compulsion. The same threat may constitute compulsion for one person and not for another. Moreover in the case of murder, threat of beating and confinement is not compulsion whereas in the case of drinking and larceny it constitutes compulsion. The jurists

[20] Ibn Nujaym, *al-Baḥr al-Rā'iq,* vol. 3, p. 80
[21] 'Awdah, *al-Tashrī' al-Jinā'ī al-Islāmī,* vol. 1, pp.563-64
[22] Qur'ān, 16:106
[23] 'Awdah, *al-Tashrī' al-Jinā'ī al-Islāmī,* vol.1, p.565

concur that the threat of railing, vituperation and calumniation is not compulsion.[24]

The order of a competent authority will be treated as compulsion if it implies punishment of death, grievous hurt or imprisonment for the disobedient. But in the case of an order given by an official who is not vested with powers is not treated compulsion.[25]

According to Imām Mālik, Imām Shāfi'ī and Imām Aḥmad threat to destroy property also constitutes compulsion provided the said property is substantial. The quantum or value of such property is relative to the person and his status. A specific quantum of property may constitute compulsion for one person but may not for another.[26]

According to Imām Abū Ḥanīfah threat to destroy property is not compulsion because the object of the threat is a person and not property. However, some Hanafites opine that threat to destroy such part of the property whose destruction may involve substantial loss to the owner does constitute compulsion.[27]

2. Threat should be of immediate nature. It should be such a threat that if the person under compulsion does not do the desired act at once, it will be translated into action immediately. If the threat does not require immediate action, it will not be deemed a threat liable for compulsion, since it will provide for the person under compulsion time enough to make arrangements for his protection.
3. The person causing the threat must be powerful enough to carry out what he threatens to do. It is not necessary that the person threatening should be in authority such as an officer or a public servant.
4. The person under compulsion must believe that if he does not perform the act he is being threatened to do, the threat held out to him will be carried out.

It is pertinent to mention that contrary to the state of compulsion, the state of necessity does not affect the offences of

[24] Ibn Qudāmah, *al-Mughnī*, vol.3, p.261
[25] Ibn 'Ābidīn, *Radd al-Muḥtār*, vol.3, p.322
[26] Ibn Qudāmah, *al-Mughnī*, vol.3, pp.261-62
[27] Ibn Nujaym, *al-Baḥr al-Rā'iq*, vol.3, p.82

murder or hurt. However the state of necessity is effective in an offence exclusively related to eating and drinking. For instance eating of carion or swines' flesh and drinking of blood are allowed in a state of necessity provided that the commission of such acts is confined to the fulfilment of necessity.

If a person compels another person to kill a person by threatening him with death etc and the person being compelled kills that person, there is a difference of opinion among the jurists in this case. According to Imām Abū Ḥanīfah the compeller will be liable to intentional murder and not the compelled one because the action of a compelled person has no liability. He bases his view on a *ḥadīth* of the Prophet (p.b.u.h) who said, "My Ummah has been exempted from what they do by mistake, forgetfulness or under compulsion". The compelled offender in such a case, however, will be liable to *ta'zīr* to be fixed according to the circumstances of the case. But according to Imām Mālik, Imām Shāfi'ī and Imām Aḥmad both the compeller and the compelled will be liable to intentional murder because the compeller is the real cause of the death of the victim and the compelled actually kills him in order to save himself which is not allowed in a murder case due to the sanctity of human blood. Some of the Shāfītes opine that the offender in a such case will be punished with *ta'zīr* because compulsion creates doubt which removes the punishment of *qiṣāṣ* i.e. death. However, compulsion is effective in offences other than intentional murder and it removes punishment from the person under compulsion.

Causing death as a part of one's lawful duty

The Islamic law has imposed certain duties on the public authority and to discharge these duties is the responsibility of the public servants who are appointed by the Government. Thus if a public servant causes death to any person in the due discharge of his duty, he shall not be accountable for that on criminal ground. However, the public servant must remain within the limits of his duties failing which he may be liable for criminal accountability to the extent of his violating such limits to be determined under the circumstances of the case. The general rule of Islamic law is that if a public servant does anything in the due discharge of his duties he will not be accountable for that on criminal grounds even if the act he does is one forbidden by Islam, such as murder. If a policeman fires on a mob on the order of his officer and causes the death of any person or persons he will not be liable for any accountability for that. Similarly if a judge who passes the order of causing death to an offender and the law enforcing persons execute that punishment, neither judge nor the executors shall be liable for accountability on criminal grounds. However, the command of the person in authority should not be inconsistent with the doctrines of Islam while the person subject to his command should not obey him in contravention of the injunctions of Islam. The Holy Prophet said, "No created being should be obeyed in violation of the creator's command". None can make anything lawful what Allah has made unlawful.

Willingness to be killed

If a person permits or desires another person to kill him and he kills him on the basis of such permission, there is a difference of opinion among the jurists on this point. According to Imām Abū Ḥanīfah permission of the victim to be killed does not warrant the validity of the homicide. The Ḥanafis, however, hold that permission creates doubt and nullifies *qiṣāṣ*. The offender will be liable to *diyat*. According to the preferred view of Imām Mālik, permission of the victim does not warrant homicide and as such the offender shall be liable to *qiṣāṣ*. Some Mālikīs, however, consider permission as giving rise to doubt which removes *qiṣāṣ*. There are two views among Shāfi'īs, one that permission creates doubt and removes *qiṣāṣ* and the other that permission of the victim invalidates both *qiṣāṣ* and *diyat* but does not make the act of homicide lawful. According to Imām Aḥmad there is no responsibility on the person who kills such a person because this was the right of the victim and he has given his consent before his death.[28] The later jurists have preferred the view of Imām Mālik.

Abetment and instigation in murder

If a person abets, induces, instigates or conspires in the commission of an intentional murder but does not take practical part in the killing of the victim, he will not be liable to intentional

[28] 'Awdah, *al-Tashrī' al-Jinā'ī al-Islāmī,* vol.2 pp.88-89

murder. Anyhow abetment in murder is in itself a crime in Islamic criminal law and is liable to *ta'zīr* to be fixed according to the circumstances of the case. Abetment is sometimes effective and sometimes ineffective and it bears several shapes and different stages with respect to the commission of the offence. According to Imām Mālik an abettor will be subject to intentional murder if he is present at the time of the occurrence of the offence in an active position.[29]

If one person seizes another person without having the intention to cause his death and meanwhile another person causes his death by a fatal attack, the first person will not be liable for *qiṣāṣ* while the second person will be liable for *qiṣāṣ*. The first person will be liable for seizing the victim and will be punished with *ta'zīr*.

Limitation of intention

According to Imām Abū Ḥanīfah and Imām Aḥmad there is no difference in the intention of causing death of a specific person and the intention of causing death of an unspecified person, among a gathering or in a locality provided the intention is to cause death of some person. The offender in both cases will be liable for *qiṣāṣ* i.e. death. But according to Imām Shāfi'ī if a person intends to cause the death of a specific person and he then kills him, he will be liable to intentional murder but if he does not intend to cause the death of a specific person and causes death of an unknown or unspecified person, he will not be liable to intentional murder but will be liable to murder by mistake or quasi-intentional murder.[30]

Mistake in intention

If a person intends to cause death of a specific person but after causing death it appears that the victim is another person and is not the person whom he intended. Then there is a difference of opinion in this case. According to Imām Mālik and Imām Aḥmad he is liable to intentional murder because he has intended to cause the death of a person and completed his intention by causing death even though the victim is not the person whom he had intended to

---

[29] Ibid., vol.2, p.260

[30] Ibid., vol.2, pp.126-29

kill. But according to Imām Abū Ḥanīfah and Imām Shafi'ī he is liable to murder by mistake because he had no intention of causing death to the victim and the act was committed by mistake.[31]

General conditions

It is the unanimous view of all jurists that it is a condition for incriminating a person for any criminal act, including intentional murder, that the offender be an adult and sane. It is based on the *ḥadīth* of the Prophet (p.b.u.h) who said, Three persons have been exempted from any liability, namely:

(i) The minor until he attains puberty
(ii) The insane until he attains sanity and
(iii) The sleeping person until he awakes.[32]

Thus if a minor, insane or sleeping person causes the death of any person even by using a deadly weapon, he shall not be liable to intentional murder but shall be liable to a suitable *ta'zīr* as the court deems fit in the circumstances of the case.

It is pertinent to mention here that according to the jurists a minor becomes an adult either by attaining the age of majority or attaining puberty. Regarding age Imām Mālik, Imām Shāfi'ī and Imām Aḥmad opine that a minor becomes an adult by attaining the age of 15 years whether male or female and Imām Abū Ḥanīfah is of the view that a male minor becomes an adult by attaining the age of 18 years while a female minor becomes an adult by attaining the age of 17 years. Puberty is attained by a male minor when his sex glands become functional with the discharge of semen and it is attained by a female minor when her menses start or she becomes pregnant.[33] Further, sane means to be in good and proper sense and as such if the sense of a person is befogged and he cannot differentiate between wrong and right, and does not understand what he speaks, he will not be considered sane whether he becomes so by madness, intoxication, disease or is so by nature.

The Holy Qur'ān states:

---

[31] Ibid., p.89
[32] Sayyīd Sābiq, *Fiqh al-Sunnah,* vol.3, p.410
[33] 'Awdah, *al-Tashrī' al-Jinā'ī al-Islāmī,* vol.1, pp.599-603

يَا أَيُّهَا الَّذِينَ آمَنُواْ لاَ تَقْرَبُواْ الصَّلاَةَ وَأَنتُمْ سُكَارَى حَتَّى تَعْلَمُواْ مَا تَقُولُونَ

O you who believe! Approach not prayers with a mind befogged until you can understand all that you say. (4:43)

Causing death in self-defence

The right of self-defence has been recognized in Islamic law. If a person attacks another person with the intention of causing his death and the other in self-defence attacks him and causes his death, he will not be liable for intentional murder. The Holy Qur'an states:

فَمَنِ اعْتَدَى عَلَيْكُمْ فَاعْتَدُواْ عَلَيْهِ بِمِثْلِ مَا اعْتَدَى عَلَيْكُمْ

And one who attacks you, attack him in like manner as he attacks you. (2:194)

It has been related on the authority of Y'alā Ibn Umayyah that his servant was involved in a brawl with someone. One of them took the hand of the other and bit it. The latter withdrew his hand from the mouth of his rival with the result that two of the latter's teeth were dislocated. He went to the Holy Prophet and complained to him. The Prophet declared his teeth not liable for any compensation and said, "Do you think that the man should have left his hand in your mouth to be bitten by you". It has been related in *Sunan* al-Bayhaqī that in the period of Ḥaḍrat 'Umar a man from Ḥudhayl tribe became the guest of a person and he tried to coerce a girl into having sexual intercourse. The girl in self-defence beat him with a stone which caused his death. Ḥaḍrat 'Umar did not order the payment of *diyat.*[34]

The jurists concur that the act of a person in his self-defence is not an offence and is not subject to any civil or criminal liability. However, if he crosses the limits prescribed for such defence, his act becomes an offence liable to criminal and civil liability.[35]

---

[34] Al-Bayhaqī*, al-Sunan al-Kubrā,* vol.7, p.337

[35] 'Awdah, , *al-Tashrī' al-Jinā'ī al-Islāmī,* vol.1, pp.488-89

According to the preferred opinion of Imām Abū Ḥanīfah, Imām-Mālik and Imām Shāfi'ī, the right to kill a person in self-defence limits the case to an attack on the body of that person or the body of another person. But some jurists extend the right of legal defence to the defence of the property and allow a person to kill the person who takes away his property forcibly and such a person has no other means to prevent him except to kill him. It is based on a *ḥadīth* related on the authority of Abū Hurayrah that a person came to the Holy Prophet and said, "Oh Prophet! What should I do when a person takes away my property?" The Prophet said, "Don't give him your property". He said, "What should I do if he quarrels with me?" The Prophet said, "Quarrel with him." He said, "If he kills me?" The Prophet said, "You are then a martyr". He said, "If I kill him?" The Prophet said, " He will be in hell."[36]

Conditions of legal-defence

Jurists have unanimously described the following conditions for the validity of legal defence whether of body or honour or property of one self or of another person;

1. The act of the aggressor must be transgression.
2. Transgression is actually committed.
3. It is not possible for the defender to defend himself otherwise.
4. The quantum of force used to deter the wrong should be commensurate with the need to do so.

1. The act of the aggressor must be transgression

It is necessary for the justification of the legal defence that the act which is being contemplated should be transgression failing which defence shall not be allowed against it. For instance, a father, a husband or a teacher beats his son, wife or pupil respectively for the purpose of correction, or the official executioner beheads the man who is sentenced to death by decapitation, in such cases there is no transgression. There is no limit of transgression and it varies in various cases. However, the defender is restricted by the

---

[36] Sayyed Sābiq, *Fiqh al-Sunnah,* vol.2, p.488

condition that he should defend himself with a force which is just sufficient for the purpose.

According to Imām Mālik, Imām Shāfi'ī and Imām Aḥmad transgression may not necessarily be a punishable offence. It is sufficient that the act is illegal. It is also not necessary that the aggressor should be criminally accountable and the legal defence is allowed in case the aggressor is a lunatic or a child. But according to Imām Abū Ḥanīfah legal defence is only justified when the act of transgression constitutes a punishable offence and the aggressor should be one who is accountable on criminal grounds.[37]

The aggressor is not allowed to counter the defensive act of the victim on the ground that he is acting in self-defence, because it is he who originally commits transgression and is therefore, the object of the defensive action of the victim. It is based on the decision of Ḥaḍrat 'Alī in the case of a woman who hid her paramour on the wedding night in her bedroom. When her husband entered the room the paramour assaulted him but the husband in self-defence killed the paramour, whereupon the bride killed her husband. She asserted that she committed the homicide in her defence. But Ḥaḍrat 'Alī decided that she was guilty of killing her husband and sentenced her to death. The caliph did not take into consideration the plea that she acted in her own defence or the defence of someone else. But if the action taken in defence is in excess of what is required, the excessive action will in itself be considered transgression and the aggressor will be allowed to defend himself against the excessive action in self-defence.[38]

It is relevant to point out that it is not necessary that transgression should continue till the exercise of the right of defence, because the person under aggression cannot wait for the aggressor to attack. He should rather be the first to act in order to deter the act of the aggressor.

If an aggressor being armed with weapons confronts the aggrieved, the probability of his intended transgression will be determined by the conjecture of the latter. If he assumes that the aggressor is going to attack him although he may not have done so

---

[37] Ibn Qudāmah, *al-Mughnī,* vol.7, p.264

[38] 'Awdah, *al-Tashrī' al-Jinā'ī al-Islāmī,*. vol. 1, p.480

as yet, it will be presumed that he would strike the aggrieved person. But if the aggrieved person thinks that the aggressor will not strike him, then it will be taken for granted that he will not do so. However, it is necessary that the conjecture of the aggrieved person should be the highest level of probability so that it may warrant action in self-defence. If his conjecture consists of a mere notion of being attacked, there will be no justification for defence.[39]

It is vital to ascertain the beginning and end of transgression, for defence begins with the beginning of transgression and ends with the end thereof. The state of defence does not arise from a mere wish or intention of the aggressor to transgress. It arises when transgression is started or is probably presumed to be started.

2. Transgression is actually committed

The state of legal defence arises when transgression is actually committed or is probably to be committed. Thus any transgression to be committed in future cannot give rise to the state of defence in the present. Any intimidation to commit transgression does not occasion any act of defence, because it does not pose an impending danger to be counted immediately. The aggrieved in such a case has enough time to defend himself by other legal means such as lodging a report with a law-enforcing agency.

3. It is not possible for the defender to defend himself otherwise

Another condition for the exercise of the right of self-defence is that no other possible method is available to the aggrieved to protect himself against the aggressor. If there is any method other than counter attack which can be adopted to deal with the aggressor, it is obligatory on the aggrieved to adopt it. If an aggrieved does not adopt any other method and counter attacks the aggressor, he shall himself be deemed a transgressor. It is not permitted to an aggrieved person to resort to violence, if he can get

[39] Imām Shāfi'ī, *al-Umm*, vol.6, p.27

the help of the people or police in time, or can defend himself without adopting violent means.[40]

4. The quantum of force used to deter the wrong should be commensurate with the need to do so

One of the conditions for the validity of the exercise of the right of defence is to act in defence with a force commensurate with the indispensable need. If the force used exceeds the limit of need, it ceases to be defence and gains the status of transgression itself. If the attack of the aggressor can be deterred by a lesser force, it should be used and not more than that because the main aim of the action against the aggressor is defence. Thus, if the attack of the aggressor can be repelled with the use of a stick, it would be needless to repel it with the use of anything made of iron. Similarly, when the aggressor receives a grievous injury at the hands of the defender and is not able to proceed with his wrongful act, it would not be allowed to subject him to further violence, because the transgression committed by him is done away with. Any possible measure in defence may be taken up in the event of willful attempt on one's life or an attack on one's family or property. If defence is possible by raising a hue and cry in order to call people for help, such a mode of defence should preferably be adopted instead of using force. But if no help is forthcoming and the attack can be repelled by the use of hands, then it is lawful to use one's hands.[41]

The defender is not allowed to be the first to act with the intention of killing or wounding the aggressor, unless he is sure that defensive action against him is not possible without doing so and that the use of such a force in defence is indispensable. The defender should adopt the method which he is inclined to think for cogent reasons requires the least force irrespective of the severity of the attack of the attacker. In case of a scuffle specially when the attackers comprise a group, every member of the group may be dealt with in a different manner according to the role played by him. In such a case all the factors have to be taken into account in the assessment of the requisite force indispendable for defence.

---

[40] Ibn Qudāmah, *al-Mughnī* , vol.10, p.353

[41] 'Awdah, *al-Tashrī' al-Jinā'ī al-Islāmī,* vol.1 , pp.482-87.

However, if the defender uses force in the exercise of the right of defence in excess of what is absolutely essential, he will be responsible for the use of excessive force. For instance, if the attacker can be prevented from attacking by threatening him, but the defender inflicts a blow on him, the defender shall be accountable for murder if he kills the attacker who can be forced to desist from transgression by only injuring him.[42]

Transgression and defence are co-related. The moment transgression begins the state of defence starts and when transgression ends the state of defence correspondingly ceases. Any act done by the defender after the end of transgression would entail accountability on his part. But transgression would not be deemed to have come to an end in case the attacker gets away with the property of the defender. The defender in such a case is allowed to use as much force as is necessary to snatch away his property from the attacker. If it is not possible to recover the property without killing the attacker, the defender will be within his rights to do so. Moreover, if the defender while exercising the right of his defence, causes harm or injury to a person other than the attacker, he shall be accountable for that accordingly.

Further the jurists extend the right of self-defence even in a case when a minor or insane person or an animal attacks a person and allow such a person to kill the minor, insane or animal if he cannot escape himself without killing the attacker. This is the opinion of Imām Mālik, Imām Shāfi'ī and Imām Aḥmad and according to them the offender in this case shall not be subject to any civil or criminal liability. But according to Imām Abū Ḥanīfah the offender in this case shall be subject to civil liability and shall be liable for *diyat* of the minor or insane or the price of the animal, as the case may be.[43]

The jurists, however, agree that the defender in case of causing the death of the aggressor in self-defence must produce sufficient evidence that he has killed the victim in self-defence and is within his rights, failing which he shall be subject to the

[42] Ibid., pp.485-86
[43] Ibid., p.476

discretion of the heirs of the victim either to demand *qiṣāṣ* or pardon him or make any compromise.[44]

Proof of intentional murder

The jurists concur that the offence of intentional murder is proved either by the confession of the offender or by the testimony of two adult, sane, male and reliable eye witnesses.

The confession of the accused must be with his free consent without any coercion. The offender must be adult and sane. The confession must be explicit with respect to the time, place and weapon used and the method adopted for the commission of the murder of the victim. The confession must be before a competent court.

The witness after being adult and sane must be a credible person. A credible witness is a witness who abstains from major sins and is not notorious. A famous Ḥanafī jurist, Abū Bakr al-Jaṣṣāṣ, after producing various opinions of the jurists about the admissibility of the evidence of a witness, writes, "It seems that everyone of them has based the matter of the admissibility of the evidence on what is more likely in his opinion that it is to be accepted and relied upon.[45] The majority of the jurists are of the view that the witnesses in the case of the proof of an intentional murder should be male. The evidence of a blind person is not acceptable in intentional murder. According to the majority of the jurists the evidence of a dumb and deaf person is not acceptable in a murder case while some opine that his evidence is acceptable if he can write and give written evidence. The witness must not be a person who is blamed for a close relation with the victim or enmity with the offender. The testimonies of the witnesses must not contradict each other and must be consistent in time, place, weapon and method used for causing the death of the victim. The witness must not have been punished for false accusation of *zina* or of giving false evidence in any other case in a court. The witness should not be an interested witness. A non-Muslim is a competent witness in a case of intentional murder if the offender is

---

[44] Sayyid Sābiq, *Fiqh al-Sunnah,* vol.2, p.488
[45] Al-Jaṣṣāṣ, *Aḥkām al-Qur'ān,* vol.1, p.506

non-Muslim.[46] If any of the witnesses retracts his testimony at any stage before the execution of the punishment of death, the offender shall not be punished with death but shall be punished with *ta'zīr*. Similarly when the heirs of the victim make compromise with the offender or waive the right of *qiṣāṣ*, the offender shall not be punished with death.

Ibn Taymiyyah, Ibn Qayyim, Ibn Ḥazm and some later jurists are of the view that the evidence of women is also acceptable for the proof of intentional murder liable to *qiṣāṣ* specially where no male witness is available in such a case like the case of the murder of a woman in a women's hostel or in a place that is exclusively for women. The jurists further opine that any intentional murder can also be proved by circumstantial evidence if it reaches a degree of certainty and beyond any reasonable doubt, for example, a man comes out from an empty house with fear and haste and with a bloodstained knife in his hand and immediately thereafter some persons go into that house and find a dead man with his throat recently cut, there is no doubt that that man is the murderer of this dead person.[47] If the court is satisfied on any evidence on record other than that of two witnesses and the confession of the accused that the accused is the person who has murdered the victim, it may grant him death punishment as *ta'zīr*.

Qasamah (joint oaths)

One of the sources of proof of a murder is *qasamah*. *Qasamah* is derived from *qasam* which literally means to take oath and it means an oath repeated 50 times by fifty persons or less at the place of crime or the relatives of the victim in a case of murder wherein the offender is not known.

It is based on a *ḥadīth* related on the authority by Sahl bin Abī Hasmah and Rafi'a bin Khadīj that Muḥaysah bin Mas'ūd and 'Abd Allāh bin Sahl went to Khaybar and separated from one another in trees of fates (belonged to Jews). 'Abd Allāh bin Sahl was murdered and Jews of (Khaybar) were accused. 'Abd al Raḥmān Ibn Sahl, the brother of 'Abd Allāh and his two cousins named Muhaysah and Huwaysah came to the Holy Prophet. When

---

[46] 'Awdah, *al-Tashrī' al-Jinā'ī al-Islāmī*, vol.2, pp.396-407
[47] *Majallah al-Aḥkāam, al-'Adliyyah*, section 1741

'Abd al-Raḥmān started explaining the occurrence of the incident, the Prophet said, "Your elder should speak". On this Muhaysah and Huwaysah informed the Prophet of the incident. The Prophet said to them, "You have to take fifty oaths against any one of them (Jews) so that he will be incriminated (for this offence)". They said, "How can we take oath when we have not witnessed anyone." The Prophet said, "the Jews will take fifty oaths for the proof of their innocence". They said, "They are non-Muslims (and we cannot reply on their oaths)". Thus Prophet paid them *diyat* from his own account i.e. Bayt al-Māl.[48]

Qasāmah (joint oaths) was in practice in pre-Islamic period and it was retained in Islam to the extent of a case of the murder wherein murdered is found in a specific private locality and his murderer is not known at all. It is the opinion of the majority of the jurists. But according to some earlier jurists like Abū Qalabah, Salim Ibn 'Abd Allāh, Ḥakam Ibn 'Utaibah, Qatadah, Sulayman Ibn Yasar, Ibrahim Ibn 'Ulayyah, Muslim Ibn Khalid and 'Umar Ibn Abdul 'Azīz *qasāmah* has not been retained by Islam and is not to be practised in any event.[49]

According to Imām Abū Ḥanīfah, *qasāmah* is proceeded with to assert the innocence of an individual suspected to have killed a person. It shall only be practised in a case when a murdered person is found in a place which is either in the private ownership of any person or is considered to be in the exclusive use of certain residents of such locality and the offender is not known. Thus, if the corpse of the murdered person is found in a public place like a mosque, park, main road, market, main bridge etc. or there is any serious presumptive evidence against the accused, *qasāmah* will not be undertaken. The procedure of oaths shall be that fifty persons of that locality or place shall take oaths and each of them will have to state in his oath that he has neither killed the victim nor has he any knowledge as to who has killed him. If the number of such persons is less than fifty, they shall take the oath as many times as may be required to make up the number of the fifty oaths. And when they take such oaths, they shall be liable to *diyat*

---

48 Abū Dawūd, *Sunan*, vol.2, pp.484-85

49 Ibn Rushd, *Bidāyat al-Mujtahid,* vol.2, p.419

payable by them and their *'āqilah* to the heir or heirs of the victim.[50]

But according to Imām Mālik, Imām Shāfi'ī and Imām Aḥmad the procedure of *qasāmah* is carried out to ascertain the guilt of the accused on the basis of certain indications *(lawth)* that he has committed this murder. Thus, if there is no certain indication or serious presumptive evidence against the accused that he has committed the offence, *qasāmah* shall not be proceeded with. Moreover fifty oaths shall be taken by the heirs of the victim and each of them will have to state in his oath that the accused against whom a serious presumptive evidence is available, is the one who has committed the murder. When they take such oaths, according to Imām Mālik the accused shall be liable to *qiṣāṣ* and according to Imām Shāfi'ī and Imām Aḥmad the accused and his heir shall be liable to pay *diyat* to the heirs of the victim.

If the heirs of the victim refuse to take oaths, the accused shall be asked to take fifty oaths and if he takes fifty oaths stating that he has neither killed him nor assisted in or instigated his murder, he shall be released.[51]

It is pertinent to mention here that the institution of *qasāmah* did not function much even in the days when Islamic criminal law had a certain practical application.

It is pertinent to reproduce here the opinion of 'Umar bin 'Abd al-'Azīz which has been related by Bukhārī as under:

> "Narrated Abū Qalabah: Once 'Umar bin 'Abd al-'Azīz sat on his throne in the courtyard of his house so that the people might gather before him, then he admitted them and (when they came in), he said, "What do you think of *al-Qasāmah?* They said, "We say that it is lawful to depend on *al-Qasāmah* in *Qiṣāṣ* as the previous Muslim Caliphs carried out *qiṣāṣ* depending on it".Then he said to me, "O Abū Qalabah! What do you say about it." He let me appear before the people and I said, "O Chief of the Believers! You have the Chief of the army staff and the nobles of the Arabs. If fifty of them testified that a

---

50 Al-Kāsanī, *Badā'i' al-Ṣanā'i'*, vol.7, pp.288-92

51 Wahbah al-Zuhaylī, *al-Fiqh al-Islāmī*, vol.7, pp.404-7

married man had committed illegal sexual intercourse in Damascus but they had not seen him (doing so), would you stone him?" He said, "No". I said, "If fifty of them testified that a man had committed theft in Hums, would you cut off his hand though they had not seen him". He replied, "No". I said, "By Allah, Allah's Apostle never killed anyone except in one of the following three situations:

(i) A person who killed somebody unjustly, was killed (in *Qiṣāṣ)*

(ii) A married person who committed illegal sexual intercourse and

(iii) A man who fought against Allah and his apostle and deserted Islam and became an apostate."

The people said, "Didn't Anas bin Mālik narrate that Allah's apostle cut off the hands of the thieves, branded their eyes and then, threw them in the sun?" I said, " I shall tell you the narration of Anas. Anas said," Eight persons from the tribe of Ukl came to Allah's apostle and gave the pledge of allegiance to Islam (became Muslims). The climate of the place (Madinah) did not suit them, so they became sick and complained about that to Allah's apostle. He said (to them), "Won't you go out and drink camel's milk and urine (as medicine)?" They said "Yes". So they went out and drank the camel's milk and urine and after they became healthy, they killed the shepherd of Allah's apostle and took away all the camels. This news reached Allah's apostle, so he sent (men) to follow their tracks and they were captured and brought (to the Prophet). He then ordered the cutting of their hands and feet, and their eyes were branded with heated pieces of iron, and then he threw them in the sun till they died. I said "What can be worse than what those people did? They deserted Islam committed murder and theft". Then Anbasa bin Sa'īd said, "By Allah, I have never heard a narration like the one today." I said, "O Anbasa! You deny my narration?" Anbasa said, "No, but you have related the narration in the way it should be related. By Allah, these people are in welfare as long as this Sheikh (Abu Qalabah) is among them" I added, "Indeed in this event there has been a tradition set by Allah's apostle." The narrator added, "Some

Ansari people came to the Prophet and discussed some matters with him. A man from amongst them went out and was murdered. Those people went out after him and saw their companion swimming in blood. They returned to Allah's apostle and said to him "O Allah's apostle we have found our companion who had talked with us and gone out before us, swimming in blood (killed)". Allah's apostle said to him, "Whom do you suspect or who do you think has killed him?" They said, "We think that the Jews have killed him". The Prophet sent for the Jews and asked them "Did you kill this (person)?" They replied, "No". He asked the Al-Ansars, "Do you agree to let fifty Jews take an oath that they have not killed him?" They said, "It matters little to the Jews to kill us all and then take false oaths". He said, "Then would you like to receive the *Diyat* after fifty of you have taken an oath (that the Jews have killed your man)? They said, "We will not take the oath". Then the Prophet himself paid them the *Diyat* (Blood money)". The narrator added, "The tribe of Hudhayl repudiated one of their men (for his evil conduct) in the pre-Islamic period of ignorance. Then at a place called al-Batha (near Makkah), the man attacked a Yemenite family at night to steal from them but a man from the family noticed him and struck him with his sword and killed him. The tribe of Hudhayl captured the Yemenite and brought him to 'Umar during the Ḥaj season and said," He has killed your companion". The Yemenite said, "But these people had repudiated him (i.e. their companion)." 'Umar said, "Let fifty persons of Hudhayl swear that they had not repudiated him". So forty nine of them took the oath and then a person belonging to them, came from Sham and they requested him to swear similarly, but he paid one thousand dirhams instead of taking the oath. They called another man in his place and the new man shook hands with the brother of the deceased. Some people said. "The fifty men who had taken false oaths *(al-Qasāmah)* set out, and when they reached, it was raining so they entered a cave in the mountain and the cave collapsed on those fifty men who had taken the false oath, and all of them died except the two persons who had shaken hands with each other. They escaped death but a stone fell on the leg of the brother of the deceased and it broke, whereupon he survived for one year and then died". I further said, "Abdul Malik bin Marwan sentenced a man to death in *Qiṣāṣ* (equality in punishment) for murder basing his judgement on *al-Qasāmah*, but later on he regretted that judgement and ordered that the names of the fifty persons who had taken the oath (*al-Qasamah*), be erased from the register, and he exiled them to Syria.[52]

2 Quasi-intentional murder

Quasi-intentional murder means someone intentionally makes another person the direct object of some action, not usually fatal, and he dies as a result of that action. Thus quasi-intentional murder consists of three elements:

(i) the offender must have the intention of causing bodily harm to the victim and have no intention of causing his death;

(ii) the weapon or the act of the offender is not likely to cause death in the ordinary course of nature and

(iii) the victim dies as a result of the act of the offender.

For example, if a person in order to cause hurt strikes another person with a stick or small stone which usually does not cause death of a human being, but that person dies as a result of that act, the offender is said to have committed quasi-intentional murder. It is based on a *ḥadīth* of the Prophet (p.b.u.h) who said, "If a person kills another by throwing a stone, striking with a whip or a staff, its *diyat* will be one hundred camels". This *ḥadīth* relates to the causing of death by such a stone, whip or staff which would not be ordinarily sufficient to cause death and as such from the use of such a weapon no conclusion of intentional murder can be drawn. Thus the Prophet did not consider this murder as murder liable to *qiṣāṣ* i.e. death and considered it quasi-intentional murder liable to *diyat*.

It is also necessary for incriminating a person for quasi-intentional murder that the victim be a protected person. Thus if a person with the intention of causing hurt strikes an unprotected person and he dies as a result of that, he will not be liable to quasi-intentional murder. Similarly, the victim must be a living human being at the time of the commission of the offence. So if a person with the intention of causing bodily harm strikes a dead person or

[52] Al-Bukhārī, *Saḥīḥ*, vol.2, pp.25-26

an animal and that animal dies of that act, he will not be liable to quasi-intentional murder.

Quasi-intentional murder is proved either by the confession of the accused without coercion or by the evidence of two adult, sane and reliable witnesses or any other authentic evidence which, in the opinion of the course, is sufficient to prove the guilt.[53]

Quasi-intentional murder can be pardoned by the heir or heirs of the victim with or without compensation.

3. Murder by mistake

Murder by mistake means someone, without intention to cause death of, or cause harm to a person, causes the death of a person either by mistake of intention or by mistake of act, for instance a person mistakes another person for a wild beast, and kills him or someone hits another person unluckily while shooting at a target so that he dies. Murder by mistake contains three elements:

(i) the offender must have no intention to cause death or harm to the victim.

(ii) the offender must have committed some fatal act and

(iii) the victim must have died as a result of the act of the offender.[54]

Sometimes murder by mistake is committed by some negligence of the offender and sometimes it is committed without his negligence. When it is committed by negligence, the offender will be punished for such negligence.

The victim must be a living human being and a protected person failing which the offender will not be liable to murder by mistake.

Murder by mistake is proved either by the confession of the accused of his own free will without any coercion or by the evidence of two witnesses or by any other authentic evidence which is sufficient to prove the guilt.

Murder by mistake can be pardoned by the heir of the victim with or without compensation. The court may, after the pardoning

53 'Awdah, *al-Tashrī' al-Jinā'ī al-Islāmī*, vol.2, p.95-97;185-186

54 Al-Kāsanī, *Badā'i' al-Ṣanā'i'*, vol.7, p.269-72

of the convict, award *ta'zīr* to him, if it deems it necessary in the circumstances of the case.

4. Murder equivalent to mistake

According to Imām Abū Ḥanīfah the fourth kind of murder is murder equivalent to mistake. It is a murder in which the factor of deliberation is lacking in the action like murder by mistake. For instance someone falls upon another from a roof and kills him. The offender in such a murder is not liable to intentional murder. Imām Mālik, Imām Shafi'ī and Imām Aḥmad include it in murder by mistake and do not consider it an independent kind of murder. Abū Bakr al-Jaṣṣāṣ, a Ḥanafī jurist, has also favoured the opinion of the three Imāms in this matter. Some later Hanafīs also favour the opinion of the three Imāms.[55]

5. Indirect murder

According to Imām Abū Ḥanīfah the fifth kind of murder is indirect murder i.e. someone brings about the death of another person without doing anything directly against him. For instance a person digs a well in a thoroughfare without any intention to cause the death of someone and a person falls into it and dies therein. According to Imām Abū Ḥanīfah the offender in this case will be liable to indirect murder and if the person who dies is a protected person, the penalty will be the payment of *diyat* to be paid by the *aqilah* of the accused. But other Imāms do not consider it an independent kind of murder and include it in murder by mistake because the person who digs the well has no intention to cause the death of the person who falls into it.[56]

---

[55] Abū Bakr al-Jaṣṣāṣ, *Aḥkām al-Qur'ān,* vol.2, p.223

[56] 'Awdah, *al-Tashrī' al-Jinā'ī al-Islāmī,* vol.2, p 9

Chapter Three

Punishments of Murder

Punishment of intentional murder

The punishment of intentional murder is *qiṣāṣ* (retaliation) i.e. death. The Qur'ān says:

> يَا أَيُّهَا الَّذِينَ آمَنُواْ كُتِبَ عَلَيْكُمُ الْقِصَاصُ فِي الْقَتْلَى الْحُرُّ بِالْحُرِّ وَالْعَبْدُ بِالْعَبْدِ وَالأُنثَى بِالأُنثَى فَمَنْ عُفِيَ لَهُ مِنْ أَخِيهِ شَيْءٌ فَاتِّبَاعٌ بِالْمَعْرُوفِ وَأَدَاء إِلَيْهِ بِإِحْسَانٍ ذَلِكَ تَخْفِيفٌ مِّن رَّبِّكُمْ وَرَحْمَةٌ فَمَنِ اعْتَدَى بَعْدَ ذَلِكَ فَلَهُ عَذَابٌ أَلِيمٌ
>
> Oh you who believe! Retaliation is prescribed for you in the matter of murdered. The free for free, the slave for slave, the woman for woman. If any remission is made by the brother of the slain, then grant any reasonable demand and compensate him with handsome gratitude. This is a concession and a mercy from your Lord and after this whoever exceeds the limits, shall be in grave penalty. (2:178)

In pre-Islamic Arab society when a woman of a higher family or race was killed by a person of a lower family or race, the heirs of the woman killed a male person of the offender or the offender himself if he was male. Thus the people of rich and strong tribes did not equate their woman to a woman of a lower or poor tribe. Similarly the people of higher tribes equated their slave to a free man of a lower or poor tribe and thus when a free man of a lower tribe killed a slave of a higher tribe, the owner of the slave kille the free man of the lower tribe believing his slave to be equal to a free person. Thus the above verse declared that all free men, free women and slaves are equal in matter of murder meaning thereby that if a woman murders another woman she shall be given the punishment of *qiṣāṣ* i.e. death, irrespective of her relation to any tribe or race. Similarly if a slave murders another slave, he shall be given the punishment of *qiṣāṣ* i.e. death irrespective of the status and race of his owner. The Islamic law thus prescribed *qiṣāṣ* i.e. death in matter of intentional murder irrespective of the cast, colour, sex, race and status of both the offender as well as the victim. Moreover the pagan Arab continued the revenge of a murder to generations.[1]

'Abd Allāh Yusuf 'Alī, while commenting on the above verse writes:

Our law of equality only takes account of three conditions in civil society:

(i) free for free
(ii) slave for slave and
(iii) woman for woman

Among free men or women, all are equal; you cannot claim that because a wealthy, or high-born, or influential man is killed, his life is equal to two or three lives among the poor or the lowly. Nor, in cases of murder, can you go into the value or abilities of a slave. A woman is mentioned separately because her position as a mother or an economic worker is different. She does not form a third class, but is a category of the other two classes. One life having been lost, do not waste many lives in retaliation; at most, let the law take one life under strictly prescribed conditions, and shut the door to private vengeance or tribal retaliation. But if the aggrieved party consents (and this condition of consent is laid down to prevent worse evils), forgiveness and brotherly love is better, and the door of Mercy is kept open. In western law, no felony can be compounded".[2]

---

[1] Wahbah al-Zuhaylī, *al-Fiqh al-islāmī*, vol.6, p.270

[2] 'Abdullah Yusuf 'Alī, *English Translation and Commentary of the Holy Qur'ān*, p.70.

This verse shows that according to Islamic law, murder is a compoundable offence. It allows the heirs of the victim in a murder case to pardon the murderer, if they deem it proper. In that case, the court shall not award the death penalty. Of course, the offender will have to pay compensation money for it if the heirs of the victim demand it.

The Qur'an further says:

وَلَكُمْ فِي الْقِصَاصِ حَيَاةٌ يَا أُولِي الأَلْبَابِ لَعَلَّكُمْ تَتَّقُونَ.

In the Law of Equity there is (saving of) life to you, O you men of understanding; that you may restrain yourselves. (2:179)

This verse refutes those people who go to the other extreme and advocate total abolition of capital punishment. If it is inhuman to insist on retaliation *(qiṣāṣ)* without paying any heed to all other considerations, it is equally inhuman to encourage murder by totally abolishing capital punishment, as has been done in many Western countries. That is why Allah Almighty declared that there is life in the law of retribution. If a society does not pay due regard to the sanctity of life and tries to protect the murderer, it sets a premium on crime and puts in danger the lives of many innocent people. If the offenders of murder are allowed to enjoy their life freely, they are not only given a licence to kill others but also to endanger the lives of so many innocent people in society. Moreover, it is a reflection on the moral and social attitudes of the people who condone murder and killing of innocent people and disgracing the sanctity of life.

The Qur'an also says:

وَكَتَبْنَا عَلَيْهِمْ فِيهَا أَنَّ النَّفْسَ بِالنَّفْسِ وَالْعَيْنَ بِالْعَيْنِ وَالأَنفَ بِالأَنفِ
وَالأُذُنَ بِالأُذُنِ وَالسِّنَّ بِالسِّنِّ وَالْجُرُوحَ قِصَاصٌ فَمَن تَصَدَّقَ بِهِ فَهُوَ
كَفَّارَةٌ لَّهُ وَمَن لَّمْ يَحْكُم بِمَا أنزَلَ اللّهُ فَأُوْلَئِكَ هُمُ الظَّالِمُونَ

We ordained therein for them: "Life for life, eye for eye, nose for nose, ear for ear, tooth for tooth and wounds equal for equal." But if anyone remits the retaliation by way of charity, it is an act of atonement for himself. And if any fail to judge by (the light of what God has revealed) they are (no better than) wrong doers. (5:45)

وَلاَ تَقْتُلُواْ النَّفسَ الَّتِي حَرَّمَ اللَّهُ إِلاَّ بِالحَقِّ وَمَن قُتِلَ مَظْلُومًا فَقَدْ جَعَلْنَا لِوَلِيِّهِ سُلْطَانًا فَلاَ يُسْرِف فِّي الْقَتْلِ إِنَّهُ كَانَ مَنْصُورًا

Nor take life which God has made sacred except for just cause. And if anyone is slain wrongfully, we have given his heir authority (to demand *Qiṣāṣ* or to forgive); but let him not exceed bounds in the matter of taking life; for he is helped (by the Law) (17:33)

The Holy Prophet (p.b.u.h) has also ordained that the punishment of murderer is death as *qiṣāṣ*. The following *aḥādīth* are worth mentioning:

We shall kill the person who kills another person.[3]

It has been related that in the period of the Prophet (p.b.u.h) a Jew robbed a girl of her ornaments and then killed her by hitting her head within two stones. The Prophet ordered to hit his head within two stones and was thus killed by hitting his head within two stones.[4]

The killing of a Muslim is not permissible except in three cases, namely, (i) when he kills another person; (ii) when he commits *zinā* after marriage and (iii) when he becomes apostate.[5]

Whoever intentionally causes death to a person shall be liable for *qiṣāṣ* i.e. death unless the victim's heirs forgive him.[6]

The jurists of all schools of thought concur that the person who commits intentional murder shall be punished with death as *qiṣāṣ*. *Qiṣāṣ* means to give such punishment to the offender as he has caused to the victim. In the case of an offence of intentional

---

[3] Ibn Athīr, *Jami' al-Uṣūl*, vol.3, p.189
[4] Muslim, *Ṣaḥīḥ*, p.219
[5] Abū Dawūd, *Sunan*, vol.2, p.187
[6] Ibid., p.192

murder *qiṣāṣ* means death of the offender and in the case of hurt it means to cause similar hurt to the offender as he has caused to the victim. *Qiṣāṣ* is the basic punishment in the case of intentional murder. Compensation and other punishments are not basic punishments but are secondary punishments.

The punishment of *qiṣāṣ* and its execution

The Holy Qur'ān says:

وَمَن قُتِلَ مَظْلُومًا فَقَدْ جَعَلْنَا لِوَلِيِّهِ سُلْطَانًا فَلاَ يُسْرِف فِّي الْقَتْلِ

> And if anyone is slain wrongfully, we have given his heir authority (to demand *qiṣāṣ* or to forgive); but let him not exceed bounds in the matter of taking life. (17:33)

The Holy Prophet said, "The heir of the victim in a murder case or the victim in case of hurt has three choices, namely:

(i) to take *qiṣāṣ* from the convict,
(ii) to pardon him or
(iii) to take *diyat* or compensation".[7]

The Islamic criminal law has conferred the right of *qiṣāṣ* on the heir of the victim. It is based on human nature as well as the interests of both individual and the community. It is the nature of every human being that he craves to retaliate in person the wrong done to him. Thus the Islamic criminal law first authorises the heir to retaliate the death of the victim and has thus left the offender within his reach and to his discretion. But at the same time it has authorised the heir of the victim to pardon the offender in lieu of compensation or otherwise, this is the spirit which ensures maintenance of peace and tranquility between human groups. The object in bestowing the right of *qiṣāṣ* on the victim's heir is to purge the inner self, resolve the dispute between rival parties, maintain peace and security, reduce the incidents of crime and forestall the possibility of excess in the application of death punishment. However, to take *qiṣāṣ* is a right and not an obligation. Heirs of the victim in a murder case means the persons

---

[7] Ibid., p.477-78

who are entitled to their shares in the estate of the victim whether male or female and whether they have actually got the shares in the inheritance or not. This is the view of Imām Abū Ḥanīfah, Imām Shāfi'ī and Imām Aḥmad. But according to Imām Mālik an heir of the victim in a murder case means his male agnate heir only such as son, father or brother.

Thus, the execution of the punishment of death is open to the heirs of the victim. According to Imām Abū Ḥanīfah and one view of Imām Aḥmad the convict shall be beheaded with a sword or another similar weapon, and according to Imām Mālik, Imām Shāfi'ī and one view of Imām Aḥmad, the convict, if possible, shall be killed in the same way as he has killed the victim. However, if the heirs of the victim agree that the convict should be killed in a way other than that he has used for the death of the victim, it is permissible. The jurists, therefore, allow the use of any weapon or any other mode for the execution of punishment of death in intentional murder which causes the death of the convict with least pain or suffering to him.[8]

If the convict is a pregnant woman, the execution of the punishment shall be postponed until the birth of the child or miscarriage. And if there is no alternate arrangement for the maintenance of the child, the execution of the punishment shall be postponed until the expiration of a period of two years after the birth of the child and during this period she may be released on bail or kept in jail as in simple imprisonment. Before the execution of the punishment of death, a medical officer shall have to examine the convict and certify that he is medically fit for such punishment.

The punishment of death in intentional murder shall be executed when the heirs of the victim demand it. If the heirs of the murdered person are more than one, all must express this desire, and if one of them remits retaliation, the remission affects all and the convict shall be subjected to *diyat* to be paid to the other heirs if the one has pardoned him without anything and if he has pardoned him against *diyat,* he shall also be liable for his portion in the *diyat.* If one of them is a minor, insane or absent, punishment shall be delayed until he becomes an adult, sane or

[8] 'Awdah, *al-Tashrī' al-Jinā'ī al-Islāmī,* vol. 2, p.146-47

returns from the journey and expresses his desire for retaliation of the convict. This is the view of Imām Shāfi'ī and Imām Aḥmad. But according to Imām Abū Ḥanīfah and Imām Mālik in case an heir is a minor or mad, the punishment should not be delayed and when the adult heirs demand it, it should be implemented forthwith. They base their view on the will of Ḥaḍrat 'Alī to his elder son, Ḥaḍrat Ḥassan when he was attacked by Ibn Muljim wherein he said, "Imprison him. If I survive, I shall exercise my right to deal with him as I choose. But if I die, kill him as he killed me". Ḥaḍrat Ḥassan later on killed him in the absence of some minor heirs of Ḥaḍrat 'Alī. Further they opine that in case of an absent heir, the punishment of retaliation shall be delayed till he is present and expresses his desire for retaliation of the convict. The convict will be kept in prison during the waiting period.

According to Imām Mālik the right of retaliation or its pardoning is first vested in the son of the murdered, then grandson and if he has no son or grandson, then any close male relative on the father's side like father, brother etc. But according to Imām Abū Ḥanīfah, Imām Shāfi'ī and Imām Aḥmad the right of retaliation or its pardoning vests in the legal heirs of the murdered person who are entitled to inherit his property whether he has left property or not irrespective of whether they are male or female. And if a murdered person has no relative or heir, then the government shall be his avenger of blood (*walī).*[9]

The right of the punishment of *qiṣāṣ* vests in the heir or heirs of the murdered person but they are not allowed to execute the punishment as it amounts to disturbing the peace in society and affects the authority of the Islamic state. The jurists have agreed that the execution of the punishment should be carried out by the government through trained staff and under an organised institution after getting permission from the avengers of blood (*walis).* The Government is allowed to execute the punishment of death in intentional murder by any means which easily and rapidly causes the death of the convict. It is pertinent to reproduce the commentary of Abdul Mājid Daryabadi on verse 2:178. He writes:

> "*Qiṣāṣ* (retaliation) is not a synonym of naked vengeance that every individual may take it himself from

[9] Al-Kasānī, *Badā'i al-Ṣanā'i'*, vol 7

> another individual. On the other hand it is the name of an organized, civilized and systemized form of punishment in criminal law. It is collective law for the whole Ummah. The duty of its execution falls on the government or its delegated officers."[10]

The punishment of *qiṣāṣ* may not be executed until all the heirs of the victim are present, either personally or through their representatives authorized by them in writing in this behalf. However, if any of the heirs or all of them fail to be present after being informed of the date and place of the execution, the punishment will be executed in their absence.

If a person, with the intention of causing death, causes the death of the two or more persons, he shall be punished with death and his death shall be the punishment of all the deaths he has caused without any further liability.[11]

Exceptions from the punishment of *qiṣāṣ* i.e. death

The person who commits intentional murder shall be exempted from the punishment of *qiṣāṣ* in the following cases. However, the offender in such cases shall be punished with *diyat* or *ta'zīr* to be determined by the legislator or court.

(i) Father killing his son

According to Imām Abū Ḥanīfah, Imām Shāfi'ī and Imām Aḥmad if a father, with the intention of causing death, causes the death of his son, he shall not be liable to *qiṣāṣ* i.e. death. They base their view on a *ḥadīth* of the Prophet (pbuh) who said, "A father shall not be punished with *qiṣāṣ* for causing death to his son."

Similar is the case of the grandfather, mother, and grandmother who shall not be punished with death for causing intentional murder to his/her grandson or son. The Daughter is also like a son in this matter.[12]

But according to Imām Mālik if a father, with the intention of reformation, causes the death of his son, he shall not be liable to

---

[10] 'Abdul Mājid Daryabadi, *English Translation and Commentary of Holy Qur'ān,* p.156

[11] Kasānī, *Badā'i al-Ṣanā'i'*, vol.7, p.239

[12] Ibid., p.235

the punishment of death. This is meant by the *hadīth* relied upon by Imām Abū Ḥanīfah and others. But if a father, with the intention of causing death, causes the death of his son not for his reformation but otherwise, he shall be liable to the punishment of retaliation i.e. death like any other person. Similar will be the case with the grandfather, mother and grandmother.[13]

(ii) Difference in religion

According to Imām Mālik and Imām Shāfi'ī, if a Muslim, with the intention of causing death, causes the death of a non-Muslim, he shall not be liable to *qiṣāṣ* i.e. death. They base their view on a *ḥadīth* wherein the Prophet (p.b.u.h) said, "A Muslim shall not be subjected to *qiṣāṣ* for causing death to a non-Muslim" But according to Imām Abū Ḥanīfah if a Muslim, with the intention of causing death, causes the death of a non-Muslim, he shall be punished with *qiṣāṣ* i.e. death. He bases his views on a *ḥadīth* in which the Prophet (pbuh) ordered the execution of a Muslim who had intentionally caused the death of a non-Muslim and said, "I am responsible for the redress of a non-Muslim resident of the Islamic state (*dhimmī*)". He further argues that the *ḥadīth* relied upon by Imām Mālik and Imām Shafi'ī is about such non-Muslims who are at war with the Muslims and have no contractual obligations and guarantees. Moreover the Qur'ān says, *"life for life"*, which includes the murder of a non-Muslim by a Muslim.[14] The difference of the jurists is due to the varied derivations from the Shariah texts and the more correct derivation is the one which declares Muslims and non-Muslims equal, for it is in harmony with the generality of the Shariah texts and is in accord with the principle of equality for the two individuals guilty of the same offence.

(iii) Minor or insane offender

If a minor or insane person who intentionally causes the death of a person he shall not be liable to *qiṣāṣ*. However, the jurists opine that his *aqilah* if any, shall be liable for *diyat* to be paid to the heirs of the victim.

---

[13] Saḥnūn, *al-Mudawwanah,* vol.7, p.106-108

[14] 'Awdah, *al-Tashrī' al-Jinā'ī al-Islāmī,* vol.2, p.122-123

(iv) Pardon of *qiṣāṣ* by the heir or heirs of the victim

The heir or heirs of the victim in an intentional murder can pardon the punishment of *qiṣāṣ* of the convict either against *diyat* or without anything.[15] This is the view of Imām Shāfi'ī and Imām Aḥmad. But according to Imām Abū Ḥanīfah pardoning of *qiṣāṣ* means to pardon *qiṣāṣ* without taking anything. The Holy Qur'ān states:

يَا أَيُّهَا الَّذِينَ آمَنُواْ كُتِبَ عَلَيْكُمُ الْقِصَاصُ فِي الْقَتْلَى الْحُرُّ بِالْحُرِّ وَالْعَبْدُ بِالْعَبْدِ وَالأُنثَى بِالأُنثَى فَمَنْ عُفِيَ لَهُ مِنْ أَخِيهِ شَيْءٌ فَاتِّبَاعٌ بِالْمَعْرُوفِ وَأَدَاءٌ إِلَيْهِ بِإِحْسَانٍ ذَلِكَ تَخْفِيفٌ مِّن رَّبِّكُمْ وَرَحْمَةٌ فَمَنِ اعْتَدَى بَعْدَ ذَلِكَ فَلَهُ عَذَابٌ أَلِيمٌ

Oh you who believe! The law of retaliation is prescribed for you in cases of murder. The free for free, the slave for slave, the woman for woman. But if any remission is made by the brother of slain, then grant any reasonable demand and compensate him with handsome gratitude. This is a concession and mercy from your Lord. After this whoever exceeds the limits shall be in grave penalty. (2:178)

وَكَتَبْنَا عَلَيْهِمْ فِيهَا أَنَّ النَّفْسَ بِالنَّفْسِ وَالْعَيْنَ بِالْعَيْنِ وَالأَنفَ بِالأَنفِ وَالأُذُنَ بِالأُذُنِ وَالسِّنَّ بِالسِّنِّ وَالْجُرُوحَ قِصَاصٌ فَمَن تَصَدَّقَ بِهِ فَهُوَ كَفَّارَةٌ لَّهُ

We ordained therein for them: "Life for life, eye for eye, nose for nose, ear for ear, tooth for tooth and for wounds retaliation. But if anyone remits the retaliation by way of charity, it is an act of atonement for himself.(5:45)

وَمَن قُتِلَ مَظْلُومًا فَقَدْ جَعَلْنَا لِوَلِيِّهِ سُلْطَانًا فَلاَ يُسْرِف فِّي الْقَتْلِ

[15] Abū 'Abd Allāh Muḥammad al-Qurṭubī, *al-Jāmi' li Aḥkām al Qur'ān*, p.255

> And if anyone is slain wrongfully we have given his heirs authority (to demand retaliation or to forgive): but let him not exceed bounds in the matter of taking life. (17:33)

The Holy Prophet has also declared that the heirs of a victim in a murder case are authorized to pardon the offender with or without compensation. Some of the relevant *ḥadīth* are as under:

> "It has been related on the authority of Anas bin Malik who said, "I have seen the Prophet (pbuh) that whenever a case punishable with retaliation was referred to him, he directed for pardoning therein".[16]

> "It has been related on the authority of Abū Shuraih al-Khuzai that the Holy Prophet said, "The heir of a victim in a murder case or the victim in the case of hurt has three options, namely (i) to take *qiṣāṣ* from the convict, (ii) to pardon him or (iii) to take *diyat* and he is not entitled to any other choice."[17]

> "It has been related on the authority of Abū Hurairah that a person was killed in the period of the Holy Prophet and the case was referred to the Prophet. The Prophet called for the heir of the victim and referred the matter to him. The offender said "I swear by Allah that I had not intended to kill him". The Prophet said "If he is true in his oath and even then you kill him, you will enter hell". The heir of the victim pardoned him".[18]

In one *ḥadīth* there are two options for the heir or heirs of the victim in a murder case, namely:

(i) to take *qiṣāṣ* or
(ii) to take *diyat*

The jurists thus concur that the legal heir of the victim in case of an intentional murder is allowed to pardon the *qiṣāṣ* of the

---

[16] Muḥammad ibn 'Alī Shawkānī, *Nayl al-Awṭār,* vol.7, p.33
[17] Abū Dawūd, *Sunan,* vol.2, p.477-78
[18] Ibid.

convict either without anything or with *diyat* or any valuable thing.

According to Imām Mālik only the close male relatives of the victim on the father's side like the son, father, brother, uncle or the woman who is the direct heir of the victim have the right to pardon the *qiṣāṣ* of the convict. But according to Imām Abū Ḥanīfah, Imām Shāfi'ī and Imām Aḥmad all legal heirs whether male or female have the right to pardon *qiṣāṣ*.[19]

Further according to Imām Abū Ḥanīfah and Imām Mālik the pardoning of the punishment of retaliation against *diyat* is subject to the consent of the convict failing which it will not be effective. But according to Imām Shāfi'ī and Imām Aḥmad the consent of the convict for paying *diyat* is not necessary and when the heir of the victim agrees to pardon the convict against *diyat,* the convict has to accept it. This is based on the fact that according to Imām Abū Ḥanīfah and Imām Mālik to give up the demand of the punishment of retaliation of the convict by the heir of the victim against *diyat* is not pardoning but it is compounding of retaliation while according to Imām Shāfi'ī and Imām Aḥmad it is pardoning.[20]

It is pertinent to mention here that none except the heirs of the victim has the right to pardon *qiṣāṣ* of the convict not even a ruler or his authorized representative or officer. However, a ruler can pardon the convict with the consent of the heir.

If an heir, after pardoning the convict against *diyat* or otherwise, causes his death intentionally, he shall be punished with retaliation i.e. death because the convict after being pardoned becomes protected.[21]

If a victim has more than one heir and one of them waives the punishment of retaliation, the convict shall be liable to *diyat.* When there is more than one victim, the waiver of the punishment of retaliation by the heirs of one victim shall not effect the right of retaliation of the heirs of the other victim. Where there is more than one convict, the waiver of the punishment of the retaliation against one convict shall not effect the right of retaliation against

[19] Wahbah al-Zuhaylī, *al-Fiqah al-Islāmī,* vol.5, p.288
[20] 'Awdah, *al-Tashrī' al-Jinā'ī al-Islāmī,* vol.2, p.157-58
[21] Ibid., p.161

the other convicts. Similarly, if a victim, before his death, has himself waived the punishment of retaliation of the convict, the convict shall not be punished with death. But according to Imām Mālik the convict in such a case shall be liable to *qiṣāṣ* as the victim has pardoned the offence before its commission which is not effective. The heirs of the victim who pardon the punishment of retaliation, must be adult and sane.[22]

It is important to mention here that when the heir or heirs of the victim pardon the convict, the court or Government can grant him any suitable *ta'zīr* punishment less than death punishment keeping in view the circumstances of the case. This is the view of Imām Mālik and Imām Abū Ḥanīfah. It is based on the ground that *qiṣāṣ* bears two aspects:

(i) right of Allah and
(ii) right of individuals.[23]

As a matter of fact, Imām Mālik opines that *ta'zīr* is essential in every case of intentional murder wherein *qiṣāṣ* stands invalidated or its sentence cannot be translated into action.[24]

Abdullah Yusuf 'Alī while commenting on verse 5:45, writes:

> "Even where the injured one forgives, the state or the ruler is competent to take such action as is necessary for the preservation of law and order in the society. For crime has a bearing that goes beyond the interests of the person injured".[25]

But according to Imām Shāfi'ī and Imām Aḥmad when the heir or heirs of the victim in case of intentional murder pardon the *qiṣāṣ* of the convict, he shall not be given any more punishment and shall be released forthwith. Al-Māwardī among Shafeites and Abū Ya'la among Ḥanbalis favour the opinion adopted by Imām Abū Ḥanīfah and Imām Mālik. However, *ta'zīr* is not compulsory in every case and should only be given when it is needed for

---

[22] Al-Kāsānī, *Badā'i al-Ṣanā'i'* vol.7, pp.247-48
[23] Wahbah, al-Zuhaylī, *al-Fiqh al-Islāmi,* vol.5, pp.291-92
[24] Al-Ḥattāb, *Mawāhib al-Jalīl,* vol.5, p.257
[25] Yusuf 'Alī, *Commentary,* p.257

public interest.[26] Moreover *ta'zīr* in such a case must be less than death.

If there is more than one heir of the victim in an intentional murder and one or some of them pardon the *qiṣāṣ* of the convict and the other demand his *qiṣāṣ*, the convict shall not be punished with *qiṣāṣ* i.e. death and he shall be liable to pay the share of *diyat* of the heirs who had not pardoned him and to those also who had pardoned against *diyat.*

v. Compromise for removing *qiṣāṣ*

The jurists concur that intentional murder is a compoundable offence and the heir or heirs of the victim are authorized to make a compromise for the release of the offender from *qiṣāṣ* against any valuable thing agreed upon between the parties whether the thing agreed upon is more in value or less, or whether it is paid on the spot or on deferred basis. The difference between waiver and compromise is that waiver is usually made without taking any compensation while compromise is made against any valuable thing. Compromise has been encouraged in Islam in all matters. The Holy Qur'ān says:

وَالصُّلْحُ خَيْرٌ

And compromise is better. (4:128)

The Holy Prophet said, "He who commits intentional murder, remains at the discretion of the heirs of the victim who have three options: (i) to kill him (ii) to demand *diyat* comprising 30 camels three years old, 30 camels four years old and 40 pregnant she-camels or (iii) to make compromise on anything to be taken by them".[27]

Thus compromise with the convict is open to the heirs of the victim at any stage and against anything they mutually agree upon. The amount is to be given or paid to them as agreed upon in the compromise. The thing on which compromise is made between the convict and the heirs of the victim is called *Badal al-Sulh* (بدل الصلح)

Some jurists further opine that the guardian of a minor or insane heir of a victim is not allowed to make a compromise for

---

[26] Ibn Qudāmah, *al-Mughnī,* vol.7, p.745

[27] Al-Tirmidhī, *al-Jāmi',* vol,2, p.212

the removal of *qiṣāṣ* on less than the amount of *diyat* so as to protect the interests of the heir.

When the heirs of the victim make a compromise with the convict, the convict shall be released forthwith according to Imām Shāfi'ī and Imām Aḥmad. But according to Imām Abū Ḥanīfah and Imām Mālik he may be punished with *ta'zīr* if it is required in the circumstances of a case or in public interest. Imām Mālik, in case of waiver and compromise, fixes *ta'zīr* punishment as imprisonment for one year and whipping 100 strokes.

All other conditions for the pardoning of *qiṣāṣ* shall apply to the compromise as well. It is relevant to mention that if the heirs of the victim in intentional murder make a compromise on *diyat,* such *diyat* shall be paid by the convict himself and not by his *aqilah.* Similarly, whenever a convict in an intentional murder is punished with *diyat,* he himself shall be liable for its payment to the heirs of the victim.

If a convict dies before the execution of the punishment of *qiṣāṣ,* all his liabilities cease and his heirs are not liable for anything as punishment for his offence. This is the view of Imām Abū Ḥanīfah and Imām Mālik. But according to Imām Shāfi'ī and Imām Aḥmad *diyat* is to be paid from his property to the heirs of the victim.[28]

It is pertinent to mention that pardon of *qiṣāṣ* in case of intentional murder may either be with or without compensation and a compromise is not required.

Denial of inheritance

The convict in intentional murder shall be deprived of the inheritance in the property of the victim if he is his heir. The Prophet said, "A murderer has no right in the inheritance (of the murdered)". Further according to Imām Mālik the convict in intentional murder and quasi-intentional murder is deprived of inheritance in the property of the murdered but not in murder by mistake. According to Imām Abū Ḥanīfah a murderer who causes the death of the murdered directly is deprived of the inheritance in the property of the murdered irrespective of whether the murder is intentional murder, quasi-intentional murder or murder by

---

[28] 'Awdah, *al-Tashrī' al-Jinā'ī al-Islāmī,* vol.2, p.156-57

mistake. However, a child and person of unsound mind shall not be deprived of the inheritance. The preferable opinion of the Shafeite school is that the murderer stands disinherited in all cases, whether the murder is intentional or unintentional, whether he is sane or insane or a minor or adult. But according to Imām Aḥmad only unjustifiable murder annuls the right to inheritance and legitimate murder does not stand in the way of inheritance, for instance, killing in self defence or as *qiṣāṣ*. The later jurists, however, opine that only in the case of an intentional murder the offender will be deprived of the inheritance of the victim if he is his heir and not in the case of quasi-intentional murder or murder by mistake. Similarly the murderer shall be deprived of the will of the murdered if he has made a will for him in his property.[29]

Punishment of quasi-intentional murder

(i) The punishment of quasi-intentional murder is *diyat* and *ta'zīr*.

It is based on a *ḥadīth* of the Prophet (pbuh) who said, "If a person kills another by throwing a stone, a whip or with a staff, its *diyat* (blood money) will be one hundred camels". This *ḥadīth* relates to the causing of death by a stone, whip or staff which would not ordinarily be sufficient to cause death and as such from the use of such a weapon no conclusion of intentional murder can be drawn. The *diyat* payable in quasi-intentional murder is heavy and will be paid either in lump sum or in instalments to the heirs of the victim within a period of three years.[30]

According to Imām Abū Ḥanifah, Imām Shāfi'ī and Imām Aḥmad *diyat* of quasi-intentional murder is payable by the *'āqilah* of the convict. It is based on a *ḥadīth* of the Prophet (pbuh) related on the authority of Abū Hurairah that in the period of the Prophet (pbuh) two women of Huzayl tribe fought with one another. One of them hit the other with a stone which caused the death of that woman as well as the child in her womb. The Prophet (pbuh) ordered that *diyat* should be paid by the *'āqilah* of the convict (woman) to the heirs of the victim and a slave to be freed for the

[29] Ibid., pp.185-87

[30] Al-Kāsānī, *Badā'i' al-Ṣanā'i'*, vol.7, p.254

death of the child in the womb of the mother. As this was a quasi-intentional murder, the Prophet (pbuh) ordered for the payment of *diyat* by the *'āqilah* of the convict.[31] In another *ḥadīth* the Prophet said, "*Diyat* in quasi-intentional murder wherein murder is caused with a stick or stroke is one hundred camels including forty pregnant she-camels.[32] The heirs of the victim in quasi-intentional murder can remit the whole of *diyat* or a portion thereof and can also make a compromise with the convict as well on any valuable thing.

(ii) Expiation

The convict in a quasi-intentional murder will also be liable for expiation. Expiation is to free a believing slave and if one cannot afford it, he should fast for two consecutive months. This should not be imposed by the court.

(iii) *Ta'zīr*

The convict in a quasi-intentional murder, in addition to the punishment of *diyat* etc. may also be punished with *ta'zīr* if it is required in the interest of the public or the circumstances of the case.[33]

Punishment of murder by mistake

The punishment of murder by mistake is *diyat* (blood money). The Qur'ān says:

وَمَن قَتَلَ مُؤْمِنًا خَطَئًا فَتَحْرِيرُ رَقَبَةٍ مُّؤْمِنَةٍ وَدِيَةٌ مُّسَلَّمَةٌ إِلَى أَهْلِهِ إِلاَّ أَن يَصَّدَّقُواْ

> He who has killed a believer by mistake must set free a believing slave and pay *diyat* (compensation) to the deceased's family unless they remit it freely. (4:92)

The payment of *diyat* in murder by mistake is the liability of the *aqilah* of the convict. The *diyat* in murder by mistake will be

---

[31] Abū Dawūd, *Sunan* vol.2, p.497

[32] Ibid., p.492

[33] 'Awdah, *al-Tashrī' al-Jinā'ī al-Islāmī,* vol.2 p.200

paid to the heirs of the victim either in lump sum or in equal instalments within a period of three years.

If a murder by mistake is committed because of the negligence of the accused for example a driver was driving a vehicle at a high speed in a populated area or he was not following traffic rules and thereby killed a person in an accident, he shall be punished with *ta'zīr* for his negligent driving while *diyat* will also be paid by his *'āqilah* to the heirs of the victim.

The convict in murder by mistake will also be liable for expiation i.e. to set free a believing slave and if he cannot afford it, he should fast for two months. The punishment of expiation will, however, not be given by the court.

The heirs of the victim in murder by mistake can remit the whole or a portion of *diyat.*[34]

Diyat and its value

Diyat means prescribed compensation to be paid to the heirs of the victim in cases of murder by mistake and quasi-intentional murder or to the victim in cases of certain hurts. The Holy Qur'ān states:

وَمَن قَتَلَ مُؤْمِنًا خَطَئًا فَتَحْرِيرُ رَقَبَةٍ مُّؤْمِنَةٍ وَدِيَةٌ مُّسَلَّمَةٌ إِلَى أَهْلِهِ إِلاَّ أَن يَصَّدَّقُواْ

> He who killed a believer by mistake must set free a believing slave and pay *diyat* (compensation) to the deceased's family unless they remit it freely. (4:92)

The Holy Prophet says, "Whoever is killed inadvertently as by flogging or beating with a stick or being hit by a stone, his *diyat* is hundred camels".

The value of *diyat* is one hundred camels. The Holy Prophet, in a letter to Amr bin Ḥazm wrote, "In the matter of murder the *diyat* is one hundred camels."[35]

Ḥaḍrat 'Umar, in his caliphate, declared that as the price of a camel is very high, *diyat* is prescribed as 1,000 dinars for the people of gold i.e. the people of Egypt and Syria and 12,000

---

[34] Ibn Qudāmah, *al-Mughnī,* vol.9, pp.209-14

[35] Nasai, p.372

dirhams for the people of silver i.e. the people of Iraq, two hundred cows, two thousand sheep or two hundred pairs of garments for concerned people.[36]

According to Imām Abū Ḥanīfah, Imām Mālik and the old opinion of Imām Shāfi'ī the value of *diyat* is determined in any of the three things i.e. camels, gold and silver. But according to Imām Aḥmad it is determined in any of the six things i.e. camels, gold, silver, cows, sheep and garments.[37] Further the jurists concur that the value of *diyat* in gold is 1000 dinars which is equal to 4250 grams of gold. But as far as the value of *diyat* in silver is concerned according to Imām Mālik, Imām Aḥmad and Imām Shāfi'ī the value of *diyat* is 12,000 dirhams, but according to Imām Abū Ḥanīfah the value of *diyat* is 10,000 dirhams. As the price of gold is very high in some countries, the value is determined in silver therein. But in other countries gold is the base of the determination of the value of *diyat*. If the *diyat* is paid in gold or silver then it is equal for all kinds of murder, and if it is paid in the form of camels then *diyat* to be paid in murder by mistake is twenty she-camels one year old, twenty two years old, twenty he-camels two years old, twenty she-camels three years old and twenty she-camels four years old. *Diyat* in intentional murder is twenty five she-camels one year old, twenty five two years old, twenty five three years old and twenty five four years old. According to one *ḥadīth diyat* in quasi-intentional murder is one hundred camels out of which forty must be pregnant. Sometimes due to severity of a murder liable for *diyat*, the *diyat* is made heavier which includes the camels of a determined type and higher age.[38]

Diyat in the modern Muslim countries is determined in gold or silver due to the non-availability or extremely high price of the camels therein. The legislator has to determine the value of the prescribed quantity of gold and silver from time to time in the prevailing currency.

According to Imām Abū Ḥanifah the amount of *diyat* in intentional murder should be paid by the convict either in lump

---

[36] Al-Bayhaqī, *al-Sunan al Kabrā*, vol.7, p.268
[37] Ibn Qudāmah, *al-Mughnī*, pp.759-61
[38] Ibid., vol.7, p.759

sum or in instalments. But according to other jurists, *diyat* in intentional murder should be paid by the convict forthwith in lump sum or as agreed upon in the pact of compromise. The amount of *diyat* shall be paid to the heirs of the victim according to their respective shares in the inheritance.[39]

And if there is no *'āqilah* of the offender or his *'āqilah* cannot bear the payment of *diyat, diyat* shall be paid by the Government.[40] *Diyat* in quasi-intentional murder and murder by mistake shall be paid by the *'āqilah* of the convict either in lump sum or in instalments within a period of three years.

Diyat is a fixed compensation and the court can neither enhance nor diminish it. *Diyat* for a quasi-intentional murder is different from that intended for murder by mistake. It is also different for various hurts. There is no difference between the *diyat* of a child and an adult, the weak and the strong, the young and the old, the ruler and the ruled. *Diyat* is also liable in an offence of intentional murder wherein *qiṣāṣ* is not liable. *Diyat* in an intentional murder and quasi-intentional murder is heavy while in the case of murder by mistake it is light. Moreover *diyat* is necessary even if the offender is a minor or insane and in such a case the *diyat* will be paid by the family of the offender to the victim or his heirs as the case may be.

According to the majority of the jurists, *diyat* in case of a female victim is half of that of a male victim in any kind of murder. They rely on a *ḥadīth* of the Prophet who said, "*diyat* of a woman is half of that of a man". But according to some jurists like Ibn Ulayyah and Abū Bakr al-'Āsim the *diyat* of a man and a woman is equal. They rely on the *ḥadīth* related on the authority of Amr bin Ḥazm wherein the words are "ف النفس المومنة ماءة من ابل" [In the murder of a Muslim (man or woman) are one hundred camels] and they consider the *ḥadīth* relied upon by the majority of the jurists as weak and unreliable.[41] However, according to

---

[39] 'Awdah, *al-Tashrī' al-Jinā'ī al-Islāmī*, Vol.2, pp.179-83

[40] Council of Islamic Ideology, Pakistan, *Draft Law of Qiṣāṣ and Diyat* 1981, p.22

[41] Wahbah, al-Zuhaylī, *al-Fiqh al-Islāmī,* vol. 7, pp.310-11

some later jurists there is no difference in the *diyat* of a male and a female and it has been preferred by the later jurists.

No member of an *'āqilah* shall be made liable to pay more than 44.55 grams of silver or 6.35 grams of gold or their value in the prevailing currency as *diyat* annually. Where an *'āqilah* is made liable for the payment of *diyat,* the convict shall be deemed to be a member of such *'āqilah* and shall pay the proportional share of the *diyat.* Women and children are not liable to pay *diyat.* If a convict or his *'āqilah* liable for the payment of *diyat* fails to pay *diyat* or any part thereof within the specified period, it shall be recovered with force from them.[42]

It is relevant to mention that full *diyat* is paid not only for the loss of life, but also for the destruction of any single member or joint in the body, privation of complete sight or complete hearing, loss of sexual power, hurt on head which permanently reduces the intelligence quotient of the brain of the victim and cutting of part of the nose or the whole of it, resulting in permanent disfiguring of the face. In these cases the *diyat* is paid by the convict to the victim.

It is also pertinent to mention that if the victim of murder by mistake or quasi-intentional murder has been insured by an insurance company in accordance with the Islamic principles, the amount payable to him by such company on his accidental death as insurance benefits may be deducted from the amount of the *diyat.* In case the amount of such insurance benefits is equal to or more than the amount of *diyat, diyat* may not be paid to the victim in such a case. Similarly if the victim of murder by mistake is a rich person, *diyat* may not be paid in such a case. The offender shall, however, be punished for his negligence in such cases with imprisonment and fine as deemed fit according to the circumstances of the case.

Institution of *'āqilah*

'Āqilah (عاقلة) in term of Islamic criminal law means agnatic male relatives of a person on his father's side, or an institution or

[42] Al-Kāsānī, *Badā'i' al-Ṣana'i',* vol. 7, pp.355-59

organization from which he receives or expects to receive support or help.

In pre-Islamic Arabs when a person of a tribe committed murder, the whole tribe specially its adult and sane male members were obliged to pay *diyat* (blood money) irrespective of whether the offender killed the victim intentionally or unintentionally. It was based on the principle that the people of the family and tribe being in a position to influence the actions of the offender should be reminded of their duty of keeping the offender and similar other persons under control and check their criminal activities. This was a form of collective fine on the relatives and supporters of the offender which was a successful method in a homogenous society of the Arabs. But Islam changed this concept and imposed the payment of *diyat* on *'āqilah* only in unintentional murder and quasi-intentional murder.

It has been related that in the period of the Holy Prophet (pbuh), two women from Hudhayl tribe quarreled with each other, one of them who was pregnant was killed by the other with a stone, which hit her in the womb. The Prophet said that *diyat* shall be paid to the heirs of the victim by her *'āqilah* i.e. agnates.[43]

According to Imām Mālik, Imām Shāfi'ī and Imām Aḥmad *'āqilah* means the agnate relatives of a person on the father's side such as brothers, nephews, uncles, cousins. It does not include son, father, maternal relations, husbands and other relatives who are not paternal. But according to later Ḥanafīs *'āqilah* means the institution or organization to which a person belongs and from which he receives or expects to receive help or support such as the army, ministry, university, or bank. If a person does not belong to any institution or organization then his *'āqilah* is his paternal relative, tribe or anyone from whom he receives or expects to receive help or support. If a person has no *'āqilah* or his *'āqilah* cannot bear the burden of *diyat,* the Government will pay *diyat.*

According to Imām Mālik and Imām Abū Ḥanīfah the offender shall be included in his *'āqilah* as a member and shall be liable for the payment of his share in *diyat.* But according to Imām Shāfi'ī and Imām Aḥmad, the offender is not liable for any portion of *diyat* at all and the whole *diyat* will be paid by his *'āqilah.*

---

[43] Shawkānī, *Nail al-Awṭār,* vol.6, p.369

There are two opinions in case the offender has no *'āqilah* or if he is destitute or the number of his family members is so small that they cannot bear the burden of the *diyat:*

- The first opinion is that the Government will take the place of *'āqilah.* If there is no *'āqilah* at all or there is *'āqilah* but the persons concerned are poor, then the *diyat* will be paid by the Government. If the number of the family members is small and can not pay the whole *diyat,* the balance will be paid by the Government. This is the opinion of Imām Mālik and Imām Shāfi'ī. The apparent position of the Ḥanafites and the Ḥanbaleites is also the same.
- The second opinion is that *diyat* will be recoverable from the assets or property of the offender, for in reality the offender alone is responsible for the payment of *diyat.* The family bears the burden simply by way of helping him. Hence if there is no family, the obligation of the payment of *diyat* would revert to the origin. This opinion has been quoted by Imām Muḥammad with reference to Imām Abū Ḥanīfah. Some of the Hanbaleites also subscribe to this opinion.[44]

The payment of *diyat* by *'āqilah* was in force till the period of Ḥaḍrat 'Umar. But in the period of Ḥaḍrat 'Umar, when he saw that the structure of society had changed, he declared in the presence of *ṣaḥābah* (companions of the Prophet) that lists (*dīwān)* of the persons serving in the army should be drawn up in various districts. The persons whose names contained in those *diwan* owed one another mutual assistance and had to contribute to the payment of *diyat* if any of them committed murder unintentionally.

It is pertinent to mention here that some later Ḥanafī jurists like Ibn 'Ābidīn opine that in the modern world the offender himself shall be liable for the payment of *diyat* alone if he is rich and can afford it. If he is a person with ordinary means, he can be held liable for the payment of a portion of *diyat,* to the extent that can afford it, and if he is too poor to pay *diyat,* then *diyat* shall be

[44] 'Awdah, *al-Tashrī' al-Jinā'ī al-Islāmī,*.vol.1, pp.677-79 see also Wahbah Al Zuhaylī, *al-Fiqh al-Islāmī,* vol.7, p.322-26

paid by the Government from the fund maintained for this purpose. Ibn 'Ābidīn further states that the people of one profession in a specific area may contribute a small amount to a fund from which *diyat* will be paid in case anyone of them causes death to a person by mistake.[45]

Bearing the burden of *diyat* by the family would mean that those who are not guilty have to bear the brunt of the offender's crime, whereas it is said in the Holy Qur'ān;

أَلَّا تَزِرُ وَازِرَةٌ وِزْرَ أُخْرَى

That no bearer of burden can bear the burden of another. (53:38)

But the question of *diyat* is an exception to this rule. The reason for this is, the circumstances of the offender and the victim's party. On these grounds such an exception is the demand of justice and guarantee of the recovery of the dues. The exception in question is warranted on the following grounds:

1. If this rule is applied in its entirety to this question and obliges every offender to bear the consequences of his act, the result would be that only the well-to-do would be liable to punishment, who are small in number and the poor could not be awarded any punishment who are in majority. Consequently if the offender is affluent, the victim or his lawful guardian will receive *diyat* in full and in case he happens to be of moderate means, *diyat* could be recovered partially but if he is indigent, as is mostly the case, the victim will get no *diyat* at all. Thus there will be no justice between the offenders and the victim. It is for this reason that exemption must be given from the general rule relating to the problem under discussion.
2. Although *diyat* constitutes a punishment yet it is also the pecuniary right of the victim or his rightful guardian. Allowance has been made in *diyat* for serving as a fair compensation for the offence. Now if the rule mentioned above is extended to this case and the accused is declared liable to the payment of *diyat* alone, then a large number of

---

[45] Ibn 'Ābidīn, *al-Durr al-Mukhtār,* vol.5, p.456

victims will not be able to recover *diyat* for the amount fixed for full *diyat* is beyond the financial means of a common man. The value of a hundred camels come to more than a thousand dinar. Obviously, full amount of *diyat* is not within the means of an average individual. Hence, if the rule in question is applied in its entirety in this case and holds only the offender responsible for the results of his act, the victim's party will not be able to recover what is due to them. In this context, therefore, exemption from the general rule alone would ensure the realization of their dues by the aggrieved party.

3. The impact of the burden on *'āqilah* (family) is associated with unintentional offences. The offences committed unintentionally owe themselves to inattention and carelessness and both these weaknesses are the result of the lack of right guidance and bad training. Therefore, the people who will be held responsible for the guidance and training of the individuals are those related to the offender by blood. As the individual is influenced by the members of his family and bears close affinity to them in all matters, his negligence and carelessness would be attributed to the influence of the family. Family, in its turn, is subject to the impact of the society. Hence negligence and carelessness would be finally treated as social legacy.

Hence, it is necessary that the family and the society both should bear the consequences of the individual's mistakes. If the *'āqilah* cannot afford to do so, then the society as a whole should bear the burden thereof.

Inattention and carelessness spring from the consciousness of honour and power and this state of mind stems from the conjunctions of the family and the society, for it has been observed that those who have no family are more careful and cautious than those with a family and those with a small family are more careful and cautious than those having a larger family. Hence, it is necessary for the family and the society that they should bear the brunt of the individual's inadvertence because they are the ultimate source of the carelessness and negligence resulting in his grave mistake. The family system and the social system both stand on the firm basis of natural sympathy and mutual cooperation. It is therefore, incumbent on every individual or the family to co-operate with and help all the other members of the family and this is also obligatory for every individual of the society. Making the family first and then the society bear the consequence of an individual's inadvertence brings effectively into play the spirit of mutual help and fellow-feeling. In fact it renews and reaffirms this spirit each and every moment. Thus whenever an individual commits unintentional offence, the offender contacts the members of his family, and the family members in their turn contact members of other families and co-operate in this way in the collection of the *diyat.* As unintentional crimes are very common, reciprocal expression of sympathy and mutual contact and co-operation among the individuals of the society continues unbroken.

4. As a result of burdening the offender and his family with payment of the *diyat* due from him, the offenders, in general, are treated in a humane manner, their punishment is mitigated and they are not wronged or oppressed. The reason for this is that the offender whose family bears the burden of his *diyat* may at some stage himself play the role of bearing the burden of the *diyat* due from another individual and since to err is human, it is also most likely that the offender would share the burden of the *diyat* of another family member to the same extent as this member bears the burden of the offender's *diyat.*

5. The fundamental principle of the *Sharī'ah* is to protect the life of the people and to prevent loss thereof without any reason. That is why *diyat* has been prescribed in lieu of life and its loss without any rhyme or reason. Now if every offender is himself held responsible for the payment of his *diyat* and he is unable to pay it, the victim's life would turn out to have been lost. Hence, exemption from the general rule is imperative, so that the life of the people may not be lost in vain.

The question is whether the system of *'āqilah* can be established in the present time and if it can't be established what alternatives can, instead be considered. In this connection a contemporary Egyptian scholar, Abdul Qadir 'Awdah writes:

> "It is not possible to establish *'āqilah* system nowadays because it presupposes the existence of a family system. But this system has disintegrated. Whatever remains of it consists of too small a number of individuals to make them bear the burden of *diyat.* The existence of *aqilah* is possible only when the people guard their descents and relationships and cling to their paternal tribes and clans. But in most countries such a situation no longer exists. For this reason there is no alternative but to accept one of the two opinions of the jurists: either the offender be made to bear the entire burden of *diyat* or *diyat* will be paid out of Government treasury.

If the whole burden of *diyat* is placed on the shoulders of the offender, the victim's life would have been wasted (i.e. the offender will not be able to pay *diyat*) because the offenders are generally poor. Obviously this is not consistent with the *Shariah.* Besides, there is no justice and equality in such a situation.

On the other hand, if the second opinion is accepted, the Government will be required to bear the burden of *diyat.* This would meet the requirement of justice, security of life would be ensured and the aim of the *Shariah* fulfilled. Hence the burdening of the Government should not stand in the way of the achievement of the objectives of the *Sharī'ah.* The Government may rather levy a tax or earmark certain amounts realized through certain fines for the payment of this kind of compensations. Moreover, if modern states assume the responsibility of providing social security for the indigent, they are liable to take upon themselves the responsibility of the payment of compensation to the oppressed heirs of the victim.

Some European countries like Germany, Italy and Yugoslavia have adopted this concept and have earmarked a special fund for the purpose known as the *mulct* fund. In this fund those fines are deposited which the courts impose. Income from this fund is reserved for the payment of the *mulct* of those offenders whose possessions and assets are not sufficient to pay the *mulct* due from them.

The part of *'āqilah* system adopted by some European countries is meant to achieve the objectives which the *Shariah* takes into account. Now if the system could be established in its present form in Europe, it is actually our own system which ought to be established among the Muslims, so that the aims of the *Sharī'ah* may be fulfilled under our circumstances".[46]

> Another contemporary scholar, Wahbah al-Zuhaylī, writes; The old tribal system does not exist nowadays and the structure of the Government treasury has changed and the social system is now different than that existing in the days of pre-Islamic Arabs. Moreover, the family system has also changed and everybody bears his own burden only and does not bear the burden of his family or tribe members. In this situation *diyat* cannot be imposed on *'āqilah* nowadays. *Ḍiyat* can, however, be imposed on the offender only as some Ḥanafī jurists have opined.[47]

The Government may impose a small additional fee on the issue and renewal of a driving licence and the amount so collected should be deposited in *diyat* fund. Moreover, the persons belonging to one profession or organization may contribute to a *diyat* fund and whenever any of them commits murder by mistake, *diyat* may be paid from this fund.

It is thus concluded from the above discussion that nowadays *'āqilah* cannot be held responsible for the payment of *diyat*. The offender can be held responsible for the payment of *diyat* if he is rich and can afford it. But if the offender is poor, he cannot be held responsible for the payment of *diyat* and *diyat* in such a case should be paid from some other source. And if the offender is a man of ordinary means he shall be held responsible to such portion of *diyat* which he can afford.

---

[46] 'Awdah, *al-Tashrī' al-Jinā'ī al-Islāmī,* vol.1, pp.677-78

[47] Wahbah al-Zuhaylī, *al-Fiqh al-Islāmī*, vol.6, p.326

Chapter Four

Hurts and their punishments

Another heinous crime in Islamic criminal law is causing hurt to a person. "Hurt" means to cause bodily pain, harm, disease, infirmity or injury to any person or impair, disable or dismember any limb or organ of his body, without causing his death. Thus hurt in short is any bodily harm which is less than death. Hurts are of two classifications, namely:

(i) intentional hurt and
(ii) hurt by mistake

This is the view of Imām Abū Ḥanīfah and Imām Mālik. But according to Imām Shāfi'ī and Imām Aḥmad there are three classifications of hurt, namely:

(i) intentional hurt,
(ii) quasi-intentional hurt and
(iii) hurt by mistake or unintentional hurt.[1]

Jurists have divided the hurts into five main kinds

1. To cut or amputate totally any limb or organ of the body of another person like amputation of hand, foot, finger, eye, ear, lip etc.

2. To destroy or permanently impair the functioning or power of a limb or an organ of another person.

3. To cause hurt on the head or face of any person which does not amount to the total amputation or destroying of the head or face. It is called *Shajjah*, and is of eleven kinds as follows:

---

[1] Wahbah al-Zuhaylī, *al-Fiqh al-Islāmī*, vol.6, p.332

i. *Hārisah*, if only the skin has been cut or separated.
ii. *Dāmiyah*, if blood has flowed.
iii. *Bāḍiah*, if the flesh has been injured.
iv. *Mutalāḥimah,* if the flesh has been penetrated.
v. *Simhāk*, if the membrane enters the flesh and the bone is injured.
vi. *Muḍiḥah*, if the bone has been uncovered.
vii. *Hāshimah*, if the bone itself has been injured.
viii. *Munaqqilah,* if the bone is broken, so that the fragments are separated.
ix. *Mamunah* or *Āmmah*, if the membrane of the brain has been injured.
x. *Dāmighah*, if the brain is injured.
xi. *Dāmi'ah*, if the blood is uncovered but does not flow.[2]

4. To cause hurt on any part of the body of a person other than the head or face leaving a mark of the wound whether temporary or permanent. If a person causes hurt to another person and the wound enters the body cavity of the trunk, it is called *jā'ifah.* And if a person causes hurt to another person and the wound does not enter the body cavity of the trunk, it is called *ghayr jā'ifah* and such hurt either causes rupturing of the skin with which bleeding starts or cutting the flesh without exposing the bone or lacerating the flesh without exposing the bone or fracture of a bone without dislocating it or fracturing and dislocating the bone.[3]

5. Hurts other than the hurts mentioned above.

Punishments of intentional hurts

The punishment of hurt, when it is caused intentionally, is *qiṣāṣ* (retaliation) if the victim is a protected person and causing similar hurt to the same part of the body of the convict is possible. The Qur'ān says:

---

[2] Ibid., p.351-58

[3] 'Awdah, *al-Tashrī' al-Jinā'ī al-Islāmī*, vol.2, pp.204-9

وَالْعَيْنَ بِالْعَيْنِ وَالأَنفَ بِالأَنفِ وَالأُذُنَ بِالأُذُنِ وَالسِّنَّ بِالسِّنِّ وَالْجُرُوحَ قِصَاصٌ

Eye for eye, nose for nose, ear for ear, tooth for tooth and for wounds retaliation. (5:45)

وَإِنْ عَاقَبْتُمْ فَعَاقِبُواْ بِمِثْلِ مَا عُوقِبْتُم بِهِ وَلَئِن صَبَرْتُمْ لَهُوَ خَيْرٌ لِّلصَّابِرِينَ

And if you do catch them out, catch them out not worse than they catch you out: But if you show patience, that is indeed the best (course) for those who are patient. (16:126)

It has been related on the authority of Anas bin Mālik that Rābi'a daughter of Nadar broke the front teeth of a girl. They imposed *arsh* (compensation) on them but the victim refused and demanded *qiṣāṣ*, so her brother Anas bin Nadar came to the Prophet and said, "Oh Prophet! You will break the front teeth of Rabi'a, for the sake of Allah, please don't break her front teeth". The Prophet said, "Oh Anas, Allah has prescribed *qiṣāṣ*". But meanwhile the victim pardoned her *qiṣāṣ*. The Prophet said, "There are some persons if anyone of them swears in Allah for any act, Allah expiates him".[4]

The term *qiṣāṣ* in hurt means punishment by causing similar hurt at the same part of the body of the offender as he has caused to the victim. There are some conditions for *qiṣāṣ* in hurt which, in short, are as under:

1. The offender must have caused hurt to the victim intentionally.

2. The offender must be adult and sane.

According to Imām Shāfi'ī the victim must be a Muslim. Thus if a Muslim causes hurt liable to *qiṣāṣ* to a non-Muslim he will not be punished with *qiṣāṣ* but will be punished with compensation accordingly. But according to Imām Abū Ḥanīfah the hurt of a Muslim and non-Muslim is equal and as such if a Muslim causes

[4] Sayyid Sābiq, *Fiqh al-Sunnah*, vol.2, p.456

hurt liable to *qiṣāṣ* to a non-Muslim he will be punished with *qiṣāṣ* and vice-versa. The later jurists have preferred this opinion.

1. There must be equality in the relevant organ or limb of the victim and the offender. Thus the right hand shall not be amputated in *qiṣāṣ* for the left hand and a fit hand will not be amputated in *qiṣāṣ* for a damaged or paralysed hand etc.

2. There must be complete equality in the severity of the hurt and thus no such hurt will be caused to the offender which causes more harm to him than what he has caused to the victim.[5]

As causing a similar hurt to the offender as he has caused to the victim is difficult in many hurts, *qiṣāṣ* will only be applied when the organ has the joint and limit known in the body like finger, hand etc. if dismembered totally or any such hurt which can easily and clearly be caused to the offender without causing him anymore harm than he has caused to the victim. The Holy Prophet said, "There is no *qiṣāṣ* in fracture of the bone". In another *ḥadīth* the Prophet said, "There is no *qiṣāṣ* in *mamūnah, jā'ifah and munaqqilah.*"[6]

The jurists further agree that *qiṣāṣ* shall not be applied in the following hurts:

(i) If full nose is cut since it would require cutting the nasal bones.

For the same reason if the cutting of the limb involves cutting of the bone too or cutting of a finger from a place other than the joint.

(ii) If the eye is gouged.

(iii) If only a part of a limb is cut.

(iv) In cutting of tongue.

(v) If an additional finger of the victim is cut.

---

[5] Ibid., pp.456-57

[6] Ibid.,

(vi) In the cutting of the skin, the head or the body or cutting the flesh of the cheek, belly or back or in the cutting of hair.[7]

The jurists also concur that the execution of the sentence of *qiṣāṣ* (retaliation) in hurts should be preceded by medical examination in order to find out whether equality can be maintained without causing the convict an additional injury and to make sure that no bone would be affected.

With all these conditions and exceptions the punishment of *qiṣāṣ* in hurts is given in rare cases only and instead the punishment of compensation or imprisonment or both is given in general cases of hurts keeping in view the circumstances of the case.

If an offender, at the instance of the victim, causes hurt to him, he shall not be punished with *qiṣāṣ* (retaliation) and shall be punished with compensation accordingly. Similarly if a person causes hurt to an unprotected person, he shall not be liable to *qiṣāṣ* (retaliation) but shall be liable to imprisonment or fine or both if it is required in the circumstances of a particular case. Further if a victim in a case of hurt dies before the execution of the punishment of *qiṣāṣ* (retaliation), the offender shall not be punished with *qiṣāṣ* (retaliation) but shall be liable to compensation accordingly.[8]

In the case of a hurt where *qiṣāṣ* is not applicable due to some legal grounds, the offender may be made liable for compensation and may also be made liable for *ta'zīr* if it is required under the circumstances of a particular case.

Hurt by Mistake

If a person, without intention of causing hurt, causes hurt to another person, he shall not be punished with *qiṣāṣ* (retaliation) but shall be punished with compensation accordingly and may also be liable to *ta'zīr* if the offence has been committed partly due to his negligence or it is required for public interest.

There are many hurts for which compensation has been fixed in the *Sunnah* of the Prophet (pbuh) and the jurists, with some

---

[7] Wahbah, al-Zuhaylī, *al-Fiqh al-Islāmī*. vol.6, pp.342-48

[8] 'Awdah, *al-Tashrī' al-Jinā'ī al-Islāmī*, vol.2, pp.290-91

minor differences, have approved them. Fixed compensation is called *arsh* (ارش) while unfixed compensation is called *daman* (ضمان) or *arsh ghayr muqaddar* (ارش غير مقدر). Some of these hurts and their compensations are as under:[9]

S.No	Hurt	Compensation
1.	Destruction or amputation of any member or joint in the body	Full *diyat* if the member or joint is single such as nose, tongue etc.
2.	Permanent impairing of the powers of member or joint	Half *diyat* if the members are in pairs and damage is caused to one of them such as eyes, ears, hands, feet.
3.	Cutting of one lip	Half *diyat*
4.	Privation of complete sight or complete hearing	Full *diyat*
5.	Cutting of nose-part or whole, resulting in permanent disfiguring of the face	Full *diyat*
6.	Loss of sexual power	Full *diyat*
7.	Loss of tooth other than milk tooth	5% *diyat*
8.	Loss of one finger or thumb whether of hand or foot	5% *diyat*
9.	Hurt on head or face in which bone is exposed	5% *diyat*
10.	Hurt on face or head with fracture of the bone without dislocation	10% *diyat*
11.	Hurt on face or head with dislocation of bone	15% *diyat*
12.	Fracture of the skull when the wound touches membrane of the brain	1/3 *diyat*

[9] Al-Jazīrī, *Kitāb al-Fiqh 'alā al-Mazāhib al-Arba'ah*, vol.5, pp.335-62

13.	Hurt on head which permanently reduces the intelligence quotient of the brain of the victim	Full *diyat*
14.	Hurt other than on head or face which enters the body of the trunk	1/3 *diyat*

The compensations of the hurts other than those mentioned above have not been fixed and have been left to the legislators and judges to fix them according to the prevailing circumstances. The maximum amount of compensation may be fixed and it may be left to the judge to impose such amount as he thinks fit in view of the circumstances of each case and the financial position of the convict as well as the offender. Any prescribed or non-prescribed compensation shall be paid to the victim and if he dies, to his heirs according to their respective shares in the inheritance of the victim.

Pardoning or compounding in matters of hurts

An adult and sane victim in case of hurt is authorised to pardon *qiṣāṣ* (retaliation) with or without compensation, or compound it by anything agreed upon by the parties. The offender shall, after pardoning or compounding, not be punished with *qiṣāṣ* (retaliation) and shall be liable for the payment of compensation mutually agreed upon in compounding of *qiṣāṣ* (retaliation). If the victim is a minor or insane, then his guardian shall have the right of *qiṣāṣ* (retaliation) and its pardoning or compounding.[10]

Hurt to a pregnant woman causing miscarriage

If a person intentionally causes hurt to a pregnant woman which causes miscarriage, he shall be liable for *diyat* if the child is born alive and dies later on. And if the child is born dead, the offender shall be liable for 1/20 of *diyat* and shall also be liable for *ta'zīr* to be determined in the circumstances of the case. In case the offender has caused the hurt by mistake, 1/20 of the *diyat* shall be paid by his *'āqilah* in lump sum or within a period of one year.

---

[10] 'Awdah, *al-Tashrī' al-Jinā'ī al-Islāmī*, vol.2, pp.257-59

And if the child in miscarriage is such whose organs or limbs have not been formed and the miscarriage has not been caused in good faith for the purpose of saving the life of the woman, the offender shall be liable for *ta'zīr* to be determined in the circumstances of the case.[11]

Hurt caused jointly by two or more persons

If two or more persons jointly cause hurt to any person which is liable to *qiṣāṣ* (retaliation) and their acts cannot be distinguished or identified as to whose act was sufficient to cause such hurt and whose act was not of them shall be liable to *qiṣāṣ*. And if their acts can be identified then each of them shall be liable for the hurt he has caused to the victim. This is the opinion of Imām Aḥmad. But according to Imām Mālik and Imām Shāfi'ī all of them shall be liable for *qiṣāṣ as* if they have jointly caused hurt to the victim. But according to Imām Abū Ḥanīfah when two or more persons jointly cause hurt liable to *qiṣāṣ* to a person, *qiṣāṣ* shall applied to all of them and all of them shall be liable to pay jointly the compensation for such hurt.[12] And if two or more persons jointly cause hurt to a person which is liable for compensation, such compensation shall be payable by all of them in equal shares and if any *ta'zīr* is considered suitable, each of them shall be liable to *ta'zīr*.

Execution of the punishment of *qiṣāṣ* (retaliation) in hurt

Before the execution of the punishment of *qiṣāṣ* (retaliation) in the matter of hurt, an authorised medical officer may examine the convict and make sure that the execution of *qiṣāṣ* (retaliation) shall neither cause the death of the convict nor shall it exceed the hurt caused by the convict to the victim. And if the medical officer is of the opinion that there is danger of the death of the convict in the execution of the punishment or a similar hurt cannot be caused to the convict that he has caused to the victim the punishment of *qiṣāṣ* (retaliation) shall not be executed and the convict shall be liable for compensation and may also be liable for *ta'zīr* if required in the circumstances of the case. And if the convict is a

---

[11] Wahbah, al-Zuhaylī, *al-Fiqh al-Islāmī,* vol.6, pp.362-67

[12] Sayyed Sābiq, *Fiqh al-Sunnah*, vol.2, p.458

pregnant woman, the execution of the punishment shall be postponed till the birth of the child or miscarriage and during this period she should be released on bail or kept in jail as in simple imprisonment. After the birth of the child or miscarriage, the woman may be subjected to the execution of punishment at a suitable time.

Proof of crime of hurt

The crime of hurt liable to *qiṣāṣ* (retaliation) is proved either by the confession of the accused without any coercion or by the testimony of two adult, sane and credible witnesses. The crime of hurt liable for compensation whether prescribed *(arsh muqaddar)* or unprescribed *(ḍamān)* and the crime of hurt by mistake is proved by the confession of the accused or by the testimony of two witnesses or one witness or circumstantial evidence or any other evidence which proves the guilt to the satisfaction of the court.

Liability of hurt cause by an animal

If an animal causes hurt to a person, the owner of such animal shall be liable for its compensation provided he was either riding the animal at that time or was present to take care of it. But, if the owner was not present at that time, he shall not be responsible for anything. Similarly if an animal causes damage to any property, the owner of such an animal shall be liable for its compensation provided he was present with his animal at that time. But, if the owner was not present with his animal at that time, he shall not be responsible for anything. However, other circumstances may also be looked into in incriminating the owner of the animal in such cases along-with his own position.[13]

[13] Ibid., vol.2, p.483

Chapter Five

Crimes Liable to *Hudūd*
(Part I)

Introduction

Ḥadd literally means boundary or limit which separates one thing from another. The watchman is called *ḥaddad* as he prevents the public from entering the place which he protects and separates. In terms of Islamic criminal law *ḥadd* means the punishment fixed either by the Holy Qur'ān or *Sunnah* of the Holy Prophet for a crime as the Right of Allah. Fixed punishments are known as *ḥudūd* because they are meant to prevent crimes and they have fixed limits for punishments. The idea of 'limit' is thus basic both to the literal as well as the technical meanings of *ḥadd.* The classification of *ḥadd* as the right of Allah signifies that it is meant to be a mandatory punishment which requires fulfillment and no one, including the victim, judge, legislator or ruler has the authority to decrease, increase, alter, pardon or suspend it. The punishment of *qiṣāṣ* is not *ḥadd* because it has been fixed as the right of individuals and it is for this reason that it can be pardoned by the victim or his heirs. *Ḥadd* also means the crime for which punishment has been fixed either by the Holy Qur'ān or *Sunnah* of the Prophet as the Right of Allah.[1] The following are the crimes liable to *ḥadd* in Islamic criminal law:

i) *Zinā* (Adultery or fornication).
ii) *Qazf* (Accusation of *zinā).*

---

[1] 'Awdah, *al-Tashri' al-Jinā'i al-Islāmī,* vol.2, p.343

iii) Theft.
iv) *Ḥarābah* (Robbery and dacoity).
v) Drinking intoxicating liquor.
vi) Rebellion.
vii) Apostasy.

I. *Zinā* (Adultery or Fornication)

A crime liable to *ḥadd* in Islamic criminal law is *zinā* (adultery and fornication). *'Zinā'* means willful sexual intercourse between a man and a woman who are not, and do not suspect to be, validly married to each other. Jurists usually define it as sexual intercourse between a man and a woman who are not, and do not suspect to be, in a state of legal matrimony. *Zinā* has been prohibited in Islam. Qur'ān says:

لاَ تَقْرَبُواْ الزِّنَى إِنَّهُ كَانَ فَاحِشَةً وَسَاء سَبِيلاً

And come not near to adultery: For it is a shameful (deed) and an evil, opening the road (to other evils). (17:32)

'Abdullah Yusuf 'Alī, while commenting on the above verse, writes, "adultery is not only shameful in itself and inconsistent with any self-respect or respect for others, but it opens the road to many evils. It may destroy the basis of the family; it works against the interest of children born or to be born; it may cause murders and feuds and loss of reputation and property and also loosen permanently the bonds of society. Not only should it be avoided as a sin but any approach or temptation to it should be avoided."[2]

The Qur'ān, while describing the qualities of the believers, says:

وَالَّذِينَ لَا يَدْعُونَ مَعَ اللَّهِ إِلَهًا آخَرَ وَلَا يَقْتُلُونَ النَّفْسَ الَّتِي حَرَّمَ اللَّهُ إِلَّا بِالْحَقِّ وَلَا يَزْنُونَ وَمَن يَفْعَلْ ذَلِكَ يَلْقَ أَثَامًا

Those who invoke not with God any other god, nor slay such life as God has made sacred, except for just cause,

---

[2] Yusuf 'Alī, *Commentary*, p.703

nor commit fornication, and any that does this meets punishments. (25:68)

يَا أَيُّهَا النَّبِيُّ إِذَا جَاءَكَ الْمُؤْمِنَاتُ يُبَايِعْنَكَ عَلَى أَن لَّا يُشْرِكْنَ بِاللَّهِ شَيْئًا وَلَا يَسْرِقْنَ وَلَا يَزْنِينَ وَلَا يَقْتُلْنَ أَوْلَادَهُنَّ وَلَا يَأْتِينَ بِبُهْتَانٍ يَفْتَرِينَهُ بَيْنَ أَيْدِيهِنَّ وَأَرْجُلِهِنَّ وَلَا يَعْصِينَكَ فِي مَعْرُوفٍ فَبَايِعْهُنَّ وَاسْتَغْفِرْ لَهُنَّ اللَّهَ إِنَّ اللَّهَ غَفُورٌ رَّحِيمٌ

O Prophet! When believing women come to you to take the oath of fealty to you, that they will not associate in worship any other thing whatever with God, that they will not steal, that they will not commit adultery (or fornication) that they will not kill their children, that they will not utter slander, intentionally forging falsehood and that they will not disobey you in any just matter – then do you receive their fealty. (60:12)

Islam is very strict in prohibiting *zinā* because it leads to confusion of lineage, child abuse, the breaking-up of families, bitterness in relationships, the spread of venereal diseases and a general laxity in morals.

The prohibitions of approaching *zinā*

Islam has not only prohibited *zinā* but it closes all avenues of approach to it and has thus prohibited every step and every means leading to it. Accordingly, whatever excites passions, opens ways for illicit sexual relations between a man and a woman and promotes indecency and obscenity is prohibited and their violation is punishable with *ta'zīr.*

Khalwat (Proximity)

Islam prohibits *khalwat* between a man and a woman who are not related to one another to the degree of *mahram* relationship. *Khalwat* literally means proximity which denotes a man and a woman who are neither married to each other nor *mahram* to each other being alone together in a place in which there is no fear of intrusion by anyone else, so that an opportunity exists for sexual intimacy such as touching, kissing, embracing or even for intercourse. The Holy Prophet said, "Whoever believes in God and the Last Day must never be in proximity with a woman without there being a *mahram* with her, for otherwise satan will be the third person (with them)[3]. *Mahram* relationship means a relationship either by marriage or by close blood ties of such a degree that marriage is permanently prohibited. With reference to a woman, a *mahram* is either her husband or any male relative with whom her marriage is permanently prohibited, such as her father, grandfather, son, brother, uncle or nephew. The reason for the prohibition of *khalwat* is to protect the man and the woman from wrong thoughts and sexual feelings which naturally arise when they are alone together without the fear of intrusion by a third person. Thus if a man who is found in retirement with and in suspicious proximity to a woman who is neither married to him nor is related to him at the degree of *mahram,* both the man and woman shall be liable for *ta'zīr.* In the same way if a man lives with a woman who is not married to him or related to him at the degree of *mahram* in a place like spouses, both shall be liable for *ta'zīr.* Similarly if a man takes a woman out of her natural or lawful guardian, without the consent of the guardian, both shall be liable for *ta'zīr.*

Lustful looking at the opposite sex and display of women's adornment

In order to close the avenue of approach to adultery, Islam has prohibited looking at a member of the opposite sex with desire, for the eye is the key to the feelings. The Holy Qur'ān says:

قُل لِّلْمُؤْمِنِينَ يَغُضُّوا مِنْ أَبْصَارِهِمْ وَيَحْفَظُوا فُرُوجَهُمْ ذَلِكَ أَزْكَى
لَهُمْ إِنَّ اللَّهَ خَبِيرٌ بِمَا يَصْنَعُونَ وَقُل لِّلْمُؤْمِنَاتِ يَغْضُضْنَ مِنْ
أَبْصَارِهِنَّ وَيَحْفَظْنَ فُرُوجَهُنَّ وَلَا يُبْدِينَ زِينَتَهُنَّ إِلَّا مَا ظَهَرَ مِنْهَا
وَلْيَضْرِبْنَ بِخُمُرِهِنَّ عَلَى جُيُوبِهِنَّ وَلَا يُبْدِينَ زِينَتَهُنَّ إِلَّا لِبُعُولَتِهِنَّ أَوْ
آبَائِهِنَّ أَوْ آبَاءِ بُعُولَتِهِنَّ أَوْ أَبْنَائِهِنَّ أَوْ أَبْنَاءِ بُعُولَتِهِنَّ أَوْ إِخْوَانِهِنَّ أَوْ

3 Aḥmad ibn Ḥanbal, *al-Musnad,* vol.2, p.286

بَنِي إِخْوَانِهِنَّ أَوْ بَنِي أَخَوَاتِهِنَّ أَوْ نِسَائِهِنَّ أَوْ مَا مَلَكَتْ أَيْمَانُهُنَّ أَوِ التَّابِعِينَ غَيْرِ أُولِي الْإِرْبَةِ مِنَ الرِّجَالِ أَوِ الطِّفْلِ الَّذِينَ لَمْ يَظْهَرُوا عَلَى عَوْرَاتِ النِّسَاءِ وَلَا يَضْرِبْنَ بِأَرْجُلِهِنَّ لِيُعْلَمَ مَا يُخْفِينَ مِن زِينَتِهِنَّ

> Tell the believing men that they should lower their gazes and guard their sexual organs; that is purer for them indeed. Allah is well-acquainted with what they do.
> And tell the believing women that they should lower their gazes and guard their sexual organs and not display their adornment, except that which is apparent of it, and that they should draw their head coverings over their bosoms and not display their adornment except to their husbands or their fathers or their husbands' fathers or their sons or their husbands' sons or their brothers or their brothers' sons or their sisters' sons or their women or those whom their right hand possess or male servants who lack sexual desire or children who are not aware of women's nakedness and that they should not strike their feet in order to make known what they hide of their adornment. (24:30-31)

'Lowering the gazes' does not mean that in the presence of the opposite sex the eyes should be shut or that the head should be bowed towards the ground, but it means to avert one's gaze from the faces of the passers-by and not to caress the attractive features of the members of the opposite sex with one's eyes.

The Holy Prophet (pbuh) said, "The eyes also commit *zinā* and their *zinā* is the lustful look".[4]

The Prophet (pbuh) has forbidden that any person should look at the *'awrah* (secret organs) of another, whether of the same or of the opposite sex and whether with or without desire. The Prophet (pbuh) said, "A man should not look at the awrah (secret organs) of another man nor a woman of a woman, nor should a man go under one cloth with another man, nor a woman with another woman."[5]

---

[4] Al-Bukharī, *Ṣaḥīḥ,* vol. 1, p.382
[5] Abū Dāwūd, *Sunan*, vol.2, p.179

Thus any joint sexual act of a man and a woman who are not validly married to each other lesser than intercourse such as kissing, lying on one bed, be in suspicious proximity are offences liable for *ta'zīr*.

Prohibition and meaning of *zinā*

The jurists of all schools of thought unanimously agree that *zinā* is prohibited in Islam. They further define *zinā* as willful sexual intercourse of a man and a woman who are not validly married or mistakenly believe that they are married to each other and both of them are adult and sane and have the intention and knowledge of making illicit sexual intercourse. Penetration is necessary to constitute sexual intercourse that amounts to the crime of *zinā* liable to *ḥadd*.

Parties to *zinā* must be *muḥsan*

One of the basic conditions for *zinā* liable to *ḥadd* is that both parties must be *muḥsan*. *Iḥsān* (احصان) literally means fortress, protection, inaccessibility and in technical terms it means sexual intercourse of an adult and sane man and an adult and sane woman during a valid marriage. Thus if a man who marries a woman but has not yet had sexual intercourse with her, shall not be considered *muḥsan* for the purpose of the punishment of *zinā* and shall be liable for the punishment of hundred stripes if they commit zinā. Similarly if a man marries a woman through an irregular contract for example without witnesses or during iddat from her previous husband and has sexual intercourse with her, he shall not be considered muhsan. Similarly if a man marries a woman lawfully and has intercourse with her during her menstruation, he shall not be considered *muḥsan*.

In the same way if a man has intercourse with his minor or insane wife, he shall not be considered muḥsan. The intercourse must be in the vagina i.e. the pudendum of the woman and not through the unnatural way. Thus if a man marries with a woman and makes intercourse through her rectum, he she shall not be considered *muḥsan*.[6]

---

[6] 'Awdah, *al-Tashri' al-Jinā'ī al-Islāmī*, vol.2, pp.390-92

According to some shia jurists, *muḥṣan* (محصن) means a man and a woman who being lawfully married to one another are in a position to fulfill the sexual requirements of one another. If either one of the spouses is not in a position to fulfill the sexual requirements of the other spouse, neither shall be considered *muḥṣan*. Thus if a man marries a woman and later on divorces her, he does not remain a *muḥsan* provided he has no other wife. Similarly if one of the spouses dies, the other does not remain muḥsan. In the same way if both the spouses have been living separately for a considerable period of time or if one of them is suffering from a disease that he or she is unable to fulfill the sexual requirements of the other spouse, the other spouse shall not be considered muḥsan during this period. But according to Imām Abū Ḥanīfah, Imām Mālik, Imām Shāfi'ī, Imām Aḥmad and some shia jurists a man who marries a woman through a valid contract and has sexual intercourse with her, he becomes muhsan even if he later divorces his wife or his wife dies or remains separated from him for a considerable period of time. Similarly a woman who has sexual intercourse with her husband in a valid contract of marriage, becomes *muḥsan* even if she is divorced later on or her husband dies or she remains separated from her husband for a considerable period of time.

It is pertinent to mention here that according to Imām Abū Ḥanīfah, a non-Muslim cannot become muḥsan and as such the punishment of rajm (stoning to death) is not applicable to him. Moreover, if a Muslim marries a non-Muslim woman (Jew or Christian) he shall not become muḥsan even if he he had intercourse with her during such a valid marriage. But according to Imām Shāfi'ī and Imām Aḥmad, Islam is not a condition for becoming *muḥsan*.[7]

According to Shaikh Muḥammad Abduhu and his disciple Rashīd Riḍā the punishment of rajm is only applicable to the offenders who at the time of committing the offence were party to a valid marriage. As for the offender who had married once but is

---

[7] Wahbah al-Zuhaylī, *al-Fiqh al-Islamī,* vol.7, p.

not married any more, he or she should be punished lightly or at most equal to that of the unmarried offender.[8]

Abū Zahrah has concluded from his own enquiry into this issue that there is no clear text to determine that a woman who has been divorced or a man whose wife has died should be classified as *muḥsan*. Abū Zahrah further states that muhsan is a person who is protected, in the case of a woman, by her husband and in the case of a man, by his wife, and where there is a separation, or divorce, they no longer qualify as *muhsan* or *muḥsanah* in the same way as they are no longer married Somewhat like a traveller who is no longer a traveller after returning from his journey, or a sick person who is no longer sick after recovery from sickness.[9]

Zinā under coercion

If a person, whether male or female, is coerced to commit zinā and thereupon he or she commits *zinā*, he or she shall not be liable to any punishment whether *ḥadd* or *ta'zīr*. However, the person who causes coercion shall be liable for punishment. It has been related that a woman was coerced to commit *zinā* in the period of the Holy Prophet. The Prophet didn't implement *ḥadd* on her.[10] It has also been related that in the period of Ḥaḍrat 'Umar, a thirsty woman demanded water from a shepherd in the desert. The shepherd told her that unless she has sexual intercourse with him, he would not give her water. The woman agreed under coercion to have sexual intercourse with him. When this matter was referred to Ḥaḍrat 'Umar, he asked Ḥaḍrat 'Alī about his opinion thereon. Ḥaḍrat 'Alī said that she was coerced. So Ḥaḍrat 'Umar released her and gave her some compensation.[11] In such cases the coerced party shall not be subjected to any punishment. Coercion, however, should be proved it to the satisfaction of the court by the person alleging coercion.

---

[8] Muḥammad Rashīd Riḍā, *Tafsīr al-Manār,* vol.5 p.25

[9] Abū Zahrah, *al-Jarīmah wa al-'uqūbah*, pp.101,102

[10] Al-Tirmidhī, *al-Jāmi'* vol.2, p.219

[11] 'Awdah, *al-Tashrī' al-Jinā'ī al-Islāmī,* vol.2, pp.364-65

Zinā committed by minor or insane

If a minor or insane man has illicit sexual intercourse with an adult and sane woman, he shall not be liable to *ḥadd* of *zinā* but shall be liable for *ta'zīr*. Further according to Imām Aḥmad the woman in such a case shall also not be liable to *ḥadd* for *zinā* because any sexual intercourse with a minor or insane person is not considered *zinā* and as such the woman shall also not be liable to *ḥadd* for *zinā*. However she may be given any *ta'zīr* punishment. This is also the opinion of Imām Abū Ḥanīfah. But according to Imām Shāfi'ī the woman shall be liable for *ḥadd* of *zinā*. And according to Imām Mālik the woman shall be liable for *ḥadd* of *zinā* in the case of intercourse with an insane person but not in the case of a minor. If an adult and sane man commits zinā with a minor or insane girl who is mature, he shall be liable for the *ḥadd* of *zinā* because the waiver of *ḥadd* from the minor or insane person does not affect the liability for *ḥadd*. This is the unanimous opinion of the jurists. However, the minor girl in such cases must be in a position that sexual intercourse can be had with a similar girl failing which the opposite side will not be liable for *ḥadd* and will be liable for *ta'zīr* because sexual intercourse with or by a minor is not considered *zinā* and is not liable to *ḥadd*. Some jurists opine that as zinā is a joint offence by a male and a female, the waiver of ḥadd from one party creates doubt in the commission of the offence of the other party and as such the other party also becomes liable for *ta'zīr* and not for *ḥadd*.[12]

Sexual intercourse under mistaken belief

If a person commits *zinā* under mistake, he shall not be liable to the *ḥadd* for *zinā*. Mistake sometimes arises in the contract of the marriage, for example, a man has sexual intercourse with a woman with whom he has made a contract of marriage without witnesses or without the consent of a guardian or for a limited period (mat'ah). So in all these cases he is not liable to *ḥadd* of *zinā* though he believes that such a contract of marriage is prohibited. It is based on the reasoning that there is a difference of opinion among the jurists with respect to the permissibility of these

---

[12] Ibid., p.356-58

contracts of marriage which create doubt. Similarly if a man makes a contract of marriage with a woman with whom his marriage is permanently prohibited and thereafter has sexual intercourse with her, he shall not be liable for *ḥadd* of *zinā* provided he was not aware of the prohibition of such a contract of marriage. But if he knows about the prohibition of such a marriage, he shall be liable for *ḥadd* of *zinā*. This is the opinion of the majority of the jurists. But according to Imām Abū Ḥanīfah, if he knows about the prohibition of such a contract of marriage even then he shall not be liable for *ḥadd* of *zinā* because a contract of marriage creates doubt which removes *ḥadd*. However, in such a case, the offender shall be liable to severe *ta'zīr*.[13] The jurists further concur that intercourse between a man and a woman who have made an irregular contract of marriage which lacks some of the conditions of marriage is not zinā liable to any punishment. They argue that the purpose of any contract of marriage is to avoid *zinā* and as such sexual intercourse after contracting marriage is not the offence of *zinā* even though such a contract is not valid.[14]

Mistake sometime arises in respect of a wife, for example, intercourse with the wife who has been divorced with two or three divorces and is still in *'iddat* period. Thus if a person has sexual intercourse with his divorced wife in *'iddat*, he shall not be liable for *ḥadd* of *zinā*. The husband is responsible for the maintenance of his divorced wife during iddat and she is not allowed to contract marriage with another person during iddat. However, the husband may be liable for a light punishment as *ta'zīr*.

Similarly when a man finds a woman other than his wife lying on his bed at night and he considers her his wife and has sexual intercourse with her, or a blind man invites his wife to come to his bed for intercourse and a woman other than his wife comes to his bed and he has sexual intercourse with her, in such cases the offender shall not be liable for *ḥadd* and may be liable to suitable *ta'zīr* if it is required in the circumstances of a particular

---

[13] Wahbah, al-Zuhaylī, *al-Fiqh al-Islāmī*, vol.6, p.33

[14] Al-Kasānī, *Badā'i' al-Ṣanā'i'*, vol.7 p.36

case. The woman in such cases shall be liable to *ḥadd* if she has had intercourse willfully without any mistake.[15]

Claim of previous husband

When a woman in good faith believes that her husband has divorced her and contracts marriage with another man and later on her first husband claims that he has not divorced her, her sexual intercourse with her second husband shall not be considered zinā and they shall not be punished for that even though it is later on proved that her first husband had not divorced her. Moreover, the children of the second husband from this wife shall be their legitimate children. It is based on the reasoning that any sexual intercourse between a man and a woman who are married to each other is not *zinā* even though such a marriage is not properly valid. Further the first husband should have denied divorce well in time specially at the time of the second marriage of his wife but when he remains silent and thereafter claims that he has not divorced his wife, it is based on malice and it creates doubt in his claim which renders the second marriage valid specially for the purpose of the permissibility of sexual intercourse and legitimacy of the children. Similarly if the first husband was not present at the time of the second marriage of his wife or was not aware that it had taken place but when he became aware he claimed that he has not divorced his wife, even then the sexual intercourse of his wife with her second husband is not *zinā* and they shall not be punished for that because the second marriage has been contracted in good faith and marriage is contracted for avoiding *zinā*.

However, the authenticity of the claim of the first husband that he has not divorced his wife will be decided separately on the basis of the available evidence which in no case affects the permissibility of sexual intercourse of the second husband with his wife and the legitimacy of their children. It is pertinent to mention here that any complaint or claim made after a lapse of time is based on malice and it cannot be based for the illegitimacy of any right created therewith in good faith though later on it is proved that such complaint or claim is genuine.

---

[15] Wahbah, al-Zuhaylī, *al-Fiqh al-Islāmī,* vol.6, p.33

Penetration must be of the penis of a man into the vagina of a woman

One of the basic conditions of *zinā* liable to *ḥadd* is that a man who had illicit sexual intercourse with a woman must have penetrated his penis into the vagina of the woman. Thus if a man has sexual intercourse through the rectum of the woman or indulges himself in lustful touching of the thighs or other part of her body, they shall not be liable for *ḥadd* of *zinā* but shall be liable for *ta'zīr*. This is the opinion of Imām Abū Ḥanīfah. But according to Imām Mālik, Shāfi'ī and Aḥmad it is *zinā* liable to *ḥadd* whether a man penetrates his penis into the vagina of a woman or into her anus like sodomy.[16]

Zinā with a dead woman

Another condition of *zinā* liable to *ḥadd* is that the woman accused of committing zinā must be alive at the time of the commission of the offence. Thus if a man has sexual intercourse with a dead woman, he shall not be liable for the *ḥadd* of *zinā* but shall be liable for *ta'zīr*. The jurists, however, concur that a severe punishment in such a case should be given to the offender as *ta'zīr* because he has disgraced the dead body of a woman and has also committed the offence of *zinā* liable to *ta'zīr*.[17]

Sexual intercourse with animals

Zinā means willful illicit sexual intercourse between a man and a woman who are not validly married to each other and not of the animals or of a human being and animal. Thus if a man has sexual intercourse with an animal, he shall not be liable to *ḥadd* but shall be liable to *ta'zīr* if it is required under the circumstances of the case. Similarly if a woman has intercourse with an animal, she shall not be liable to *ḥadd* of *zinā* but shall be liable for *ta'zīr* if it is required under the circumstances of the case. This is the unanimous preferred opinion of the jurists.[18]

---

[16] Ibn Qudamah, *al-Mughnī*, vol.10, p.160

[17] Ibn Humām, *Fatḥ al-Qadīr*, vol.6, p.152

[18] Ibn Qudamah, *al-Mughnī*, vol.10, p.163

Zinā with the consent of a woman

If a man has illicit sexual intercourse with a woman with her consent and invitation and even with the permission of her husband or guardian *(walī)* both shall be liable to *ḥadd* for *zinā*. This is based on the reasoning that *zinā* has been prohibited by Allah and His Prophet and as such it cannot be made permissible by anyone else.[19]

Zinā committed by a dumb person

If a dumb person commits *zinā*, he or she shall not be liable to *ḥadd* of *zinā* even his or her offence is proved either by the testimony of four witnesses or by his or her confession. This is the opinion of Imām Abū Ḥanīfah. He argues that the dumb cannot claim any doubt or mistake which may exist in the commission of his offence. Moreover the written confession of a dumb person or his confession by intelligible signs is not like his oral confession and as such that is not sufficient for the proof of *zinā* liable to *ḥadd*. He will, however be liable for *ta'zīr*.[20]

But according to Imām Mālik, Imām Shāfi'ī and Imām Aḥmad if the *zinā* of a dumb person is proved by the testimony of four credible witnesses, he or she shall be liable to *ḥadd* for *zinā*. Similarly if he confesses his offence by his own writing or intelligible signs, he shall be liable to *ḥadd* for *zinā*.[21]

Denial of one party in *zinā*

If one of the parties denies the commission of zinā and the other confesses it, ḥadd shall not be implemented on both of them. This is one opinion among Hanafis. They argue that the denial of one party creates doubt in the commission of the offence by the other party because *zinā* is a joint offence of the two parties and thus it removes *ḥadd* of *zinā*. Both will, however, be liable for *ta'zīr* to be determined on the basis of other evidence if any and the circumstances of the case. But according to Imām Mālik, Imām Shāfi'ī, Imām Aḥmad and Zaydīs the one who confesses to the

---

[19] Ibid.,p.156

[20] Al-Kasānī, *Badā'i al-Ṣanā'i'*, vol.7, p.50

[21] Ibn Qudamah, *al-Mughnī,* vol.10, p.171

commission of the offence shall be liable for the *ḥadd* of *zinā* as the refusal of the other party does not affect his confession and confession is a conclusive proof against the confessor if it is otherwise authentic.[22]

Claim of one party to be spouse

If any of the accused man and woman in the offence of *zinā* claims that he or she is the spouse of the other and the other confesses to have committed *zinā*, both of them shall not be liable for the *ḥadd* of *zinā* but shall be liable for *ta'zīr* because the claim of being a spouse creates doubt which leads to the waiver of *ḥadd*. This is the opinion of Imām Abū Ḥanīfah.[23]

But according to Imām Mālik and Imām Shāfi'ī the one who confesses the commission of the offence of *zinā* shall be liable for *ḥadd* of *zinā* unless the other party proves the contract of marriage.[24]

Claim of the parties to be spouses

If both the man and the woman accused of having committed *zinā* claim that they are husband and wife, they shall not be liable for the ḥadd of *zinā* unless there is independent evidence that they have committed zinā by proving that the woman is already married to another person or that they had not contracted marriage with one another up to the time of committing *zinā*. This is the view of the majority of the jurists. But according to Imām Mālik they have to prove that they are married failing which they shall be liable for the *ḥadd* of *zinā*.[25]

*Zin*ā with *mahram*

A man and a woman who commit *zinā* and who are *mahram* to each other and marriage between them is permanently forbidden shall be liable for *ḥadd* of *zinā*. But if *ḥadd* is not proved due to a lack of condition and no evidence is available, then a severe *ta'zīr* may be awarded to the offenders.

---

[22] Ibid., p.174
[23] 'Awdah, *al-Tashrī' al-Jinā'ī al-Islāmī*, vol.2, p.372
[24] Ibid., p.173
[25] Ibn Qudamah, *al-Mughnī*, vol.10, p.162

Sodomy

According to Imām Abū Ḥanīfah sodomy is not an offence liable for *ḥadd* of *zinā* but it is an offence liable for *ta'zīr* because it has a different meaning than that of *zinā* and it does not affect the parentage of the children etc. like *zinā* and it is for this reason that there was a difference of opinion among the companions of the Prophet about its punishment and different punishments have been prescribed for it by different companions of the Prophet. But according to Imām Mālik, Imām Shāfi'ī, Imām Aḥmad and Zaydīs sodomy is an offence liable for *ḥadd* of *zinā* because it is prohibited sexual intercourse like *zinā* and a similar word has been used for both *zinā* and sodomy by the Holy Qur'ān i.e. *fāhishah* (فاحشه) in verses 29:28 and 4:15.[26] Similarly lesbianism is also an offence liable to *ta'zīr*.

Rape

Rape has been discussed as a separate offence in the English law and some other contemporary laws and has not been included in *zinā* (adultery or fornication). It is based on the concept that according to English law sexual intercourse between an adult man and an adult woman is not an offence if both are willing. Rape means to force a woman to submit to sexual intercourse against her will or to have sexual intercourse with a girl who has not reached the age of consent which is usually the age of 13 years. It is called statutory rape. The Pakistan Penal Code has defined rape in section 375 which is reproduced as under:

> "375: A man is said to commit 'rape', who, except in the case hereinafter excepted, has sexual intercourse with a woman under circumstances falling under any of the 5 following descriptions :-
>
> a) against her will;
> b) without her consent;
> c) with her consent, when her consent has been obtained by putting her in fear of death or of hurt;

[26] Ibid., p.160

d) with her consent, when the man knows that he is not her husband, and that her consent is given because she believes that he is another man to whom she is, or believes herself to be, lawfully married;

e) with or without her consent when she is under 14 years of age.

Explanation: Penetration is sufficient to constitute the sexual intercourse necessary to the offence of rape.

Exception: Sexual intercourse by a man with his own wife, the wife not being under 13 years of age, is not rape."

According to some jurists, rape falls under *zinā bil-jabr* (to commit *zinā* with force) and the person who commits rape shall be liable to *ḥadd* of *zinā* accordingly and the person forced shall not be liable to punishment. But according to other jurists rape does not come under *zinā* and is an offence other than *zinā.* They argue that the ingredients of *zinā* is the willingness of the parties to have sexual intercourse without being married to each other while in the case of rape the willingness of the victim does not exist. Moreover in the case of rape the victim is usually taken away from the house or any safe place or custody forcibly and is threatened, beaten or injured. These jurists consider the offence of rape more heinous than *zinā* and liable to a severe punishment such as death or imprisonment for a long term irrespective of whether the offender is married or unmarried. The later jurists have preferred this view. According to this view the offence of rape is not an offence liable to *ḥadd* and as such it can be proved by any evidence whether confession, testimony, circumstantial evidence, documentary or any other thing which proves the guilt to the satisfaction of the court. Further the punishment of rape may be varied according to various cases, but must be severe and acts as a deterrent.

It is pertinent to mention here that as contract of marriage with a minor girl is permissible in Islam, the intercourse of a husband with his minor wife shall not be considered rape and he shall not be punished for that.

Some jurists opine that rape comes under *harabah.* But in that case it would be difficult to determine as to which punishment among the punishments of *harabah* would be prescribed for that whether death or amputation of right hand and left foot or imprisonment and why. Moreover the cases of *zinā bi al-Jabr* (*zinā* under coercion) have happened in the early period of Islam but none among the *Ṣaḥabah* or *Tābi'ūn* have considered any such cases as *harabah* and have dealt with them as cases of *zinā* under coercion i.e. *zinā bi al-jabr*. It is relevant to point out that according to some jurists the offence of *zinā bi al-jabr* (*zinā* under coercion) can be proved by the sole testimony of the victim i.e. the woman who is coerced to commit *zinā*. It is based on the following *ḥadith*: "It has been related that in the period of the Holy Prophet a woman was going to the mosque for prayers early in the morning. As it was dark a man attacked her and had illicit sexual intercourse with her forcibly and then ran away. Suddenly another man who was also going to the mosque met her and she related to him the whole story. That man went in search of the first man who was the offender. Meanwhile a group of persons met that woman and she also explained to them the whole situation. They also went in search of the real culprit. These persons while searching for the real culprit met the second man who was also searching for the real culprit and caught him. He was silent and was in a terrible situation. They brought him before that woman and she confirmed that he was the man who coerced her to commit *zinā*. Thus they brought both of them to the Prophet. The Prophet said to him, "Have you committed *zinā* with this woman forcibly." He remained silent. On the other side the woman testified before the Prophet that he was the man who committed *zinā* with her forcibly. The Prophet ordered to stone him to death. But as the real offender was present there at that time, he stood and said, "I have committed *zinā* with this woman forcibly and not this man." On this the Prophet released him.[27]

But there is a difference of opinion among the jurists on the point whether the order of the Prophet for stoning him to death in the above mentioned *ḥadīth* was solely based on the testimony of the victim or was based on other circumstances as well. 'Allamah Ibn Qayyim after relating the above *ḥadīth*, states that the order of the Prophet was based on circumstantial evidence – the silence of the accused, his being arrested by the persons who were present

---

[27] Al-Tirmidhī, *al-Jāmī'*, p.324

and the testimony of the victim who was also present.[28] But according to the majority of the jurists any offence of *zinā* liable to *ḥadd* is proved by the testimony of four-witnesses or the confession of the accused. However, the testimony of the victim shall be considered sufficient for the award of *ta'zīr* if it is corroborated with other evidence. The jurists concur that *ta'zīr* in such cases must be severe.

Punishment of *zinā*

The punishment of *zinā* in the early days of Islam was confinement to the house or corporal punishment. The Holy Qur'ān says:

وَاللاَّتِي يَأْتِينَ الْفَاحِشَةَ من نِّسَآئِكُمْ فَاسْتَشْهِدُواْ عَلَيْهِنَّ أَرْبَعةً مِّنكُمْ فَإِن شَهِدُواْ فَأَمْسِكُوهُنَّ فِي الْبُيُوتِ حَتَّى يَتَوَفَّاهُنَّ الْمَوْتُ أَوْ يَجْعَلَ اللّهُ لَهُنَّ سَبِيلاً وَاللَّذَانَ يَأْتِيَانِهَا مِنكُمْ فَآذُوهُمَا فَإِن تَابَا وَأَصْلَحَا فَأَعْرِضُواْ عَنْهُمَا إِنَّ اللّهَ كَانَ تَوَّابًا رَّحِيمًا

> If any of your women are guilty of lewdness, take the evidence of four (reliable) witnesses from amongst you against them. And if they testify, confine them to houses until death do claim them or God ordain for them some (other) way. If two men among you are guilty of lewdness, punish them both. If they repent and amend, leave them alone for God is oft-returning, most merciful. (4:15-16)

The above two verses have been interpreted differently by different commentators of the Holy Qur'ān. According to the majority of them, they relate to *zinā* committed by a man or a woman and its punishment. Abdullah Yusuf Ali while commenting on these verses writes:

> "Most commentators understand this to refer to adultery or fornication. In that case they consider that the punishment was altered to 100 stripes by the later verse XXIV.2. But I think it refers to unnatural crime between

[28] Ibn Qayyim, *I'lām al-Muwaqqi'īn*, vol.4, p. 328

women, analogous to unnatural crime between men in IV.16 below because: i) no punishment is specified here for the man, as would be the case where a man is involved in the crime; ii) the word *'Allati'*, the purely feminine plural of *'Allati'* is used for the parties to the crime; iii) the punishment is indefinite".[29]

The Holy Prophet, referring to the way promised in verse 4:15 above, said, "Take from me, Allah has prescribed for them (those guilty of *zin*ā) the way, an unmarried will be punished with hundred stripes and expulsion for one year and a married will be punished with a hundred stripes and stoning to death."[30] Later the punishment of expulsion and the punishment of hundred stripes to a married person were excluded.

The majority of the commentators, *muḥaddthīn* and jurists believe that the above verses have been abrogated by verse 24:2 which is as under:

الزَّانِيَةُ وَالزَّانِي فَاجْلِدُوا كُلَّ وَاحِدٍ مِّنْهُمَا مِئَةَ جَلْدَةٍ وَلَا تَأْخُذْكُم بِهِمَا رَأْفَةٌ فِي دِينِ اللَّهِ إِن كُنتُمْ تُؤْمِنُونَ بِاللَّهِ وَالْيَوْمِ الْآخِرِ وَلْيَشْهَدْ عَذَابَهُمَا طَائِفَةٌ مِّنَ الْمُؤْمِنِينَ

The woman and the man guilty of adultery or fornication flog each of them with hundred stripes. Let not compassion move you in their case, in a matter prescribed by God, if you believe in God and the Last Day; And let a party of the believers witness their punishment. (24:2)

The order of this verse is general for both married and unmarried persons who commit *zinā*. But the *Sunnah* of the Prophet excluded the married person from its ambit and this verse applies to unmarried persons only who commit *zinā* and prescribes the punishment of 100 stripes for each of them. Thus the *ḥadd* punishment of *zinā* for an unmarried person is hundred stripes. This is the opinion of Imām Abū Ḥanīfah. According to Imām

---

[29] Yusuf 'Alī, *Commentary,* p.183

[30] Muslim, *Ṣaḥīḥ,* p.176

Mālik, Imām Shāfi'ī and Imām Aḥmad the punishment of *zinā* for an unmarried person is hundred stripes and banishment for one year. Further, Imām Mālik exempts women from the punishment of banishment.

As far as the punishment of *zinā* for a married person is concerned, the Holy Prophet has prescribed it as *rajm* i.e. stoning to death. The Holy Prophet has given the punishment of *rajm* (stoning to death) to three married Muslims, one man and two women. It would be appropriate to reproduce these *aḥādīth* as below:

1. It has been related on the authority of Abu Hurairah and Zaid ibn Khalid that a villager came to the Holy Prophet and said, "Oh Prophet! I beseech you by Allah to decide our case according to the Book of Allah". His opponent who was more intelligent than him also requested to decide between them according to the Book of Allah and desired for permission to speak. The Prophet allowed him to speak. He said, "My son was a servant of this man (the opponent) and he committed *zinā* with his wife and I was told that my son will be stoned to death. I ransomed one hundred sheep and a slave girl. Then I asked the religious scholars who informed me that my son will be punished with hundred stripes and be expelled for one year and the wife of this man shall be stoned to death. The Prophet said, "I shall decide your case according to the Book of Allah. Your sheep and slave girl will be returned to you and your son shall be punished with one hundred stripes and be expelled for one year and ordered a person from the Aslam tribe named Unays to go tomorrow to the wife of that person and if she confesses, stone her to death." Unais then went to that woman and she confessed the commission of *zinā.* She was thus stoned to death as ordered by the Prophet.[31]

2. It has been related on the authority of Abu Hurairah who said, "A man came to the Prophet when he was in the mosque and said, "Oh Prophet! I have committed *zinā*". The Prophet turned his face from him but he repeated his statement four times by coming in front of the Prophet. When he completed

---

[31] Abū Dawūd, *Sunan*, Vol,2 , pp.218-19

four times testimony against himself, the Prophet said to him, "Are you insane". He answered in the negative. The Prophet said, "Are you married?" He answered in positive. The Prophet said, "You might have kissed her". He answered that he had intercourse with her. The Prophet said, "Do you know *zinā*"?. He answered in the affirmative. At last the Prophet ordered to stone him to death and he was stoned to death.[32] In other versions of this *ḥadīth* the Prophet asked him some additional questions also and then the Holy Prophet ordered to stone him to death after his repeated confessions for four days before the Holy Prophet.

3. It has been related on the authority of Sulaiman who relates from his father Buraidah that a woman who belonged to Ghamid came to the Prophet and said, "Oh Prophet! clean me". The Prophet told her to go back and repent. She said, "I think you get me returned as you had done in the case of Maiz Ibn Malik." The Prophet then asked her as to what had happened to her. She said that she was pregnant as a result of adultery. The Prophet said, "I will decide your case when you give birth to the child". The Prophet then gave her in the custody of an Anṣārī man. When she gave birth to the child, she came to the Prophet. The Prophet said, "I shall not punish you until someone takes the responsibility of the maintenance and nourishment of the child". A man from Anṣār stood up and offered to take the responsibility of the maintenance of the child. Thus the Prophet ordered to stone her to death and she was stoned to death.[33]

The Holy Prophet, in the early days at Madinah, ordered two Jews, a man and a woman who had committed *zinā* to be stoned to death and they were stoned to death accordingly.[34]

The Holy Prophet said, "The killing of a Muslim is not permissible except in three cases: (i) when he kills another person,

---

[32] Al-Shawqānī, *Nail al-Awṭār*, vol.7, pp.111-13

[33] Muslim *Ṣaḥīḥ*, vol.2, p.212

[34] Al-Bukhārī, *Ṣaḥīḥ*, p.332

(ii) when he commits *zinā* after being married and (iii) when he becomes an apostate."[35]

There is thus consensus of opinion among the jurists that the punishment of a Muslim married person who commits *zinā* is *rajm* i.e. stoning to death.

It is also to be mentioned here that according to Khawarij the punishment of both married and unmarried persons who commit *zinā* is a hundred stripes and they deny the punishment of stoning to death for a married person who commits *zinā*. They argue that the punishment of *zinā* has been prescribed by the Holy Qur'ān in verse 24:2 and has not differentiated between a married and an unmarried person and the *Sunnah* cannot abrogate, change or particularize any order of the Holy Qur'ān. Moreover they believe that all the cases of *rajm* that occurred in the period of the Holy Prophet happened before the revelation of verse 24:2 of the Holy Qur'ān which abrogated this punishment and prescribed the punishment of a hundred stripes for a married as well as unmarried person who commits *zinā*.

The jurists on other side argue that the *Sunnah* can particularize a general order of the Holy Qur'ān specially when it reaches the degree of *mashhūr* i.e. any saying or practice of the Prophet related by a group of the Companions (*Ṣaḥābah*) and is otherwise authentic. As the *aḥādīth* relating to the punishment of *rajm* (stoning to death) for a married person who commits *zinā* are *mashhūr* and authentic, they are sufficient to particularize the general order of verse 24:2 and exempt a married person from its ambit. Moreover the claim of abrogation of the punishment of stoning to death for a married person by verse 24:2 is not correct because Khalid Ibn Walīd, Abbas Ibn 'Abdul Muṭṭalib and Abū Hurairah were present in Madinah at the time of execution of this punishment to Maiz Ibn Malik and Ghamidiyyah and all of them came to Madina as Muslims after the sixth year of Hijrah while verse 24:2 has been revealed in the fifth year after Hijrah in the context of the scandal against Ḥaḍrat 'Ā'ishah. Khalid Ibn Walīd was on the side of the *Mushrikin* in the pact of Hudaibiyyah and embraced Islam after 6th Hijrah. Similarly Abū Hurayrah embraced Islam in the seventh year after Hijrah while Ḥaḍrat

[35] Abū Dawūd *Sunan*, vol.2, p.117

Abbas came to Madinah after the conquest of Makkah in 8th Hijrah. So all these historical facts denote that the Holy Prophet gave the punishment of stoning to death to the married persons who had committed *zinā* even after the revelation of verse 24:2. Moreover Ḥaḍrat 'Umar and Ḥaḍrat 'Alī also gave this punishment to the married persons who had committed *zinā* during their caliphate.

There is also a report, attributed to caliph 'Umar, wherein he has stated that the Qur'ānic verse 24:2 regarding 100 strokes for *zinā* was abrogated in the Qur'ān itself. A verse of the Holy Qur'ān was revealed in *Surah al-Ahzah* which expressly declared that: "When a married man or woman commits *zinā* stone them to death as a deterrence from Allah, and Allah is Most Powerful, Most Wise." According to Ḥaḍrat 'Umar although the wording of this revelation did not become a part of the Qur'ān, its ruling has nevertheless become a part of Shariah. By way of explanation it is said that the reported addition was not incorporated into the standard text of the Holy Qur'ān because it did not amount to *mutawatir* and anything less than *mutawatir* cannot, as a rule, become a part of the Holy Qur'ān. Ḥaḍrat 'Umar had said, "had it not been for people saying that 'Umar made an addition to the Holy Qur'ān, I would have added the above verse to the Holy Qur'ān. The jurists concur that the evidence in support of this verse is doubtful firstly by saying that the actual wording of the alleged verse falls short of the eloquent style of the Holy Qur'ān and then to say that there was an addition in the Surah al-Ahzab regarding stoning to death but God ordered the Prophet to eliminate it from the text of the Holy Qur'ān while retaining its ruling that it is imaginary. Thus the report of the above verse is doubtful and it cannot be taken to overrule the clear text of the Holy Qur'ān on flogging. It is further supported by the statement of Caliph 'Alī that when he stoned Sharahah to death he said, "I flogged her in accordance with the Book of Allah and stoned her in accordance with the *Sunnah* of the Prophet. It is said that Ḥaḍrat 'Ali evidently did not refer to 'Umar's report on the additional ruling by the Holy Qur'an itself.[36]

[36] Al-Alūsī, *Rūḥ al-Ma'ānī,* vol.18, p.79

It is also important to mention a narration narrated by Abū Isḥaq al-Shaybānī who asked Ibn Abi Awfa, a companion of the Holy Prophet, whether the Prophet had implemented the punishment of *rajm.* Abdullah answered in the affirmative. He then asked him whether it was before the revelation of Surah Al-Noor or after that. He answered, "I don't know". Moreover the *ḥadīth* which is based on the punishment of *rajm* imposes the punishment of whipping along with *rajm* for a married person who commits *zinā* and whipping along with expulsion for one year for an unmarried person who commits *zinā,* but the jurists do not believe in whipping with *rajm* but they consider *rajm* sufficient while Imām Abū Ḥanīfah does not consider expulsion for one year for an unmarried person as *ḥadd* but he has left it to the discretion of the judge or legislator. According to Imām Mālik a woman shall not be punished with expulsion if she commits *zinā.* Thus when a part of a punishment mentioned in a *ḥadīth* does not remain *ḥadd,* the other part of the same punishment also does not remain *ḥadd* and such a punishment remains *ta'zīr.*[37]

It is relevant to mention the opinion of some jurists who opine that the *ḥadd* punishment of *zinā* is not for the offenders who commit *zinā* for the first time but it is for the habitual offenders who have a criminal record. They argue that the words *'zaniah'* and *'zānī'* are adjectives, not verbs and adjectives do not materialize in a person without a measure of repetition. A person is not, for example, described as 'generous', 'honest' or a 'liar' merely by a single act of generosity, honesty or lying. These adjectives carry their full meanings where there is recurrence and repetition. It has been related that Maiz bin Malik, who was stoned to death by the order of the Holy Prophet, was a habitual offender and when people went for battle he entered their houses and tried to commit *zinā* with the women therein. Similarly Ghamidiyyah, a woman who was stoned to death by the order of the Prophet, was a habitual offender having committed *zinā* a number of times.[38]

The Islamic law does not make it obligatory that a person must confess his guilt of *zinā* and that those who have knowledge of it must inform the authorities about it. But if any case does

---

[37] Badr al-Dīn 'Aynī, , *Umdah al-Qārī*, vol. 23, p.291

[38] Abū Zahrrah, *al-'uqūbah*, pp.134-35

come to the notice of the authorities, there is then no room for pardoning the guilt. This is based on a *ḥadīth* of the Holy Prophet: "If any of you is guilty of any immorality, he had better remain hidden under the curtain of Allah; but if he discloses it to us, we shall certainly enforce the Law of Allah on him". Maiz Ibn Malik Aslami committed the crime of *zinā* and went to the Prophet on the advice of Ḥazzal Ibn Nu'aim and confessed his guilt. The Prophet ordered that he should be stoned to death but said to Hazzal, "Would that you had kept the matter hidden; this would have been better for you". In another incident, the Prophet said,

> "You should yourselves pardon the crimes which are liable for *ḥadd* punishment because when a crime which is liable for such punishment comes to my notice, it will become obligatory on me to award punishment."

Under the Islamic law, *zinā* is not a compoundable crime. This is based on the *ḥadīth* wherein the father of the boy who committed *zinā* with the wife of the employer gave one hundred goats and one slave girl to the husband of the woman involved and made a compromise with him. But the Holy Prophet returned those things and awarded the prescribed punishment to both the guilty ones. This shows that *zinā* is not a compoundable crime and outraged chastity cannot be compensated in terms of money under the Islamic law.

The Islamic Government shall not take action against anybody for *zinā* unless it is fully proved. If guilt is not proved, the authorities cannot pass orders for punishment, even if they have knowledge of the crime through many other sources. There was a woman in Madinah who openly practiced prostitution, according to a tradition cited in Bukharī and Ibn Mājah, but, in spite of this no punishment was given to her as there was no proof of *zinā* against her; so much so that the Holy Prophet once said, "If I were to stone anybody to death without proof, I would certainly have had this woman stoned."[39] However, *ta'zīr* punishment may be given to the offender in such cases.

---

[39] Afzalur Rahman, *Encyclopedia of Seerah*, vol.2, pp.791-92

Execution of the punishment of whipping

The execution of the punishment of whipping in Islamic law is quite different than that prevailing in the English and other contemporary laws. The word *'Jald'* is derived from *'jild'* which means skin. It signifies that whipping should be carried out in such a way that its effect should be confined to the skin only and should not reach the flesh under it. The whipping that causes deep wounds into the flesh or tears it up into pieces is against the teachings of Islam. It is based on the following traditions:

1. It has been related that once a person came to the Holy Prophet and said, "Oh Prophet! I have committed a crime *(ḥadd)* and thus implement its punishment on me." The Holy Prophet called for a fresh whip. So he was offered a fresh whip on which there was some fruit. The Holy Prophet said, "a whip less than this". Then he was offered a whip which was cut from one side. The Holy Prophet said, "a whip better than this". Then he was offered a moderate whip and thus he ordered that the person to be whipped with that and that person was whipped accordingly.[40]

2. It has been related that once a slave-woman (of Ḥaḍrat Fāṭimah) committed *zinā* and the Holy Prophet ordered Ḥaḍrat Ali to whip her. When he went for whipping, he found her in a position that her blood of childbirth was still flowing and returned without whipping her. The Holy Prophet said, "Oh 'Alī! Did you whip her". Ḥaḍrat 'Alī said, "No, when I went there I found that her blood of childbirth was still flowing". The Holy Prophet said, "Wait till her bleeding is totally stopped and then implement *ḥadd* on her".[41]

3. It has been related that Ḥaḍrat 'Umar said to an executioner, "Don't raise your hand above your head so that the whiteness of your armpit may not appear".[42]

---

[40] Abd Al-Razzāq, *al-Musannaf*, vol,7., p.329

[41] Abu Dawūd, *Sunan*, vol.2, p.282

[42] Ibn al-Ḥajar al-Asqalānī, *al-Talkhīṣ al-Ḥabīr*, vol.2, p.78

4. It has been related that Ḥaḍrat 'Alī ordered an executioner of the whipping of a person, "Whip him and give every part of the body its share and don't whip the face and shames".[43]
5. Once when Ḥaḍrat 'Umar ordered a woman to be whipped he said to the executioner of the punishment, "Whip her but do not lacerate her skin".[44]
6. It has been related that once a very thin and weak person who was ill also committed adultery with a she-slave and asked for the Holy Prophet to implement *ḥadd* on him. The Holy Prophet ordered to whip him with a branch of a tree in which hundred very small branches exist and whip him with it only one time."[45] 'Allama Shawkānī has related that the jurists have described that the width of the whip be one fine finger and its length be one yard.[46]

Based on the above traditions the jurists have derived that the main aim of the punishment of whipping is humiliation of the convict, with a reasonable pain to his body as well. Imām al-Nawawī while describing the mode of the punishment of whipping in the offences of *zinā, Qazf* and drinking wine, writes "the lash should be moderate neither a very fresh branch nor entirely dry, the application of whipping should be normal not cause severe pain, the lashes should follow one after another, the executioner should not raise his hand over his head to the extent the whiteness of his armpit appears otherwise it will be very painful, the lash should not remain on his body but be raised and applied with normal force, the lash should not be applied on the face, genitals, head and dedicated parts of the body of the convict, the convict should not be tied, the convict should not be naked but be in his normal dress provided his dress does not save him from the pain, the male should be whipped when he is standing and the female when she is sitting and is covered with her dress, the executioner should be man, the application of whipping should be continuous

[43] 'Abd al-Razzāq, *al-Muṣannaf*, vol.7, p.37
[44] Ibid., p.38
[45] Abū Dawūd, *Sunan*, vol.2, p.280
[46] Al-Shawkānī, *Nayl al-Awṭār,* vol.7, p.130

and not after intervals."[47] According to the Shafi'īs the punishment of whipping in case of *ta'zīr* offence should be less in quality and quantity than that of a *ḥadd* offence. 'Allamah Sheikh Moḥammad al-Sharbini al-Khatib while discussing the punishment of whipping in *ta'zīr* offences, writes, "If the punishment of whipping is in a *ta'zīr* offence it must be less than forty lashes and applies equally to all offences of *ta'zīr*".[48] The Ḥanafis differentiate between the quality of whipping in *ta'zīr* offence and that of *ḥadd* offence and opine that the severity in *ta'zīr* should be more than *ḥadd,* and after that the punishment of whipping in *zinā* must be more severe than that in drinking wine and the punishment of whipping in drinking wine must be more severe than that in *Qazf*."[49] They base their view on the practise of Ḥaḍrat 'Umar in case of a person who had enraged Ḥaḍrat Ummu Salmah in connection with the repayment of loan granted to one of her close relatives in which Ḥaḍrat 'Umar said, "whip him 30 strokes in such a mode to effect his skin and flow his blood". Abū Bakr Jaṣṣāṣ has, however, asserted that it is the discretion of a Kadi in case of *ta'zīr* to order the severity of the punishment of whipping keeping in view the circumstances of a particular case.[50] According to a version of Imām Shāfi'ī, the force of a lash shall be equal both in *ḥadd* and *ta'zīr.*[51]

The jurists, however, concur that a pregnant woman shall not be given the punishment of whipping until she gives birth to the child and recovers from the bleeding after childbirth. Similarly this punishment shall not be executed on a person who is ill and can't bear the severity of this punishment until he recovers from the illness. In the same way this punishment shall not be implemented in extremely cold or hot weather.[52]

It would be appropriate to reproduce section 5 of the Execution of the Punishment of Whipping Ordinance 1979 of Pakistan which relates to the mode of the execution of the

---

[47] Al-Nawawī, *Rauḍat al-Ṭālibīn*, vol.10, pp.172-73
[48] Al-Ramlī, *Mughnī al-Muḥtāj*, vol.6, p.193
[49] Al-Jaṣṣāṣ, *Aḥkām al-Qur'ān*, vol.3, pp.256-57
[50] Ibid, vol.3, pp.256-57
[51] Al-Qurṭubī, *al-Jami' li-Aḥkām al-Qur'ān*, vol.11, p.163
[52] 'Awdah, *al-Tashrī' al-Jinā'ī al-Islāmī*, vol.2, pp.448-50

punishment of whipping into conformity with the injunctions of Islam:

The following provisions shall apply to the execution of the punishment of whipping, namely:

(a) before the execution of the punishment commences, the convict shall be medically examined by the authorized medical officer so as to ensure that the execution of the punishment will not cause the death of the convict;

(b) if the convict is too old or too weak, having regard to the sentence of whipping awarded, the number of stripes shall be applied in such manner and with such intervals that the executioner of the punishment does not cause his death;

(c) if the convict is ill, the execution of the punishment shall be postponed until the convict is certified by the authorized medical officer to be physically fit to undergo the punishment;

(d) if the convict is a woman who is pregnant, the execution of the punishment shall be postponed until the expiration of a period of two months after the birth of the child or miscarriage, as the case may be;

(e) if, at the time of the execution of the punishment, the weather is too cold or too hot, the execution shall be postponed until the weather has become normal;

(f) if the punishment shall be executed in the presence of the authorized medical officer at such public place as the Provincial Government may appoint for the purpose;

(g) the person appointed to execute the punishment shall be impartial and of mature understanding;

(h) he shall apply the whip with moderate force without raising his hand above his head so as not to lacerate the skin of the convict;

(i) after he has applied a stripe, he shall raise the whip aloft and shall not pull it off;

(j) the stripes shall be spread over the body of the convict so, however, that the stripes shall not be applied on the head, face, stomach or chest or the delicate part of the body of the convict;

(k) such clothes of the convict shall be left on the body of the convict as are required by the Injunctions of Islam to be put on;

(l) the stripes shall be applied in the case of a male, while he is standing and, in the case of a female, while she is sitting; and

(m) if, after the execution of the punishment has commenced, the authorized medical officer is of the opinion that there is apprehension about the health of the convict, the execution of the punishment shall be postponed until the authorized medical officer certifies him physically fit to undergo the remainder of the punishment."[53]

The mode of the execution of the punishment of *rajm* i.e. stoning to death is that the convict should be stoned until he dies or he should be stoned first with some stones and then he should be killed by any mode of killing which causes him least pain or suffering. The punishment of *zinā* liable to *ḥadd* whether whipping or *rajm* should be executed publicly so as to act as a deterrent. The Holy Qur'ān says:

وَلْيَشْهَدْ عَذَابَهُمَا طَائِفَةٌ مِّنَ الْمُؤْمِنِينَ

And let a party of the believers witness their punishment. (24:2)

"Party"(طَائِفَةٌ) does not mean a crowd or a huge gathering but it means few persons which indicates that the execution of the punishment should be done openly. The punishment of stoning to death shall not be executed in case the convict is a pregnant woman until she gives birth to the child and there is sufficient arrangement for the maintenance of the child.

Proof of *zinā*

The offence of *zinā* is proved either by the testimony of four male Muslim eyewitnesses or by the confession of the accused.

---

[53] Section 5, *Execution of the Punishment of Whipping Ordinance, 1979, Pakistan*

a. Testimony

Testimony (شـــهاده) in technical terms means the statement of a person in or before a court that he has seen the occurrence of the offence or he has the knowledge of the right disputed in the court by uttering the word *ashhadu* (اشهد) or by use of any synonymous expression. But with respect to the offence of *zinā* liable to *hadd* such statement includes the declaration that the witness has seen the penetration of the accused man and woman while having sexual intercourse. Four eyewitnesses are required for the proof of *zinā* liable to *ḥadd*. The Holy Qur'ān says:

> وَاللاَّتِي يَأْتِينَ الْفَاحِشَةَ مِن نِّسَآئِكُمْ فَاسْتَشْهِدُواْ عَلَيْهِنَّ أَرْبَعةً مِّنكُمْ
>
> "If any of your women are guilty of lewdness; take the evidence of four witnesses from amongst you against them." (4;15)
>
> وَالَّذِينَ يَرْمُونَ الْمُحْصَنَاتِ ثُمَّ لَمْ يَأْتُوا بِأَرْبَعَةِ شُهَدَاء فَاجْلِدُوهُمْ ثَمَانِينَ جَلْدَةً
>
> ...and those who accuse chaste women of adultery and produce not four witnesses (in support of their allegation), flog them with eighty stripes. (24:4)
>
> لَوْلَا جَاؤُوا عَلَيْهِ بِأَرْبَعَةِ شُهَدَاء فَإِذْ لَمْ يَأْتُوا بِالشُّهَدَاء فَأُوْلَئِكَ عِندَ اللَّهِ هُمُ الْكَاذِبُونَ
>
> Why did they not bring four witnesses to prove it (the allegation of *zinā*)? When they have not brought the witnesses, such men, in the sight of Allah, are liars. (24:13)

The Holy Prophet has also confirmed the condition of four witnesses for the proof of *zinā* liable to *ḥadd*. It has been related on the authority of Saad Ibn Ubadah who said to the Prophet, "Oh Prophet! If I see a person (committing *zinā*) with my wife, I should wait till I produce four eyewitnesses". The Prophet said, "Yes".[54]

It has been related that when Hilāl Ibn Umayyah accused his wife with Sharik Ibn Sahma'a before the Prophet, the Prophet said to him, "Bring four eyewitnesses or *ḥadd* of *qazf* will be implemented on you."[55] In some of the versions of this *ḥadīth* there is no mention of four witnesses. However both of these *aḥādīth* relate to the accusation of wife by the husband for which later the procedure of *li'ān* was prescribed by the Qur'ān.

The jurists thus concur that the offence of *zinā* liable to *ḥadd* is proved by the testimony of four eyewitnesses.

Further a witness in case of *zinā* must be an adult and sane both at the time of seeing the occurrence of the offence as well as giving testimony thereof in the court. It is based on the *ḥadīth* of the Prophet who said, "Three persons are exempted from any liability, namely;

i) minor until he attains puberty,
ii) the sleeping person until he awakes and
iii) insane until he attains sanity.[56]

A witness must have the power of speaking and seeing

Another condition for a witness in case of proof of the offence of *zinā* liable to *ḥadd* is that he must possess the power of speaking and seeing. Thus the evidence of a dumb and deaf is not acceptable for the proof of *zinā* liable to *ḥadd* even if his signs are intelligible or he gives his evidence in writing. This is the opinion of Imām Abū Ḥanīfah. His evidence is, however, considered as presumption liable for *ta'zīr* specially when it is corroborated with other evidence. But according to Imām Mālik and Imām Aḥmad if he can write his evidence before the court, his evidence is acceptable even for a *ḥadd* offence like *zinā,* while Imām Mālik opines that his evidence is acceptable even in *ḥudūd* if his signs are intelligible. Similarly the evidence of a blind person is not

---

[54] Al-Tirmidhī, *al-Jāmi'* p.219
[55] Ibn Mājah, *al-Sunan* vol. ?, p.346
[56] Shawkānī, *Nayl al-Awṭār*, vol.6, p.160

acceptable in *ḥudūd.* This is the unanimous opinion of all the jurists. Some jurists, however, accept his evidence in civil cases which relate to hearsay matters.[57]

A witness must be *'ādil* (credible)

Another condition for a witness in the offence of *zinā* liable to *ḥadd* is that he must be *'adil. 'Ādil* means a Muslim who abstains from major sins and does not indulge in minor sins and his good deeds are more visible than his evil deeds and is moderate in his sayings and works. The jurists have defined *adalah* (عدالہ) in different words but as a whole they concur that *'ādil* is a person who is, generally considered reliable in the society and is not notorious.[58] A famous Ḥanafī jurist, Abū Bakr al-Jaṣṣāṣ, after producing various opinions of the jurists about the admissibility of the evidence of a witness, writes, "It seems that everyone of them has based the matter of the admissibility of the testimony of a witness on what is more likely in his opinion that it is to be accepted and relied upon."[59]

Further according to Imām Abū Ḥanīfah every witness is *'ādil* (credible) and his *'adālah* (credibility) shall not be questioned unless the opposite party challenges his credibility. Thus when the *'adālah* (credibility) of a witness is challenged, the court has to satisfy itself about his credibility through *tazkiyat al-shuhud* (تذكية الشهود) or any other mode and unless his credibility is proved, his evidence shall not be accepted. It is based on a *ḥadīth* of the Holy Prophet wherein he said, "All people are *'ādil* (credible) for one another except the one on whom *ḥadd* of *qazf* has been implemented."[60] Ḥaḍrat 'Umar, in a letter to Abu Mūsā al-Ash'arī, writes, "All Muslims are *'ādil* (credible) for one another except the one who has given any false evidence or on whom *ḥadd* of *qazf* has been implemented or he is suspected with respect to his relation to the party"[61]

---

[57] 'Awdah, *al-Tashrī' al-Jinā'ī al-Islāmī,* vol.2, p. 308
[58] Ibn Ḥazm , *al-Muhalla*, vol.9, pp.393-95
[59] Al-Jaṣṣāṣ, *Aḥkām al-Qur'ān,* vol.1 p.506
[60] Ibn Athīr, *Jami' al-Uṣūl*, vol.3, p.272
[61] Shibli Numani, *al-Farooq*, p.194

But according to Imām Mālik, Imām Shāfi'ī and Imām Aḥmad, the court has to inquire about the *'adālah* (credibility) of a witness in each case even if his credibility has not been challenged by the opposite party. They argue that the Holy Qur'ān has laid down the condition of *'adālah* (credibility) for the witness in each case whether his *'adālah* has been challenged by the opposite party or not. Moreover, a judge is bound to inquire about the credibility of a witness so as to decide on his evidence irrespective of whether his credibility has been challenged by the opposite party or not. However, if a judge is otherwise satisfied of the *adalah* (credibility) of a witness, he may decide the case on his evidence without proceeding any mode of inquiry for his *adalah* (credibility)[62].

A witness to be a Muslim

The jurists concur that the evidence of a non-Muslim is not acceptable against a Muslim in the offence of *zinā* liable to *ḥadd.* They, however, differ about the evidence of a non-Muslim against a non-Muslim. According to Imām Abū Ḥanīfah the evidence of a non-Muslim is acceptable for and against a non-Muslim even in an offence liable to *ḥadd* like *zinā.* This is also the opinion of some Hanbalis like Ibn Taymiyyah and Ibn Qayyim. But according to Imām Mālik and Imām Shāfi'ī the evidence of a non-Muslim is not acceptable in any offence or right even for and against a non-Muslim.[63] The later jurists agree that the evidence of a non-Muslim is admissible in an offence liable to *ta'zīr* if it is otherwise authentic and the court is satisfied thereof.

A witness to be male

According to the majority of the jurists all the four witnesses required for the proof of the offence of *zinā* liable to *ḥadd* must be male. They opine that the evidence of a woman is not acceptable in matters of *hudūd.* It is based on the statement of Imām Zuhrī who said, "It has been in practice since the period of the Prophet and the right-guided caliphs that the evidence of a woman was not

---

[62] Ibn Ḥazam, *al-Muhalla*, vol.9, p.393
[63] Ibn Qudāmah, *al-Mughnī,* vol.12, p.53

acceptable in *ḥudūd* and *qiṣāṣ*."[64] According to Ata and Hammad the evidence of three men and two women is sufficient for the proof of the offence of *zinā* liable to *ḥadd*.[65] According to Ibn Hazam the evidence of eight women is sufficient for the proof of the offence of *zinā* liable to *ḥadd*.[66]

Ibn Taimiyyah and Ibn Qayyim opine that the evidence of a woman is acceptable even in *ḥudūd* if her evidence is, otherwise, authentic. According to Ibn Hazam the view that a woman cannot appear as witness in matters of *ḥudūd* and *qiṣāṣ* is only a juristic view and is not based either on Qur'ān or *Sunnah*. Some jurists accept the evidence of women along with the evidence of a man or men.[67] Some jurists, opine that the evidence of only women is acceptable in the offence of *zinā* liable to *ḥadd*. However, there is neither a verse of the Holy Qur'ān nor a *ḥadīth* of the Prophet which prohibits a woman to appear as a witness in a matter of *ḥudūd*.

It is relevant to point out that not accepting the evidence of women in matters of *ḥudūd* is based on their protection, sanctity and modesty and is not based on their degradation, disgrace or dishonour. It is further based on the social structure of an Islamic society wherein women are not involved in outdoor activities to such an extent as to observe the incidents of the offences of *ḥudūd* and *qiṣāṣ*.

However, the evidence of women is not rejected even in matters of *ḥudūd* and if there are only female witnesses in an offence of *zinā* liable to *ḥadd* the evidence shall be accepted if their evidence is otherwise authentic but the convict shall not be punished with *ḥadd* and shall be punished with *ta'zīr* due to the difference of opinion among the jurists which creates doubt.

Evidence must be direct

Evidence required for the proof of *zinā* liable to *ḥadd* must be direct evidence meaning thereby that the witness must have

---

[64] Al-Bayhaqī, *al-Sunan al-Kubrā*, vol.8, p.312
[65] Ibn Qudāmah, *al-Mughnī*, vol.10, p.175
[66] Ibn Ḥazam, *al-Muḥallā*, vol.9, p.395
[67] Ibn Qayyim, *Al-Turuq al-Ḥukumiyyah*, pp.37-38

observed the occurrence of the offence himself. Thus indirect evidence or hearsay evidence is not acceptable for the proof of the offence of *zinā* liable to *ḥadd*. Similarly, the letter of a judge to another judge in an offence liable to *ḥadd* is also not acceptable. Such evidence creates doubt which removes *ḥadd* punishment.[68] However, such evidence may be considered for *tà'zīr* in *ḥudūd* cases.

Evidence must not be delayed

Evidence required for the proof of the offence of *zinā* liable to *ḥadd* must not be delayed. The delayed evidence creates doubt which removes *ḥadd*. This is the opinion of Imām Abū Ḥanīfah. He bases his view on the saying of Ḥaḍrat 'Umar who said, "Those who don't give evidence at the time of the occurrence of the offence and then give evidence of that offence after a long time, their evidence is based on malice."[69] No period has been fixed for rendering an evidence as delayed and it has been left to the court to fix it in the circumstances of a case. The delayed evidence can be considered for *ta'zīr* if it is otherwise authentic or corroborated with other evidence.

But according to Imām Mālik and Imām Shāfi'ī delay in evidence does not affect its authenticity and permissibility and delayed evidence is acceptable even in *ḥudūd* if it is otherwise authentic and satisfactory.[70]

Evidence not to be based on personal interest of the witness

The evidence requires for the proof of *zinā* liable to *ḥadd* must not be based on the personal interest of the witness like his enmity with the party against which he gives evidence or his relation with the party for which he gives evidence etc. Such evidence creates suspicion which removes *ḥadd* and renders the evidence inadmissible. The Holy Prophet said, "The evidence of a suspicious and spiteful person is not admissible". In another *ḥadīth* the Prophet said, "The evidence of a traitor, traitress, adulterer and

---

[68] Ibn al-Humam, *Fatḥ al-Qadīr*, vol.4, p.171
[69] Ibid., p.162
[70] Ibn Qudāmah, *al-Mughnī*, vol.10, p.187

a rancorous person is not acceptable".[71] The Prophet said, "Remove *ḥudūd* if there is doubt".[72] Thus if there is any doubt in the evidence on any part of the offence of *zinā* liable to *ḥadd, ḥadd* punishment shall not be given but *ta'zīr* may be given.

Four witnesses are required for the proof of the offence of *zinā* liable to *ḥadd.* Thus if the number of the witnesses is less than four, *ḥadd* shall not be implemented on their evidence but *ta'zīr* shall be implemented if their evidence is otherwise authentic.

It is pertinent to mention here that according to Imām Abū Ḥanīfah, Imām Mālik and Zaydī Shia if the number of the witnesses is less than four in an offence of *zinā* liable to *ḥadd,* the witnesses shall be punished with *ḥadd* of *qazf* i.e. eighty stripes. They base their view on the practice of Ḥaḍrat 'Umar in case of Mughirah Ibn Shu'abah who was accused of committing *zinā* by Abū Bakrah, Nafi'a and Shibal and they gave evidence that they had seen him having sexual intercourse with a woman named Ummi Jamil but the fourth witness named Ziyād did not give such evidence and stated that neither the woman was fully visible to be identified nor the intercourse could be seen. Thus Ḥaḍrat 'Umar punished Abū Bakrah, Nafi'a and Shibal with *ḥadd* of *qazf* and released Mughirah because evidence against him was totally false and unauthentic.[73]

But according to Imām Shāfi'ī and Imām Aḥmad, a witness in case of *zinā* shall not be punished at all if the number of witnesses is less than four. In such a case only the accuser shall be punished. They base their view on the following verse:

وَالَّذِينَ يَرْمُونَ الْمُحْصَنَاتِ ثُمَّ لَمْ يَأْتُوا بِأَرْبَعَةِ شُهَدَاءَ فَاجْلِدُوهُمْ ثَمَانِينَ جَلْدَةً

> And those who launch a charge against chaste women and produce not four witnesses (to support their allegation), flog them with eighty stripes. (24:4)

---

[71] Abū Dawūd, *Sunan*, vol.2, p.319
[72] Al-Bayhaqī, *al-Sunan al-Kubrā*, vol.8, p.258
[73] Ibn Qudāmah, *al-Mughnī*, vol.10, p.178

It is obvious from the above verse that the punishment of 80 stripes is for those who accuse the chaste women and not for the witnesses. Moreover the Holy Qur'ān says:

وَلاَ يُضَآرَّ كَاتِبٌ وَلاَ شَهِيدٌ

And let neither scribe nor witness suffer harm. (2:282)

A witness shall not be punished at all merely on the ground that the number of witnesses in the relevant case is less than the required quantum.

It is important to note that evidence in any civil or criminal matter is only required when there is a claim or complaint launched before that in the court failing which the evidence shall not be taken. But in *ḥudūd* the evidence of a witness can be accepted even if there is no complaint lodged before that in the court because *ḥudūd* relate to rights of Allah for which all the people are responsible. So if a person accuses another person of having committed *zinā* and produces only three witnesses, he alone shall be punished with *ḥadd* of *qazf* i.e. 80 stripes and not the witnesses. However, if three persons being accusers (complainants) give evidence on the commission of the offence of *zinā* by another person they shall be punished with *ḥadd* of *qazf* not being witnesses but being accusers. In case of Mughirah, Ḥaḍrat 'Umar punished Abu Bakrah, Nafi'a and Shibl for being false accusers and not being witnesses because they were the rivals of Mughirah. Moreover, if a witness is punished merely on the grounds that the number of witnesses is less than four, it shall close the door of evidence in the offence of *zinā* liable to *ḥadd.*

Evidence must be of the penetration and must be explicit

The witness in an offence of *zinā* liable to *ḥadd* must have to give evidence that he has seen the accused in the actual state of intercourse. Any evidence which is less than that shall not be sufficient for the proof of *zinā* liable to *ḥadd.* The statements of the witnesses must be explicit as to the penetration. Moreover, there must not be any contradiction in the statements of the witnesses with respect to the significance of *zinā,* identification of the parties, time and place.[74]

The judge shall ask all these questions to his satisfiction. If there is any contradiction in the statements of the witnesses or the judge is not satisfied with their statements, *ḥadd* shall not be implemented.

Witness must not be a person punished with *ḥadd* of *qazf*

A witness in an offence of *zinā* liable to *ḥadd* must not be a person who has been punished with *ḥadd* of *qazf* because his evidence is not acceptable. The Holy Qur'ān says:

وَالَّذِينَ يَرْمُونَ الْمُحْصَنَاتِ ثُمَّ لَمْ يَأْتُوا بِأَرْبَعَةِ شُهَدَاء فَاجْلِدُوهُمْ ثَمَانِينَ جَلْـدَةً وَلَا تَقْبَلُوا لَهُمْ شَهَادَةً أَبَدًا

> And those who launch a charge against chaste women and produce not four witnesses (to support their allegation), flog them with eighty stripes and reject their evidence even after. (24:4)

Similarly the evidence of a person who has been punished for any false evidence is not admissible in an offence of *zinā* liable to *ḥadd.*

Retraction of evidence

It is necessary for a witness in an offence of *zinā* liable to *ḥadd* to remain firm to his evidence till the execution of the punishment. If a witness retracts his evidence at any stage before the execution of the punishment, his retraction shall be accepted and the *ḥadd* punishment shall be removed provided the number of the remaining witnesses is less than four.[75] However, if there is other evidence on his offence, he shall be punished with *ta'zīr*.

Judge not to decide on his own evidence

According to the majority of the jurists a judge is not allowed to decide a case of *zinā* liable to *ḥadd* by considering his own evidence along with other three witnesses. There must be four

---

[74] Muḥammad ibn Ismā'il al-San'ānī, *Subul al-Salām*, vol.4 pp.7-8
[75] Ibn Qudāmah, *al-Mughnī*, vol.10, p.182

independent witnesses other than the judge for the proof of *zinā* liable to *ḥadd.* If a judge is a witness in a case of *zinā* liable to *ḥadd,* he should not hear such a case and should appear as a witness in it before another judge.[76]

Circumstantial evidence

Is pregnancy by itself in an unmarried woman sufficient circumstantial evidence for the establishment of the crime of *zinā* liable to *ḥadd?* There is a difference of opinion on this. Ḥaḍrat 'Umar regarded it as sufficient evidence and Imām Mālik adopted it. But the majority of the jurists do not regard it as sufficient evidence for *zinā* liable to *ḥadd.* They insist that such a serious punishment should be based either on the evidence or on the confession of guilt. One of the basic principles of the Islamic law is that the benefit of the doubt should go to the accused. It is supported by the saying of the Prophet, "Avoid punishing whenever you find scope for it". The Prophet also said, "Try to avoid punishing Muslims whenever possible and if there is a way for an accused to escape punishment, let him off. An error of the judge in letting off an accused is better than one in punishing him".

Similarly according to Islamic law if a person confesses to have committed *zinā* and does not name the other party, he or she shall not be questioned about the other person with whom he or she committed *zinā.* This is because in that case two persons would have to be punished instead of one. The Islamic law is not anxious to punish people. But if the guilty person names the other party to the crime, then that party will be interrogated and also punished in case of confession or evidence. But if the other party denies it and there is no other evidence of his guilt, only the person confessing the guilt will be punished.[77]

Confession

Confession means the statement of a person before the court stating that he has committed the offence for which he is accused. It also means the evidence of a person against himself before a

---

[76] Ibid., p.191

[77] Afzalur Rahman, *Encyclopaedia of Seerah,* vol.2, p.793

court. The offence of *zinā* is proved by the confession of the accused. It is the unanimous opinion of the jurists. It is based on the *Sunnah* of the Holy Prophet that when Ma'iz bin Malik confessed four times before him that he had committed *zinā,* the Prophet ordered to stone him to death and he was stoned to death accordingly. Similarly a woman named Ghamidiyyah also confessed before the Prophet that she had committed *zinā* and insisted that she should be punished for that, the Prophet ordered to stone her to death and she was thus stoned to death.[78]

The confession must be ascertained. It has been related that when Maiz bin Malik confessed before the Prophet that he had committed *zinā,* the Prophet said to him, "Are you insane". He answered, "No". The Prophet again said to him, "You might have only kissed her". He answered, "No, I had intercourse with her". The Prophet further said to him, "Have you made penetration". He answered, "Yes". The Prophet thereafter said to him, "Do you know *zinā*?" He answered, "Yes, I have done with her illegally what a husband does with his wife legally". The Prophet also turned his face from his front but he came on the other side and repeated his confession four times separately. Thereafter the Prophet ordered to stone him to death. In some of the versions of this *ḥadīth*, the Prophet enquired from his tribesmen whether he was a reliable man. Moreover, Maiz came for four days to the Prophet and repeated his confession four times every day.[79]

The confessor must be an adult and sane person. He must be capable of self-expression. According to Imām Abū Ḥanīfah the confession of one who is deaf and dumb is not acceptable in an offence of *zinā* liable to *ḥadd* even if he can write his confession or his signs are intelligible. But according to Imām Mālik, Imām Shāfi'ī and Imām Aḥmad the confession of a deaf and dumb person is acceptable if his gestures are intelligible or he can write his confession before the court.[80]

The confession must be with the free consent of the confessor without any pressure, force, temptation or coercion. Thus a confession made under pressure, force, temptation or coercion is

[78] Al-Bukhārī, *Saḥīḥ*, vol.2, pp.248-49
[79] Al-San'ānī, *Subul al-Salām*, vol.4, pp.7-8
[80] Ibn Qudāmah, *al-Mughnī*, vol.10, p.171

not valid. The Holy Prophet said, "My Ummah has been exempted from the (liability) of the act done by mistake, forgetfulness and for which they have been forced to do".[81]

The confession must be explicit as to committing the offence. The judge has to put questions to the confessor with respect to the committing of the offence of *zinā* as was done by the Holy Prophet in case of Ma'iz bin Malik who had confessed to committing *zinā* before him. In addition to other aspects of *zinā* the confessor has to state that he has actually had intercourse with the woman.[82]

According to Imām Abū Ḥanīfah and Imām Aḥmad, it is necessary for the proof of *zinā* liable to *ḥadd* by confession that the confessor has to make four separate confessions before the court as Maiz bin Mālik had made four separate confessions before the Prophet. further according to Imām Abū Ḥanīfah, the four confessions should be made in four separate appearances of the confessor before the court whether in four or one sitting of the court while Imām Aḥmad considers that four time confessions of the confessor are sufficient to be made in one appearance and in one sitting of the court. But according to Imām Mālik and Imām Shāfi'ī only one time confession is sufficient for the proof of *zinā* liable to *ḥadd* because confession is an information and it does not need repetition. They base their view on the *ḥadīth* of the Holy Prophet (pbuh) wherein Prophet (pbuh) ordered Unays to go to the woman (whose co-accused had confessed the committing of *zinā* with her), and if she confessed stone her to death. The Prophet (pbuh) did not mention four times confession in this case and thus she was stoned to death by confessing just once.[83]

The confession is a proof against the confessor only and is not a proof against his co-accused and the offence of the co-accused shall be proved either by his or her confession or by the evidence of four witnesses. It is based on the *ḥadīth* of the Holy Prophet that a man came to the Prophet and confessed that he had committed *zinā* with a woman and named her. The Prophet enquired from the woman who denied the charge. The Prophet

[81] Ibn Athīr, *Jāmi' al-Uṣūl*, vol.4, p.136
[82] Ibn Qudāmah, *al-Mughnī*, vol.10, p.168
[83] 'Awdah, *al-Tashrī' al-Jinā'ī al-Islāmī,* vol.2, p.433

implemented *ḥadd* on the man and released the woman.[84] However, the confession of the confessor is a presumption against his co-accused and may be based for *ta'zīr* when it is corroborated with other evidence. Similarly, if a man confesses to have committed *zinā* with a woman and does not identify her, he shall be punished with *ḥadd* on the basis of his confession. The Holy Prophet implemented *ḥadd* on Maiz bin Mālik because of his confession and didn't punish the woman with whom he had committed *zinā* because there was no proof against her. This is the view of Imām Mālik, Imām Shāfi'ī and Imām Aḥmad. But according to Imām Abū ḥanīfah if one party in *zinā* confesses and the other party denies the charge, none of them shall be punished with *ḥadd* because the denial of the other party creates doubt which removes *ḥadd* The confessor shall, however, be punished with *ta'zīr*.[85]

According to Imām Abū Ḥanīfah the confession must be before a court. Thus extra-judicial confession is not valid and no evidence will be accepted on that because if such confessor confesses before the court then the offence is considered proven by his confession before the court and not by the testimony of the witnesses and if he refuses to confess before the court, his refusal will be considered his retraction from his confession which is admissible in *ḥudūd* like *zinā* that relates to the rights of Allah. But according to Imām Mālik and Imām Shāfi'ī extra-judicial confession is valid if it is witnessed by two witnesses. But Imām Aḥmad considers it valid when it is witnessed by four witnesses. If the confessor retracts his extra-judicial confession, Imām Mālik considers it a withdrawal of his confession that nullifies it, but Imām Shāfi'ī does not consider it withdrawn unless the confessor contradicts himself in his confession.[86]

Retraction from confession

Retraction from confession in matters of *zinā* liable to *ḥadd* is admissible in Islamic law at any stage before the execution of the punishment and it nullifies *ḥadd* punishment. It is based on the

---

[84] Abū Dāwūd, *Sunan*, p.368
[85] Ibn Qudāmah, *al-Mughnī*, vol.10, pp.168-69
[86] Ibid.

ḥadīth of the Prophet that Mā'iz bin Malik tried to run away during the execution of the punishment but he was stoned to death. When the Prophet was informed that he had tried to run away during the execution of the punishment, he said, "Why didn't you let him run away and retract and get rid of the punishment"? Further according to Imām Abū Ḥanīfah, Imām Mālik and Imām Aḥmad retraction does not mean proper retraction but mere running away or turning away from the punishment is also sufficient to be considered retraction which nullifies the *ḥadd* punishment. But according to Imām Shāfi'ī mere running away is not sufficient but proper retraction is required so as to nullify the *ḥadd* punishment.[87]

Thus if a confessor retracts his confession at any stage before the execution of the punishment, his retraction shall be accepted and he shall not be punished with *ḥadd* and shall be punished with *ta'zīr* if there is any evidence on the record or released if there is no other evidence on the record.

II. *Qazf* (False Accusation of *Zinā*)

Qazf literally means to accuse, to defame and in technical terms it means to accuse an adult and sane Muslim of *zinā* who has never committed *zinā* or to refuse the legitimacy of a child. The Qur'ān states:

وَالَّذِينَ يَرْمُونَ الْمُحْصَنَاتِ ثُمَّ لَمْ يَأْتُوا بِأَرْبَعَةِ شُهَدَاءَ فَاجْلِدُوهُمْ
ثَمَانِينَ جَلْدَةً وَلَا تَقْبَلُوا لَهُمْ شَهَادَةً أَبَدًا وَأُولَئِكَ هُمُ الْفَاسِقُونَ
إِلَّا الَّذِينَ تَابُوا مِن بَعْدِ ذَلِكَ وَأَصْلَحُوا فَإِنَّ اللَّهَ غَفُورٌ رَّحِيمٌ {4/24}

> And those who accuse chaste woman (of *zinā*) and produce not four witnesses (in support of their allegation), flog them with eighty stripes; and reject their evidence ever after; for such persons are wicked transgressors; unless they repent thereafter and mend

[87] Ibid., p.188

> (their conduct); for Allah is oft-forgiving most merciful. (24:4,5)
>
> إِنَّ الَّذِينَ يَرْمُونَ الْمُحْصَنَاتِ الْغَافِلَاتِ الْمُؤْمِنَاتِ لُعِنُوا فِي الدُّنْيَا وَالْآخِرَةِ وَلَهُمْ عَذَابٌ عَظِيمٌ
>
> Those who slander chaste women, indiscreet but believing, are cursed in this life and in hereafter. For them is a grievous penalty. (24:23)

The intention of Islamic law is to impose a complete ban on publicity in society of people's unlawful connections and illicit relationships, for it gives birth to innumerable evils. The foremost evil in this connection is that imperceptibly it creates and spreads an immoral atmosphere. One person describes another person's affairs, whether true or false, before others and the others pass it on to still others with additions and suspicions. This starts a trend to the spread of evil passions in society. Islamic law intends to stop this evil. On the one hand, it enjoins that if a person is found involved in *zinā* and his guilt is established by authentic evidence, he should be given the extreme punishment which is not given for any other crime; and, on the other, it says that if a person accuses another of *zinā* but is unable to prove his allegation, he should be awarded eighty stripes so that he does not utter such a slander in future. Even if the accuser is an eyewitness of an immoral act, he should keep it secret and let the faith remain where it is instead of causing it to spread. However, if he has witnessed it, he should abstain from publicizing the matter in society but should bring the case to the notice of the authorities and get the criminals duly punished by the court of law.

The words of the Qur'ān as mentioned in the above verses clearly show that they do no imply a general accusation but, in particular, the accusation of *zinā* against the chastity of pure women. Then the demand that the accusers produce four witnesses in support of their accusation also shows that it relates to *zinā,* for in the entire Islamic law, producing four witnesses is the legal requirement only in case of *zinā* and in no other matter. The jurists are, therefore, agreed that this verse describes the law relating to the accusation of *zinā*, which has been termed *qazf* for convenience, so that this law is not extended to cover cases of other accusations such as theft, drinking intoxicating liquor, taking interest etc. Apart from *qazf,* the determination of punishments for other allegations can be left to the discretion of the judge, or to the legislative body or Council of the Islamic state, who can make general laws to cover other defamation cases as and when required.

It may be added here that for an act of *qazf* to be considered as punishable, it is not enough that somebody has accused somebody else of immortality without proof, but there are other conditions also which have to be fulfilled in respect of the *qazif* (accuser), the *maqzuf* (the accused) and the act of *qazf* itself. As for the accuser, he should satisfy the following conditions:

1. He should be an adult; if a minor commits the crime of slander he can be liable for *ta'zīr* but not the *ḥadd.*
2. He should possess common sense; an insane or mentally abnormal person cannot be given the *ḥadd* punishment. Similarly, a person under the influence of an intoxicant other than a forbidden intoxicant, e.g. chloroform, cannot be considered as guilty of slander.
3. He should have committed slander of his own free will or choice and not under duress.
4. He should not be the father or grandfather of the accused for they cannot be given *ḥadd* punishment.

According to the Hanafis, the fifth condition is that the accuser should not be drunk because the person who only gesticulates cannot be held guilty of slander. But Imām Shāfi'ī disputes this.

The conditions to be satisfied by the accused are as follows:

1. He should possess normal common sense i.e. he should be accused of having committed *zinā* while in the normal state of mind, for an insane person cannot possibly safeguard his chastity fully and therefore cannot be held to deserve the *ḥadd* punishment nor incur personal defamation. Likewise, the accused will not be held as deserving the *ḥadd* punishment of slander.

2. He should be adult i.e. he should be accused of having committed *zinā* while being of full age legally.
3. He should be a Muslim.
4. He should posses a pure and blameless character.

The conditions which are required in the act of *qazf* itself are:

- the accusation must be unambiguous and in clear terms:
- the vague references in which the accusation of *zinā* or illegitimacy depends upon the accuser's intention are not reliable.

Other important points regarding this matter are summarized below:

Qazf is not a compoundable offence. If the accused does not bring the case to the court, it will be a different thing but when the case is brought to the court, the accuser will be pressed to prove his accusation, and if he fails to prove it, he will be awarded the prescribed punishment. The court then cannot pardon him nor the accused himself, nor the matter be settled by making monetary compensation nor can the accuser escape punishment by offering repentance or apology. The Prophet said, "Forgive among yourselves offences that deserve the *hadd* punishment, but when a case is brought before me, the punishment will become obligatory".[88]

When a person accuses another person of *zinā* and cannot produce four witnesses in support of his allegation, he is considered to have committed the offence of *qazf* liable to *ḥadd* and if he produces four witnesses in support of his allegation, he shall not be considered to have committed the offence of *qazf* and shall not be punished at all.[89]

It is relevant to mention that though accusation of chaste women has been mentioned in the above verses of the Holy Qur'ān it includes accusation of men also because all the orders of the Holy Qur'ān are general for both men and women unless there

---

[88] Wahbahal-Zuhaylī, *al-Fiqh al-Islāmī,* vol.2, pp.77-79
[89] 'Awdah, *al-Tashrī' al-Jinā'ī al-Islāmī,* vol. 2, p.470

is an order which particularly relates to any one of them like menstruation, pregnancy etc. which relates to women only. As both men and women are equally affected with the false accusation of *zinā* in the society, the accusers of both are considered equal and both are liable to *ḥadd* of *qazf*.

According to the majority of the jurists, it is necessary for the accusation of *zinā* to become *qazf* liable to *ḥadd* if the person accused is not ill, impotent or has not committed *zinā*. Moreover, the accusation must be direct, express and explicit failing which it shall not be liable to *ḥadd*.[90]

Jurists concur that *qazf* relates to the rights of Allah as well as to the rights of individuals. Further according to Imām Abū Ḥanīfah the right of Allah is predominant in it and as such it is not heritable and the victim cannot pardon the offender after his offence is proved. But according to Imām Shāfi'ī, Imām Aḥmad and some Hanafis the right of the individual is dominant in it and as such it is heritable and the victim can pardon the offender at any stage before the execution of the punishment.

If a person accuses another person of *zinā* and cannot produce four witnesses in support of his allegation and is punished with *ḥadd* of *qazf* and later on he again accuses the same person of *zinā* falsely, he shall be punished with *ḥadd* of *qazf* for the second time. If a person accuses another person at a time more than one time and is not punished for one of them or he accuses at one time more than one person with one accusation or different accusations, he shall be liable for one *ḥadd* only.[91]

Moreover, the person who accuses must posses the power of speaking and thus the accusation of a dumb person is not liable for *ḥadd*. Similarly, if a person accuses another person by making signs without speaking any word, it shall not be *qazf* liable for *ḥadd*. The jurists further opine that accusation in writing alone does not amount to *qazf* liable for *ḥadd*.[92]

It is further required for *qazf* liable for *ḥadd* that the person accused must lodge a charge against the accuser in the court failing which no evidence shall be considered about the accusation

---

[90] Ibn Qudāmah, *al-Mughnī*, vol.10, pp.218-20

[91] Ibid.

[92] Aḥmad Fatḥī Bahnasī, , *Al-Jarā'im fi al-Fiqh al-Islāmī*, p.152

because this is his personal right like other rights of the individual.[93]

The person accused must be known and identified failing which the accusation shall not be acceptable, for example, a person says to a group of persons, "One among you has committed *zinā.*" The jurists, however opine that if a person accuses a dead person of *zinā* and any of his heirs lodges a charge against the accuser, he shall be liable for *ḥadd.*[94]

If a person refuses to recognize the legitimacy of a child and accuses his parents or one of his parents of having committed *zinā,* he shall be liable for *ḥadd* of *qazf* if he cannot produce four witnesses in support of his allegation. But if a person refuses the legitimacy of a child by accusing his grandmother or grandfather or both of *zinā,* it shall not be *qazf* liable for *ḥadd.*[95]

The person accused of *zinā* must be a Muslim and thus if a person accuses a non-Muslim of *zinā,* he shall not be liable for *ḥadd* of *qazf* but shall be liable for *ta'zīr.*[96]

Proof of *qazf*

If a person accuses another person of *zinā* or refuses to recognize the legitimacy of a child, it is proved either by the confession of the accused or by the testimony of two adult, sane, male Muslim witnesses. If the proof is less than that, it will not be liable to *ḥadd* but will be liable to *ta'zīr.* In case the accused is a non-Muslim, the evidence of a non-Muslim is acceptable against him.[97]

All the conditions laid down for the confession and testimony during the discussion of the offence of *zinā,* are applicable in case of *qazf* as well. However, delayed evidence is acceptable in *qazf* and it averts the *ḥadd* punishment from the accuser.

It is relevant to mention that according to Imām Shāfi'ī if the accused has no evidence he can demand an oath from the accuser and if he refuses to take the oath, he shall be liable for *ḥadd* of *qazf.* Similarly when the accuser has no evidence in favour of his

---

[93] Ibid., p.156

[94] Al-Sarakhsī, *al-Mabsūṭ*, vol.9, p.112

[95] Ibn Qudāmah, *al-Mughnī*, vol.10, p.222

[96] Ibid., p.210

[97] 'Awdah, *al-Tashrī' al-Jinā'ī al-Islāmī,* vol. 2, pp.470-74

allegation, he can demand an oath from the accused and if he refuses to take the oath, the charge against him stands disproved and *ḥadd* is removed from him.[98]

If any of the witnesses in *qazf* retracts his evidence or his evidence is falsified and the number of the witnesses becomes less than two, *ḥadd* punishment shall not be given to the accuser.

Punishment of *qazf* (false accusation of *zinā*)

The *ḥadd* punishment of a person who commits *qazf* (false accusation of *zin*ā) liable to *ḥadd* is whipping eighty stripes. The Qur'ān says:

وَالَّذِينَ يَرْمُونَ الْمُحْصَنَاتِ ثُمَّ لَمْ يَأْتُوا بِأَرْبَعَةِ شُهَدَاءَ فَاجْلِدُوهُمْ ثَمَانِينَ جَلْدَةً وَلَا تَقْبَلُوا لَهُمْ شَهَادَةً أَبَدًا وَأُولَٰئِكَ هُمُ الْفَاسِقُونَ

And those who accuse chaste women and produce not four witnesses (in support of their allegation), flog them with eighty stripes; and reject their evidence ever after; for such men are wicked transgressors. (24:4)

Moreover the evidence of the accuser will not be accepted after being punished for *qazf* (false accusation of *zinā*). Further according to Imām Mālik, Imām Shāfi'ī and Imām Aḥmad his evidence will be accepted if he later on repents and mends his conduct. They rely on verse 24:5 which is as under:

إِلَّا الَّذِينَ تَابُوا مِن بَعْدِ ذَٰلِكَ وَأَصْلَحُوا فَإِنَّ اللَّهَ غَفُورٌ رَّحِيمٌ

Unless they repent thereafter and mend (their conduct). (24:5)

But according to Imām Abū Ḥanīfah his evidence will not be accepted ever again even if he later on repents and mends his conduct. He argues that the rejection of his evidence, moreover, is included as a part of the punishment prescribed for the crime, as this tends to prevent the commission of it in future; and as the rejection of his evidence is a part of the punishment, this effect

---

[98] Ibid., p.490

must evidently remain after his repentance, on the same principle that the punishment itself is not remitted although he repents.[99]

Li'ān (accusation) of a wife of *zinā*

When a husband accuses his wife of *zinā* and the wife denies the accusation, it is called *li'ān* and a specific procedure has been laid down for that in Islamic criminal law. The Qur'ān says:

وَالَّذِينَ يَرْمُونَ أَزْوَاجَهُمْ وَلَمْ يَكُن لَّهُمْ شُهَدَاءُ إِلَّا أَنفُسُهُمْ فَشَهَادَةُ أَحَدِهِمْ أَرْبَعُ شَهَادَاتٍ بِاللَّهِ إِنَّهُ لَمِنَ الصَّادِقِينَ {6/24} وَالْخَامِسَةُ أَنَّ لَعْنَتَ اللَّهِ عَلَيْهِ إِن كَانَ مِنَ الْكَاذِبِينَ {7/24} وَيَدْرَأُ عَنْهَا الْعَذَابَ أَنْ تَشْهَدَ أَرْبَعَ شَهَادَاتٍ بِاللَّهِ إِنَّهُ لَمِنَ الْكَاذِبِينَ {8/24} وَالْخَامِسَةَ أَنَّ غَضَبَ اللَّهِ عَلَيْهَا إِن كَانَ مِنَ الصَّادِقِينَ

> And those who accuse their wives and have (in support) no witnesses except themselves; let the testimony of one of them be four testimonies, (swearing by Allah that he is of those who speak the truth). And yet a fifth in invoking the curse of Allah on him if he is of those who tell a lie. And it shall avert punishment from her if she bears witness before Allah four times that the thing he said is indeed false; and a fifth (time) that the wrath of Allah be upon her if he speaks truth. (24:6-9)
>
> Commenting on the above verse, Abdullah Yusuf Ali writes: The case of married persons is different from that of outsiders. If one of them accuses the other of unchastity, the accusation partly reflects on the accuser as well. Moreover, the link which unites married people, even where differences supervene, is sure to act as a steadying influence against the concoction of false charges of unchastity particularly where divorce is allowed (as in Islam) for reasons other than unchastity. Suppose a husband catches his wife in adultery. In the nature of

---

[99] Al-Marghinani, *Hedayah*, English Translation by Charles Hamilton, p.360

> things four witnesses or even one outside witness would be impossible. Yet after such an experience it is against human nature that he can live a normal married life. The matter is then left to the honour of two spouses. If the husband can solemnly swear four times to the fact and in addition invoke a curse on himself if he lies, that is prima facie evidence of the wife's guilt. But if the wife swears similarly four times and similarly invokes a curse on herself, she is in law acquitted of the guilt. If she does not take this step, the charge is held proved and the punishment follows. In either case the marriage is dissolved, as it is against human nature that the parties can live together happily after such an incident.[100]

When this verse was revealed, Allah's Messenger called both Hilāl and his wife because Hilāl had accused his wife of having committed *zinā*. Hilāl submitted his charge but his wife denied it. The Holy Prophet then said, "Let us proceed according to the Law of *Li'ān*". So Hilāl stood up first and swore oaths according to the Qur'ānic Command. The Holy Prophet reminded them again and again, "Allah knows that one of you is certainly a liar; then, will one of you repent?" Before Hilāl swore for the fifth time, the people who were present there said to him, "Fear Allah, the punishment of the world is lighter than that of the hereafter. The fifth oath will make the punishment obligatory on you." But Hilāl said that Allah, who had protected his back (from punishment) in this world, would also spare him in the hereafter. After this, he swore the fifth oath, too. Then the woman began to swear the oaths. Before she swore the fifth oath, she was also stopped and counseled, "Fear Allah, the worldly punishment is easier to bear than the punishment of the hereafter. This law of oath will make the Divine punishment obligatory on you". Hearing this, the woman hesitated a little. The people thought that she was going to make the confession. But instead of that, she said, "I do not want to put my clan to disgrace forever" and swore for the fifth time, too. At this, the Holy Prophet ordered separation between them and ruled that her child after birth would be attributed to her and

---

100 Yusuf Alī, *Commentary*, p.897

not to the man; that nobody after that would blame her or her child; that anybody who accused either of them would incur the punishment of slander; and that she had no right left to claim maintenance, etc. from Hilāl during her legal waiting period, because she was being separated neither on account of divorce nor due to the husband's death.

There was another case of *li'ān* regarding Uwaimir and his wife. Both swore and neither repented; they were told to exercise *li'ān.* Afterwards, the Holy Prophet enforced the divorce to separate them, and said, "There shall be separation between the husband and the wife if they exercise *li'ān.*" Then this became established in the *Sunnah* that the couple who swore against each other would separate, never to marry again. The details of this case are that it happened before the revelation of this verse. When the husband of a woman could not produce four witnesses, this verse was revealed. Then the Prophet called them. Sahl said that they cursed one another in the mosque and that he was along with the people who were with Allah's Messenger. Then when they finished, Uwaimir (the husband) said, "I shall have lied against her, Allah's Messenger, if I keep her", and pronounced her divorce three times. Allah's Messenger then said to the people, "Look, if she bears a child which is black, and has very black eyes, large buttocks and flat legs, I cannot but imagine that Uwaimir has spoken the truth about her; but if she bears a reddish child like the lizard with red spots *(wahara),* I cannot but imagine that Uwaimir has lied against her." She gave birth to a child like that described by Allah's Messenger in declaring that Uwaimir would have spoken the truth, and afterwards its lineage was traced to its mother. Ibn 'Umar reported that Allah's Messenger made a man and his wife invoke curses when the man disowned her child, and separated them and attributed the child to the woman. Then Allah's Messenger exhorted and admonished the man and informed him that punishment in this world was easier than that in the next. He then summoned the woman and exhorted and admonished her and told her the punishment in this world was easier than that in the hereafter. It is also reported by Ibn 'Umar that the Prophet told those two who were invoking curses, "Your reckoning is in Allah's hand, for one of you is lying". He then told the man that he could not remarry her, whereupon he said,

"Allah's Messenger, what about my property?" He then replied, "There is no property for you. If you have spoken the truth, it is the price of your having had the right to intercourse with her; and if you have lied against her, it is more remote still from you than she is."

Abū Hurayrah reported that a desert Arab came to Allah's Messenger and said, "My wife has given birth to a black son, and I have disowned him". Allah's Messenger asked him whether he had any camels and when he replied that he had, he asked what their colour was and was told that they were red. He asked if there was a dusky one among them and was told that there were some. He asked how he thought that had come about and was told that it was a strain to which they had reverted. Then saying that this was perhaps a strain to which the child had reverted, he did not permit him to disown him.

'Ai'shah said that Utbah Ibn Abī Waqqas enjoined his brother Abū Waqqas to look after the son of Zam's slave-girl who was his. In the year of the Victory, Sa'd took him, saying he was his brother's son but Abd Ibn Zama' claimed him as his brother. They made a simultaneous plea to Allah's Messenger, Sa'd saying, "Allah's Messenger, my brother has enjoined me regarding him", and Ibn Zama' saying, "He is my brother and the son of my father's slave-girl, being born on his bed". Allah's Messenger said, "He belongs to you, Abd Ibn Zama' for the child is attributed to the one on whose bed it is born, and the fornicator is deprived of any right". He then told Saudah binti Zama' to veil herself from him because of the resemblance to Utbah which he saw in him.

Ibn Abbas narrates a man coming to the Prophet and saying, "I have a wife who rejects no one who wishes to have intercourse with her". He said that he loved her, so the Prophet told him that in that case he should keep her. It is reported that a man got up and said, "Allah's Messenger, so and so is my son; I had illicit intercourse with his mother in the pre-Islamic period". Allah's Messenger replied, "There is no unlawful claiming of paternity in Islam. What was done in pre-Islamic times has been annulled. The child is attributed to the man on whose bed it is born and the fornicator is deprived of any right."[101]

On the basis of the above-mentioned verse of the Qur'ān and the *Sunnah* of the Prophet, the jurists have formulated the following code of rule which forms the basis of the Law of *li'ān:*

(a) The Law of *li'ān* cannot be applied mutually at home, but only in a court of law in front of the judge.

(b) The exercise of *li'ān* is not the sole right of the man; the woman also has a right to demand it in a court of law if her husband accuses her of *zinā,* or denies fatherhood of the child.

(c) *Li'ān* is not necessitated by an illusion or expression of doubt or suspicion, but only when the husband accuses his wife clearly of *zinā* or denies in plain words that the child is his.

(d) If, after accusing his wife, the husband declined to swear the oaths, the Ḥanafī verdict is that he will be awarded the *ḥadd* punishment for slander. According to Mālik and others, refusal amounts to acknowledgment which makes the *ḥadd* punishment for slander obligatory.

(e) If, after the swearing of oaths by the husband, the wife declines to take the oaths, Ḥanafī's verdict is that she will be imprisoned until she exercises *li'ān* or else confesses her guilt of *zinā.* But other Imāms says that she will be stoned to death.

If a husband denies fatherhood of a child, there is a consensus that *li'ān* becomes necessary.

(f) If the husband denies fatherhood of the child, it will be attributed to the mother alone.

(g) Neither the man nor the woman is liable to punishment.[102]

The procedure of *li'ān* is that the husband shall say before the court, "I testify by Allah Almighty that I am truthful in my accusation of *zinā* against my wife," and after he has said so four times, he shall say, "Allah's curse be upon me if I am a liar in my

---

[101] Al-Bukharī, *Saḥīḥ*, pp.272-76
[102] Al-Zuhaylī, *al-Fiqh al-Islāmī*, vol.6, pp.94-97.

accusation of *zinā* against my wife". After that the wife shall, in reply to the husband's statement, testify by Allah Almighty that her husband is surely a liar in his accusation of *zinā* against her, and after she has said so four times, she shall say that Allah's wrath be upon her if her husband is truthful in his accusation of *zinā* against her".

After the completion of this procedure the court shall order the dissolution of their marriage and thereafter they will not be allowed to marry each other in future.

The majority of the jurists opine that if there is any evidence supporting the allegation of a husband who accuses his wife of *zinā, li'ān* proceedings shall not be carried out and the case shall be tried and decided on the basis of the evidence on the record.

Chapter Six

Crimes Liable to *Ḥudūd*)

(Part II)

III Theft (سرقه)

Theft **(سرقه)** means to take away the property of another person surreptitiously without the knowledge and consent of that person. Allamah al-Kasani writes. "The ingredient of theft is to take away the property of someone surreptitiously. The Holy Qur'ān says "*But any that gains a hearing by stealth*". In this verse Allah called the gaining of hearing secretly a theft. It is for this reason that taking away the property of another person publicly and forcibly is called seizure, robbery, plunder, usurpation and not theft.[1]

Theft has been prohibited in Islam and has been declared punishable crime for which punishment has been fixed. The Holy Qur'ān says:

وَالسَّارِقُ وَالسَّارِقَةُ فَاقْطَعُوٓاْ أَيْدِيَهُمَا جَزَاء بِمَ كَسَبَا نَكَالاً مِّنَ اللّهِ
وَاللّهُ عَزِيزٌ حَكِيمٌ

> As for the thief, both male and female, cut off their hands. It is the reward of their own deeds, and exemplary punishment from Allah. Allah is Mighty wise. (5:38)

---

[1] Al-Kāsānī, *Badā'i' al-Ṣanā'i'*, vol.7, p.65

Like all other offences it is necessary for the offence of theft liable to *ḥadd* that the offender must be an adult and sane at the time of the commission of the offence and that he must have committed theft intentionally. Moreover the stolen property must be moveable property and is equal to the *nisāb* or more.

The jurists, concur that the following are the basic conditions for theft liable to *ḥadd:*

1. The offender must have taken away the stolen property surreptitiously from custody (*ḥirz*).
2. The stolen property must be of a prescribed value (*niṣāb*) or more.
3. The offender must not have any direct or indirect ownership in the stolen property and it must be owned by an individual or individuals.
4. The offender must have committed the theft with his free consent and not in a state of compulsion or dire necessity.

1. To take away stolen property surreptitiously from custody (*ḥirz*)

The first condition for the offence of theft liable to *ḥadd* is that the offender must have taken away the stolen property surreptitiously from custody (*ḥirz*).

"Surreptitious" means concealed, stealthily, clandestine, secret etc. It obviously means to take away the property of another person secretly without his knowledge and consent. Allamah Ibn Humam, while explaining the term 'surreptitiously' writes, "if theft is committed in daylight 'surreptiousness' must continue till the completion of the offence and if theft is committed at night, 'surreptiousness' is required at the start of the offence and is not needed to continue after the commencement of the offence. Thus if a person enters a house at night surreptitiously and then brings the property out of that house obviously even after quarrelling with the owner of the house, *ḥadd* shall be implemented on him. But if a person enters a house in daylight surreptitiously and commits theft and brings property openly from the house, *ḥadd* shall not be implemented on him. Moreover, if the owner is not aware of the entrance of the thief in the *ḥirz* or the thief does not know that the owner is aware of his entrance in the *ḥirz* and theft is committed, *ḥadd* shall be implemented on the thief".[2] It is for this reason that taking away the property of another person publicly is not called theft. The Holy Prophet said, "The hand of the plunderer, usurper and seizer shall not be amputated".[3]

Hirz (حرز) literally means to protect, to save, to guard and in technical terms it means an arrangement made for the custody of a property. *Hirz* is a condition for the offence of theft liable to *ḥadd* on the basis of the *ḥadīth* of the Holy Prophet who said, "Hand will not be cut if theft is committed from the fruits still hanging on the trees or on the mountain but when it is brought to the protected place then theft from it of more than *niṣāb* is liable for *ḥadd*".[4] Similarly in another *ḥadīth* the Prophet said, "He who steals a sheep from among the sheep grazing in the field (without a guard), his hand will not be cut".[5] The jurists thus unanimously agree that theft shall only be liable to *ḥadd* when it is committed from *ḥirz* (custody). They further agree that *ḥirz* (custody) is of two kinds, namely:

(a) *Ḥirz* (custody) in the form of a building where entry of the public is prohibited and where properties are kept for protection like house, godown, tent, box etc, and
(b) *Hirz* (custody) through a watchman. It is usually found in common places like a mosque, shopping centers, road etc, or in places outside the populated areas like a desert, field, garden etc.

As far as house is concerned, it is considered *Hirz* (custody) for the property inside it if its door is closed and if there is no door or the door is open then it shall not be considered *Hirz* unless there is a person or persons inside it. This is about a house situated in a populated area and if a house is situated outside the populated area, then it shall be considered *Hirz* (custody) only when there is

---

[2] Ibn al-Humām, *Fatḥ al-Qadīr*, vol.4, p.219
[3] Sayyid Sābiq, *Fiqh al-Sunnah*, vol.2, p.412
[4] Ibid., p.421
[5] Ibid

some person or persons inside it irrespective of whether it is closed or open and as such if a person commits theft from such a house and there is no watchman or any other person in it, he shall not be liable for *ḥadd* but shall be liable for *ta'zīr*. This is the opinion of Imām Shāfi'ī and Imām Aḥmad. But according to Imām Abū Ḥanīfah and Imām Mālik if a property is inside a house or a tent outside the populated area and there is no watchman or other person therein theft committed from it shall be considered theft committed from *ḥirz* and shall be liable for *ḥadd*.[6]

The jurists further differ about the grave whether it is *ḥirz* or not. According to Imām Abū Ḥanīfah a grave and dead body are not *ḥirz* and as such if a person commits a theft of the coffin of a dead from a grave, his hand shall not be cut but he shall be punished with *ta'zīr*. He relies on a *ḥadīth* in which the Prophet said, "The hand of the thief of the coffin shall not be cut". But according to Imām Mālik, Imām Shāfi'ī and Imām Aḥmad the grave is *ḥirz* and theft of the coffin from it shall be liable to *ḥadd*. They also base this on a *ḥadīth* in which the Prophet said, "He who digs a grave and commits theft of the coffin of dead body from it, we shall cut his hand". But a difference in the versions of the *ḥadīth* and a difference of opinion among the jurists amounts to the removal of *ḥadd* punishment. It is further supported by an incident that the thief of a coffin was arrested in the period of Marwan, who asked the Sahabah about his punishment. They did not say any about *ḥadd* and thus Marwan punished him with strokes and did not cut his hand.[7]

Regarding animal's if they are grazing in the pasture they shall not be considered in *ḥirz* (custody) unless they come into a protected place. If a guard goes with a queue of animals in the front and an animal is stolen from behind him it shall be considered theft from *ḥirz* (custody) provided the animals are obvious to him if he sees them. This is the opinion of Imām Mālik, Imām Shāfi'ī and Imām Aḥmad. But according to Imām Abū Ḥanīfah if a person commits theft of an animal or some property

[6] Abū Bakr al-Jaṣṣāṣ, *Aḥkām al-Qur'ān*, vol.2, p.509.

[7] Ibn Qudāmah, *al-Mughnī*, vol.10, pp.251-56

loaded on an animal from the queue of the animals, it is not liable to *ḥadd* but is liable to *ta'zīr.*[8]

Further according to Imām Abū Ḥanīfah it is necessary for the theft liable to *ḥadd* that the accused must have entered into the *ḥirz* and come out from it along with the stolen property failing which he shall not be liable to *ḥadd* but shall be liable for *ta'zīr.* Allamah Kasani writes, "Taking away the property of another person surreptitiously is of two kinds, (i) direct and (ii) indirect. As far as the direct kind is concerned offender himself takes away the property of a person and gets it out of the *ḥirz.* Thus if he enters the *ḥirz* for taking away the property and is arrested inside it before taking out the property from the *ḥirz,* his hand shall not be cut because taking away the property means to bring it in one's own possession completely by getting it out of the *ḥirz* which is not found to be so. And if he throws out the property from inside the *ḥirz* and is arrested inside the *ḥirz,* his hand will not be cut because his possession is still not completed on the property. And if he is not arrested until he brings the property out of the *ḥirz* and possess it, his hand will be cut. Similarly if two persons commit a theft in a manner that one of them enters the *ḥirz* and throws the property to his companion outside the *ḥirz,* both of them shall not be liable to *ḥadd* but shall be liable to *ta'zīr.* But if more than one person enters the *ḥirz* with common intention of collecting the property and one of them carries it out and the other get out without the property, all of them shall be liable to *ḥadd* provided the property is such that if it is divided equally among them, each one of them gets a share which amounts to or exceeds *niṣāb.* If one person commits theft of the property of *niṣāb* in more than one transaction or from more than one *ḥirz,* his hand shall not be cut because entering *ḥirz* and *niṣāb* are conditions for one theft liable for *ḥadd* and not for more than one theft. If a house is occupied by more than one family, the value of the property of each family must be of the *niṣāb* or more failing which *ḥadd* shall not be implemented. And if a person aids an offender in the commission of theft outside the *ḥirz* and does not enter the *ḥirz,* he shall not be liable for *ḥadd* but shall be liable for *ta'zīr.* Similarly one who

---

[8] Ibid., vol. 9, p.252

abets or conspires in a theft liable to *ḥadd*, shall not be liable to *ḥadd* but shall be liable to *ta'zīr*."[9]. This is the opinion of Imām Abū Ḥanīfah. But according to Imām Mālik, Imām Shāfi'ī and Imām Aḥmad entering the *ḥirz* is not necessary but what constitutes theft is to take away property from a *ḥirz*. Thus if a person commits theft by taking property from *ḥirz* without entering it by entering his hand therein and taking out the property from inside, he shall be liable for *ḥadd*.[10]

It is relevant to mention here that *ḥirz* of each thing is considered different, for example, if a person commits theft of jewellery from the house of another person and the jewellery was lying on the ground inside the house, the hand of the accused shall not be cut. But if a person commits theft of jewellery from the house of another person and brings out the jewellery from a box or other container and gets it out of the house, his hand shall be cut.

Ḥirz in the case of a watchman is only to take away the property from him surreptitiously irrespective of whether he is awake or asleep provided the property is of the *niṣāb* or more. Thus if a person takes away the property for the protection of which a watchman exists, his hand shall be cut and no other *ḥirz* shall be considered in this case but the stolen property must be of *niṣāb* or above. In case of a sleeping person anything lying under his body or lying along with him shall be considered in *ḥirz* and its theft shall be liable for *ḥadd*. It has been related on the authority of Safwan Ibn Umayyah who said that he was sleeping in the mosque and his sheet was under his head; a person took away his sheet while he was sleeping. When he got up he ran and caught the offender and brought him before the Holy Prophet. The Prophet ordered the amputation of his hand. Safwan said to the Prophet, 'I forgive him'. The Prophet said, 'Why didn't you forgive him before referring his case to me'.[11] It also indicates that *ḥadd* cannot be remitted when it is proved.

The jurists further differ about a mosque whether or not it is *ḥirz* and theft therefrom will be liable to *ḥadd*. According to Imām

---

[9] Al-Kāsanī, *Badā'i al-Ṣanā'i*, vol.7, pp.65-68
[10] Ibn Qudāmah, *al-Mughnī*, vol.10, p.259
[11] Sayyid Sābiq, *Fiqh al-Sunnah*, vol. 2, p.422

Abū Ḥanīfah, Imām Shāfi'ī and Imām Aḥmad a mosque is a common place and as such theft therefrom shall not be liable to *ḥadd* but shall be liable to *ta'zīr.* But according to Imām Mālik if there is a watchman in a mosque and the goods inside the mosque are protected, then theft therefrom of more than *niṣāb* shall be liable to *ḥadd.*

The jurists are of the opinion that if a person is permitted to enter a house and thereafter he commits theft from that house, he will not be liable to *ḥadd* but will be liable to *ta'zīr.*[12]

Similarly committing theft in general trading centers during the business hours does not amount to theft liable to *ḥadd* even if there is watchman for the properties therein. However, committing theft from these business centers at night or at such a time when admission is not allowed therein is liable to *ḥadd.*[13]

The money or any other valuable thing in the pocket of a person or attached with his dress or in his hand is considered to be in *ḥirz* (custody) and its theft shall be liable to *ḥadd* if its value reaches *niṣāb.*[14]

The jurists opine that in order to determine the *ḥirz* the custom and usage must be taken into consideration because it varies in various places and times according to the prevalent circumstances.

The stolen property must be durable, valuable and of a prescribed value (*niṣāb*) or more

Another condition for theft liable to *ḥadd* is that the stolen property must be a durable and valuable thing and must be of the value of *niṣāb* or more.

(a) Perishable foodstuffs

If a person commits theft of perishable foodstuffs like fruits, meat, milk, vegetables etc. *ḥadd* shall not be implemented on him but shall be punished with *ta'zīr.* It is based on a *ḥadīth* that Holy

---

[12] Ibn al-Humām, *Fatḥ al-Qadīr*, vol.4, p.241
[13] Al-Kāsanī, *Badā'i' al-Ṣanā'i'*, vol.7, p.75
[14] 'Awdah, *al-Tashrī' al-Jinā'ī al-Islāmī*, vol.2, p.584

Prophet said, "I shall not cut hand in foodstuffs". And Holy Prophet said, "The hand shall not be cut in theft of fruit".[15]

(b) Prohibited things

Ḥadd of theft shall also not be implemented in theft of prohibited things which are not valuable according to the injunctions of Islam like wine, pig etc. Thus if a person commits theft of wine, pig etc., he shall not be liable for *ḥadd* of theft. The jurists have included in such things all intoxicants. The offender in such a case shall be liable for *ta'zīr*[16]

(c) Common things

The Holy Prophet said, "Three things are common for all, namely, water, grass and fire".[17] The Holy Prophet said, "A hunted animal is of the person who finds it".[18] It has been related that a person who committed theft of a hen was brought before 'Umar Ibn 'Abdul 'Azīz. He intended to cut off his hand but Salamah Ibn Abdul Rahman told him that Ḥaḍrat 'Uthman said, "The hand shall not be cut in (the case of) birds". So he didn't punish him with *ḥadd*. Thus the majority of the jurists opine that *ḥadd* of theft shall not be liable in the theft of fish, birds etc. But according to Imām Mālik and Imāṃ Shāfi'ī *ḥadd* of theft shall be liable if such things are in the *ḥirz* of a person.[19]

It is relevant to mention that the theft of a human being is not liable to *ḥadd* because human being is not valuable property. Such a theft is liable to *ta'zīr*.

(d) *Nisab* i.e. prescribed value

The prescribed value (*niṣāb*) for theft liable to *ḥadd* is ten dirhams. This is the view of Imām Abū Ḥanīfah who bases on the *ḥadīth* of the Prophet (pbuh) related on the authority of Abdullah Ibn Masud that the Prophet said, "The hand of (the thief) will not be cut off for less than one dinar (ten dirhams)". But according to Imām

---

[15] Abū Dawūd, *Sunan* vol.2, p.188
[16] Ibn Qudāmah, *al-Mughnī,* vol.10, p.282
[17] Sayyid Sābiq, *Fiqh al-Sunnah,* vol.2, p.415
[18] Ibid.
[19] Al-Zayla'ī, *Tabyīn al-Haqā'iq*, vol.3, p.215

Mālik, Imām Shāfi'ī and Imām Aḥmad it is ¼ of a dinar in gold or three dirhams in silver. They rely on the *ḥadīth* related on the authority of Ibn 'Umar that the Prophet cut off the hand in *mijan* (مجن) the value of which was three dirhams. According to Imām Bāqir and some Shia jurists the *niṣāb* is three dinars of gold while some other jurists opine that it is four dinars of gold or forty dirhams of silver and some others believe it is five dirhams of silver. A contemporary Egyptian scholar, Aḥmad Fathi Bahnasi, after mentioning various opinions of the jurists about the limit of *niṣāb* for the theft liable to *ḥadd,* concludes:

(a) The jurists are not unanimous on one limit of *niṣāb.*

(b) If an Islamic state in the present world fixes a limit of *niṣāb* for theft liable to *ḥadd* keeping in view its environments and the value of its currency, it will be considered *niṣāb* according to the injunctions of Islam.[20]

It is relevant to mention here that according to the injunctions of Islam, if a person cuts one hand of another person intentionally, he shall be liable to half *diyat* if *qiṣāṣ* is not practicable therein and the value of the *diyat* is equal to the value of 4250 grams of the gold or 30630 grams of silver. It is thus clear that as cutting off the hand of the thief is a severe punishment, the *niṣāb* liable to such punishment must be a considerably high sum of money in the modern world which may be varied in various Islamic countries according to their respective circumstances but should be equal to half *diyat.*

If a person commits theft wherein the value of the stolen property is of less than the prescribed value (*niṣāb*), he shall not be liable to *ḥadd* but shall be liable to *ta'zīr.* If more than one person commits theft and the aggregate value of the stolen property is such that if it is divided equally among them, each one of them will get a share which is equal to or more than *niṣāb, ḥadd* will be implemented on all of them. And if the aggregate value of the stolen property is such that if it is divided equally among them, each one of them will get a share which is less than the prescribed value (*niṣāb*), none of them will be liable to *ḥadd,* but if anyone of

---

[20] Bahnasī, *al-'Uqūbah fī al-Fiqh al-Islāmī*, pp.102-4

them has entered the *ḥirz* (custody) and has brought out property which is more than the prescribed value (*niṣāb*), he shall be liable to *ḥadd*. Similarly if a person commits theft from the same custody (*ḥirz*) in more than one transaction and the value of the stolen property in each case is less than the prescribed value (*niṣāb*), he shall not be liable to *ḥadd* but shall be liable to *ta'zīr*. In the same way if a person commits theft from more than one custody (*ḥirz*)and the stolen property in each case is less than the prescribed value (*niṣāb*), he shall not be liable to *ḥadd* but shall be liable to *ta'zīr* though the value of the total stolen property in all cases exceeds the prescribed value (*niṣāb*).[21] This is the opinion of Imām Abū Ḥanīfah. But according to Imām Mālik, Imām Shāfi'ī and Imām Aḥmad if more than one person commit theft jointly and the value of the stolen property is equal to one *niṣāb*, all of them shall be liable to *ḥadd* provided they brought the stolen property out of the *ḥirz* jointly. They relate *ḥadd* punishment to the value of the stolen property and not to the quantity of the offenders.[22]

2. The offender must not have any direct or indirect ownership in the stolen property and it must be owned by an individual.

One of the conditions for theft liable to *ḥadd* is that the stolen property must be owned by an individual other than the offender and the offender has neither any direct or indirect share in it nor is likely to have any share therein. Thus theft committed from all public properties, properties not owned by anyone, wild birds and animals and the properties lying on roads and thoroughfares is not liable to *ḥadd*. It is on this ground that theft committed from *bayt al-mal* (public treasury) is not liable to *ḥadd* and is liable to *ta'zīr*. It has been related that one of the governors of Ḥaḍrat 'Umar asked about the punishment of the person who committed theft from *bayt al-mal* (Government treasury). Ḥaḍrat 'Umar told him not to cut off his hand as everybody has a right in *bait al-māl* (Government treasury).[23]

---

[21] 'Awdah,, *al-Tashrī' al-Jinā'ī al-Islāmī,* vol.2, p.584

[22] Ibn Qudāmah, *al-Mughnī*, vol.10, p.275

[23] Al-Shirāzī, *al-Muhadhdhab*, vol.2, p.281

Similarly if a debtor commits theft from the property of his creditor his hand shall not be cut but shall be punished with *ta'zīr* provided that the stolen property, after the deduction of the amount of loan, does not exceed *niṣāb.* In the same way if an employee commits theft from the property of his employer, his hand shall not be cut off, but he shall be punished with *ta'zīr.* On this reasoning if a partner commits theft from the joint property of all partners, his hand shall not be cut but he shall be punished with *ta'zīr* provided the stolen property, after the deduction of his share, is less than *niṣāb.* On the same grounds if a guest commits theft from the house of his host, his hand shall not be cut off but he shall be punished with *ta'zīr.*[24]

Further the jurists on the basis of suspicion opine that if one of the spouses commits theft from the property of the other spouse, his hand shall not be cut ff. And if a son or grandson commits theft from the property of his father or grandfather, or a father or grandfather commits theft from the property of his son or grandson, the hand of the offender shall not be cut. It applies to all close relatives like ascendents, paternal or maternal, descendents, paternal or maternal, brothers, sisters or their children etc.

In this way if an agent or labourer or pawner or a purchaser commits theft from the property of the owner, pawnee or seller, it shall neither be liable to *ḥadd* nor *ta'zīr.* Similarly theft committed from a mosque is not liable to *ḥadd* but is liable to *ta'zīr* because mosque is common for all and its property is *waqf* property for all Muslims. This is the view of Imām Abū Ḥanīfah, Imām Shāfi'ī and Imām Aḥmad.[25] But according to Imām Mālik the building of the mosque and the things lying therein for public use are considered *ḥirz* (custody) specially when there is a watchman for the mosque. Thus theft of valuable things from a mosque of more than *niṣāb* is liable to *ḥadd.*[26]

It is relevant to mention here that if two persons committed theft liable to *ḥadd* jointly and one of them due to some grounds was not liable to *ḥadd, ḥadd* shall not be implemented on the other co-accused as well. This is the opinion of Imām Abū Ḥanīfah who

---

[24] Al-Zayla'ī, *Tabyīn al-Ḥaqā'iq,* vol.3, pp.228-30
[25] Al-Kāsanī, *Badā'i' al-Ṣanā'i',* vol.8, pp.71-72
[26] Ibn Qudāmah, *al-Mughnī,* vol.10, p.253

argues that theft in this case is a joint offence of both of them and the removal of *ḥadd* from one of them creates doubt which amounts to the removal of *ḥadd* from the other. But according to Imām Mālik and Imām Shāfi'ī *ḥadd* shall be implemented on the one who is not exempted from *ḥadd* under the doctrines of Islam.[27]

3. **The offender must have committed theft with his free consent and not in a state of compulsion or dire necessity.**

The fourth condition for the offence of theft liable to *ḥadd* is that the accused must have committed theft with his free consent and not under compulsion or due to dire necessity.

It is based on the *ḥadīth* of the Holy Prophet who said, "My *Ummah* has been exempted from the liability of the action done by mistake, forgetfulness or under coercion". Moreover, the Holy Qur'ān has generally exempted the state of dire necessity. The Holy Qur'ān says:

فَمَنِ اضْطُرَّ غَيْرَ بَاغٍ وَلَا عَادٍ فَلَا إِثْمَ عَلَيْهِ

> But if one is forced by necessity, without willful disobedience nor transgressing due limits, then he is guiltless.(2:173)

It is obvious from the above discussions that the punishment of theft liable to *ḥadd* shall be imposed when the following conditions are fulfilled and in the absence of any of these conditions, the offender shall be liable to *ta'zi*

(a) the stolen property is of the value of *niṣāb* or more;
the property is in the *ḥirz* (protection) at the time of theft;
(b) the offender has entered the *ḥirz* (place of protection of property) and come out along with stolen property;
(c) the property is owned by an individual or individuals;
(d) the property is not a common property or government property;
(e) the property is not perishable;

---

[27] Ibid., p.293

(f) the offender and the victim are not related to each other as spouses, ascendants, descendents, brothers, sisters, children of brothers and sisters;
(g) the property is valuable according to the injunctions of Islam;
(h) the property does not belong to the host or friend of the offender;
(i) the offender and the victim are not co-sharers in the stolen property;
(j) the offender is not the lender of some property to the victim, the value of which, after deduction of the amount due to him, is less than the *niṣāb;*
(k) the offender is not in a state of dire necessity or extreme hunger or thirst;
(l) the offender does not commit the act under coercion;
(m) there is either confession of the offender or at least two credible witnesses for the proof of the offence of theft;
(n) there is no doubt in the commission of the offence
(o) where theft is committed by more than one person and the aggregate value of the stolen property is such that each one of them gets a share therein less than *niṣāb;* and
(p) where the offender return the stolen property to the victim or the victim withdraws his allegation, before the execution of the punishment.

Ḥaḍrat 'Umar in the time of famine, suspended the *ḥadd* punishment of theft during his Caliphate. Thus if a person commits theft in a state of hunger or dire necessity he shall not be punished with *ḥadd.* Similarly if a person is coerced by another person to commit theft by threatening him of death or grievous hurt and he commits theft accordingly, he shall not be punished with *ḥadd.* In the same way if a person commits theft during famine, he shall not be punished with *ḥadd* provided he is unable to purchase anything and has nothing to eat.[28]

Proof of theft liable to *ḥadd*

The offence of theft liable to *ḥadd* is either proved by the testimony of two witnesses or by the confession of the accused.

---

[28] 'Awdah, *al-Tashrī' al-Jinā'ī al-Islāmī*, vol.2, pp.607-8

Testimony of the witnesses

The jurists concur that the offence of theft liable to *ḥadd* is proved by the testimony of two male, sane and Muslim witnesses. If the number of the witnesses is less than two or there is one male and one female witness or there is circumstantial evidence against the accused, he shall be liable for the restoration of the stolen property to the victim and shall be liable for *ta'zīr*.[29]

All the conditions for a witness and testimony discussed in the offence of *zinā* liable to *ḥadd* shall apply to a witness and testimony in the offence of theft liable to *ḥadd* as well. However a witness in an offence of theft liable to *ḥadd* must have to state that he has seen the accused entering the *ḥirz* and coming out from it along with the stolen property.

It is relevant to point out that according to the majority of the jurists the testimony of the witnesses in an offence of theft liable to *ḥadd* shall not be accepted unless there is a complaint lodged by the victim or his agent before that against the accused.[30]

If the accused in the offence liable to *ḥadd* are more than one and some of them are present while others are not present, those who are present shall be liable to *ḥadd* if two witnesses give evidence on the commission of their offence, and later when the others are present the evidence against them shall be taken afresh either repeating the previous evidence if it is against all the accused or producing new evidence. They shall not be made liable to *ḥadd* on the previous evidence.[31]

Confession

The offence of theft liable to *ḥadd* is also proved by the confession of the accused before the competent court though after a lapse of considerable time. The jurists agree that delay in confession does not affect its authenticity because one cannot be doubted with respect to his own confession. The majority of the jurists opine

---

[29] Ibn Qudāmah, *al-Mughnī*, vol.10, p.289

[30] Ibid., p.299

[31] Ibn al-Humām, *Fatḥ al-Qadīr*, vol.4, p.258

that only a single confession is sufficient in an offence of theft liable to *ḥadd.*[32]

If a person confesses to have committed theft of a certain property but the victim has not lodged any complaint against him he shall not be liable to *ḥadd* but shall be liable to restore the stolen property to its owner.[33]

All the conditions for the confessor and the confession discussed in the offence of *zinā* liable to *ḥadd* shall also apply to the confessor and the confession in the offence of theft liable to *ḥadd.*

If the confessor in an offence of theft liable to *ḥadd* retracts his confession, his hand shall not be cut, but he may be liable for the compensation of the stolen property.

Punishment of theft liable to *ḥadd*

The punishment of theft liable to *ḥadd* is amputation of the right hand of the convict from the joint of the wrist. This is the opinion of Imām Abū Ḥanīfah, Imām Mālik, Imām Shāfi'ī, Imām Aḥmad and Shi'ah Zaidiyyah. But according to Shi'ah Imamiyyah the tips of the fingers of the right hand will only be cut and not its palm. The Holy Qur'ān says:

وَالسَّارِقُ وَالسَّارِقَةُ فَاقْطَعُواْ أَيْدِيَهُمَا

> And to the thief, male and female, cut off his or her hand. (5:38)

If a person commits theft liable for *ḥadd* for the second time, his left foot up to the ankle should be amputated. And if he commits theft for the third time, he shall be liable for *ta'zīr* and his hand or foot shall not be cut, but may be punished with imprisonment or fine or both, as the court deems fit in the circumstances of the case. This is the opinion of Imām Abū Ḥanīfah.[34] But according to Imām Mālik and Imām Shāfi'ī if he commits theft for the third time, his left hand shall be cut from the wrist and if he commits theft for the fourth time his right foot shall

---

[32] Al-Kāsanī, *Badā'i' al-Ṣanā'i'*, vol.7, p.82

[33] Ibid.

[34] Ibid, vol.7, p.86

be cut from the ankle. And if he commits theft for the fifth time he shall be imprisoned till death or repentance.[35] However, the second and subsequent punishments are not *ḥadd* punishments and can be altered by the legislator or judge.

Further according to Imām Abū Ḥanīfah if the stolen property is found in its original form, it shall be returned to the victim. And if the stolen property is lost or consumed while in the convict's possession and his hand is cut off, he shall not be liable to pay its compensation. But according to Imām Mālik, Imām Shāfi'ī and Imām Aḥmad the convict after his hand is cut off, has to return the stolen property to the victim if it is found in any form with him or to pay its compensation if he has lost it or consumed it.[36] The punishment of theft liable to *ta'zīr* may be fixed by the legislator or judge according to the circumstances.

It is important to mention that according to some jurists the *ḥadd* punishment of theft is not for the offenders who commit theft for the first time but it is for the habitual offenders who have a criminal record. They argue that the words *'al-sariq wa al-sariqah'* are adjectives, not verbs and adjectives do not materialize in a person without a measure of repetition. A person is not, for example, described as 'generous', 'honest' or a 'liar' merely by a single act of generosity, honesty or lying. These adjectives carry their full meanings where there is recurrence and repetition. This view is supported by the *Sunnah* of the Holy Prophet and the practice of Ḥaḍrat 'Umar. In the *ḥadīth* concerning the case of al-Makhzūmiyyah, a woman whose hand was amputated for theft, it has been related that she was known for the fact that she did not return goods that were deposited with her and things that she borrowed from others. Many Ḥanbalī scholars have gone on record to say that this was, in fact, the nature of her offence. However, it is certain that she was known for having committed similar offences and had acquired a reputation for it. Moreover according to a report when Caliph Umar al-Khattab decided to amputate the hand of a young offender, his mother said, 'Pardon him, O Commander of the believers, because it was his first time'.

---

[35] Ibn Qudāmah, *al-Mughnī*, vol.10, pp.262-64

[36] 'Awdah, *al-Tashrī ' al-Jinā'ī al-Islāmī,* vol.2, pp.618-19

To this the Caliph responded, 'Allah is too merciful to reveal the nakedness of His servant for his first failure'. This opinion needs due consideration in the present world circumstances and the punishment of amputation of hand shall not be awarded to an offender who commits theft for the first time and such an offender shall be liable to *ta'zīr.*[37]

It is further supported by the opinion of some jurists who opine that the repentance of the accused removes *ḥadd* punishment from him whether he repents before the arrest or thereafter before the execution of the punishment. But if he repeats the commission of the offence after repentance, his repentance shall not be accepted and he shall be liable for *ḥadd* punishment accordingly.

It is pertinent to mention here that if a person commits theft of the door of a house or the tent, he shall not be liable to *ḥadd* but shall be liable to *ta'zīr* because this is the theft of the *ḥirz* itself and not of the property protected therein.

IV. *Ḥarābah* (Dacoity and Robbery)

Ḥarābah (حرابـه) literally means to quarrel, to fight and in technical terms it means to take away property from a person openly by using or threatening to use force. *Ḥarābah* includes highway robbery, bloodshed, high treason, dacoity etc. *Ḥarābah* may be committed by one person or a group of persons. According to Imām Abū Ḥanīfah the person who commits *ḥarābah* must be armed with something that can be used as a weapon arm or such thing which is used as arm like stick, stone, piece of wood etc. But according to Imām Mālik and Imām Shāfi'ī only personal capability of using force is sufficient for the commission of *ḥarābah* liable to *ḥadd* irrespective of whether the offender has any arms with him or not.[38]

The difference between theft and *ḥarābah* is that theft means to take away the property of another person surreptitiously while *ḥarābah* means to take away the property of another person by using force publicly. Further all other conditions for the

---

[37] Abū Zahrah, *al-'Uqūbah*, p.134

[38] Ibn Qudāmah, *al-Mughnī*, vol.10, pp.262-64

commission of theft liable to *ḥadd* – such as that the property must be in custody, the property must be of the value of *niṣāb* and each offender has to get a share in such a property equal to *niṣāb,* the property must be valuable in the sight of the Shariah, the property must be owned by an individual and the offender has no right of ownership or share in it at all – are also necessary for *ḥarābah* liable to *ḥadd.*

It is pertinent to mention that according to Imām Abū Ḥanīfah *ḥarābah* shall be liable to *ḥadd* in case it is committed outside the population otherwise it shall be liable to *ta'zīr*. But according to Imām Mālik, Imām Shāfi'ī and Imām Aḥmad *ḥarābah* is liable to *ḥadd* whether it is committed inside the population or outside the population.[39]

Proof of *Ḥarābah*

The offence of *ḥarābah* liable to *ḥadd* is proved either by the confession of the accused or the testimony of two adult, sane and credible witnesses other than the victims. According to some jurists the offence of *ḥarābah* liable to *ḥadd* is also proved by the testimony of two victims provided they do not testify for their own property or hurt. All the conditions for the confession and testimony discussed in the offence of *zinā* liable to *ḥadd* are also applicable to the offence of *ḥarābah* liable to *ḥadd* related thereto.[40]

Punishment of *Ḥarābah*

Ḥarabah has been prohibited in Islam and has been declared a punishable crime for which punishment has been fixed by the Holy Qur'ān. The Holy Qur'ān says:

إِنَّمَا جَزَاءُ الَّذِينَ يُحَارِبُونَ اللَّهَ وَرَسُولَهُ وَيَسْعَوْنَ فِي الأَرْضِ فَسَادًا
أَن يُقَتَّلُواْ أَوْ يُصَلَّبُواْ أَوْ تُقَطَّعَ أَيْدِيهِمْ وَأَرْجُلُهُم مِّنْ خِلافٍ أَوْ يُنفَوْاْ
مِنَ الأَرْضِ ذَلِكَ لَهُمْ خِزْيٌ فِي الدُّنْيَا وَلَهُمْ فِي الآخِرَةِ عَذَابٌ عَظِيمٌ

---

39 Ibid, p.304

40 Al-Kāsanī, *Badā'i' al-Ṣanā'i',* vol.7, p.93

إِلاَّ الَّذِينَ تَابُواْ مِن قَبْلِ أَن تَقْدِرُواْ عَلَيْهِمْ فَاعْلَمُواْ أَنَّ اللَّـــهَ غَفُــورٌ رَّحِيمٌ

> The punishment of those who wage war against Allah and His Messenger (in respect of endangering the security of the state established under the Divine Law) and strive with might and main for mischief through the land, is execution or crucifixion or the cutting off their hands and feet from opposite sides, or exile, from the land; that is their disgrace in this world, and a heavy punishment is theirs in the hereafter, except for those who repent before they fall into your power; in that Allah is Oft-Forgiving, Most Merciful. (5:33,34)

This verse has laid down the following four punishments for robbery and dacoity;

(i) Death
(ii) Crucifixion
(iii) Amputation of hand and foot from opposite sides
(iv) Banishment

According to Imām Mālik it is at the discretion of the legislator or judge to choose any of these punishments for the offenders according to the circumstances.

But according to other jurists if the offender commits murder only, he shall be given death punishment. But if the offender commits murder and also takes away the property of the victim of more than the *niṣāb* of theft, he shall be given the punishment of crucifixion. Further according to Imām Abū Ḥanīfah and Imām Mālik crucifixion means that the convict shall be tied alive to a cross or a tree and his body ripped up with a spear so that he dies. But according to Imām Shāfi'ī and Imām Aḥmad crucifixion means that the convict shall first be killed with a sword or any other method and then his corpse shall be ignominiously exposed on a tree or a cross. Similarly if the offender does not commit murder but takes away the property of the victim of more than *niṣāb,* he shall be punished with amputation of his right hand from the wrist and his left foot from the ankle. And if the offender neither commits murder nor takes away any property of the victim, he shall be imprisoned for such period as the court deems necessary in the circumstances of a particular case. This is the view of Imām Abū Ḥanīfah and according to Imām Mālik, Imām Shāfi'ī and Imām Aḥmad the offender in this case shall be banished from the country for such period as the court deems necessary in the circumstances of a particular case. The view to be preferred in this connection is that the offender is to be banished to the nearest city or town within the country and to be imprisoned therein.

Repentance before arrest

It is the unanimous opinion of the jurists that if the offenders of *ḥarābah* repent before their arrest by the police or other state agency, *ḥadd* shall not be implemented on them. Repentance in this offence means expression of regret and remorse for the commission of the offence and determination not to commit the offence in future after removing the arms if any and offering submission to the concerned authorities. It is based on the following verse of Holy Qur'ān which relates to the punishment of the offenders of *ḥarābah:*

إِلاَّ الَّذِينَ تَابُواْ مِن قَبْلِ أَن تَقْدِرُواْ عَلَيْهِمْ فَاعْلَمُواْ أَنَّ اللَّـــهَ غَفُــورٌ رَّحِيمٌ

> Except for those who repent before they fall into your power; in that case, know that God is oft-forgiving, most merciful.(5:34)

However, in case of repentance before arrest the offender shall be liable for the restoration of the property taken from the owner if any and shall also be liable for *qiṣāṣ* if they have committed murder or hurt liable to *qiṣāṣ* or shall be liable to *diyat* or prescribed compensation if they have committed murder or hurt not liable to *qiṣāṣ*.

But if the offenders repent after being arrested, it shall not be effective and *ḥadd* shall be implemented on them if their offence is proved by the prescribed evidence.

Effect of repentance in *ḥudūd* other than *ḥarābah*

The jurists differ on whether repentance of an offender in an offence liable to *ḥadd* removes his *ḥadd* punishment or not. According to Imām Mālik, preferred view of Imām Shāfiʻī and Imām Abū Ḥanīfah repentance of an offender in an offence liable to *ḥadd* is not acceptable and he shall be punished with *ḥadd* punishment even if he repents. They base their opinion on the generality of verse 5:38 and 24:4 wherein the Holy Qur'ān orders for the punishment of thieves and adulterers without exception to the case of repentance. They further argue that the Holy Prophet stoned to death Ma'iz bin Malik and Ghamiddiyyah while both repented and demanded *ḥadd* punishment to be implemented on them. The Holy Prophet himself admitted that Maiz bin Malik had repented and if his repentance had been divided among seventy persons of Madinah, it would have been sufficient for them. Moreover if repentance removes the punishment then every offender will repent and thus no one shall be punished at all at least for *ḥadd*.

According to Ibn Taymiyyah and Ibn Qayyim the repentance of an offender in an offence liable to *ḥadd* is acceptable and it removes *ḥadd* punishment from the offender except when the offender himself insists that *ḥadd* punishment should be implemented on him. However, he shall be liable to *ta'zīr* in such a case.

According to an opinion among Ḥanafīs repentance of the offender in the offence of theft liable to *ḥadd* is acceptable to the extent that his hand shall not be cut off and he shall be liable for the restoration of the stolen property to the victim.

According to Imām Aḥmad, one opinion of Imām Shāfiʻī and Shia Zaidiyyah repentance of an offender in an offence liable to *ḥadd* is acceptable at any stage and it removes *ḥadd* punishment from the offender. They rely on verses 4:16 and 5:39 which are as under:

وَاللَّذَانِ يَأْتِيَانِهَا مِنكُمْ فَآذُوهُمَا فَإِن تَابَا وَأَصْلَحَا فَأَعْرِضُواْ عَنْهُمَا إِنَّ

اللّهَ كَانَ تَوَّابًا رَّحِيمًا

> If two men among you are guilty of lewdness, punish them both. If they repent and amend, leave them alone, indeed God is Oft-returning, Most Merciful. (4:16)
>
> فَمَن تَابَ مِن بَعْدِ ظُلْمِهِ وَأَصْلَحَ فَإِنَّ اللّهَ يَتُوبُ عَلَيْهِ إِنَّ اللّهَ غَفُورٌ رَّحِيمٌ
>
> If the thief repents after his crime and amends his conduct, God turns to him in forgiveness; indeed God is Oft-forgiving, Most Merciful.(5:39)

The underlined portions of the above verses denote that if the offender in case of *zinā* and theft repents he shall not be punished with *ḥadd*.

However, when an offence liable to *ḥadd* is proved, the repentance of the offender may not be sufficient to annul it. Repentance is an internal thing and it cannot be determined until it plays its role in the future conduct of an offender with which its authenticity and truth is determined. Moreover if repentance in every offence becomes effective in removing punishment from the offender, then every offender will repent and get acquittal and there would be no punishment at all for any offender. This is why some jurists opine that, the offender should be kept under observation to check whether he has actually amended his conduct or not, and if he does not amend his conduct, he may be liable for *ḥadd*.[41]

V. Drinking Wine (Intoxicating Liquors)

Drinking intoxicating liquors was permissible in the early days of Islam. As drinking was common among the Arabs and was the only means of revelry, Islam prohibited it gradually. Thus the following verse of the Holy Qur'ān was the first to be revealed to forbid intoxicating liquors;

> يَا أَيُّهَا الَّذِينَ آمَنُواْ لاَ تَقْرَبُواْ الصَّلاَةَ وَأَنتُمْ سُكَارَى حَتَّىَ تَعْلَمُواْ مَا تَقُولُونَ

---

[41] Ibn Qudāmah, *al-Mughnī,* vol.2, pp.316-17

O You who believe! Come not to prayers when ye are drunk until you understand what you say.(4:43)

In this verse Allah forbids prayer when one is intoxicated. As the five times prayers cover most of the day and night, they reduced drinking to a considerable extent. It was probably the reason that the Companions of the Holy Prophet were constrained to enquire about the real order of drinking intoxicating liquors and it was in response to their enquiry and in order to explain the cause of prohibition that the following verse was revealed:

يَسْأَلُونَكَ عَنِ الْخَمْرِ وَالْمَيْسِرِ قُلْ فِيهِمَا إِثْمٌ كَبِيرٌ وَمَنَافِعُ لِلنَّاسِ وَإِثْمُهُمَآ أَكْبَرُ من نَّفْعِهِمَا

They ask you concerning wine and gambling. Answer, in both there is great sin and some uses for men. but their sinfulness is greater than their usefulness. (2:219)

When the people were mentally prepared to give up drinking intoxicating liquors, the following verse was revealed:

يَا أَيُّهَا الَّذِينَ آمَنُواْ إِنَّمَا الْخَمْرُ وَالْمَيْسِرُ وَالأَنصَابُ وَالأَزْلاَمُ رِجْسٌ مِّنْ عَمَلِ الشَّيْطَانِ فَاجْتَنِبُوهُ لَعَلَّكُمْ تُفْلِحُونَ

O you who believe! Wine and gambling and stone pillars and divining arrows are an abomination of the work of Satan, therefore avoid them that you may prosper. (5:90)

The Holy Prophet said, "Every intoxicant is prohibited".[42] The Prophet said, "Cursed is he who drinks, purchases or sells wine or causes others to drink it".[43] It has been related that when the drinking of wine was prohibited, the people of Madinah poured out in the streets all that they possessed of the intoxicating liquors.[44] Wine in the early days of Islam was prepared from grapes, dates, honey, wheat and barley usually by fermentation. According to Imām Abū Ḥanīfah the prohibited wine (*Khamr*) is

---

[42] Aḥmad ibn Ḥanbal, *al-Musnad*, vol.2, p.69
[43] Ibid., vol.5, p.238
[44] Ibid., vol.2, pp.132-33

that which is fermented from grapes and dates and thus drinking wine prepared from other than grapes and dates or other spirits shall not be liable for punishment until the person who drinks it becomes intoxicated. But according to Imām Mālik, Imām Shāfi'ī and Imām Aḥmad every beverage that induces intoxication when taken in great quantity is forbidden and liable for punishment even when only a small quantity of it is taken with which the drinker does not become intoxicated. Thus drinking of any intoxicating liquor is prohibited whether more or less or whether fermented from grapes and dates or from any other thing and is punishable by *ḥadd* or *ta'zīr.* However, it is necessary for the *ḥadd* punishment that the accused has taken wine or other intoxicating liquor by mouth. Similarly *ḥadd* shall be implemented if the accused has consumed intoxicating liquor by mouth which has been mixed in the food he has taken. Moreover, *ḥadd* shall not be implemented on taking any solid intoxicant even by mouth.

Not only the drinking of wine and other intoxicating liquors is prohibited but their purchase and sale is also prohibited in an Islamic state and is an offence liable for *ta'zīr.*

Punishment of drinking wine

The Prophet and Caliph Abū Bakr had given the punishment of forty stripes to the drinker of wine. But in the period of Ḥaḍrat 'Umar, Khalid Ibn Walīd reported to him that people were indulging in prohibited drinks. Thereupon Ḥaḍrat 'Umar consulted the companions of the Prophet and they advised him to fix eighty stripes for that. Thus according to Imām Abū Ḥanīfah, Imām Mālik and Imām Aḥmad the *ḥadd* punishment for drinking wine is eighty stripes. But according to Imām Shāfi'ī the *ḥadd* punishment for drinking wine is forty stripes. Imām Shāfi'ī, however, opines that the *ḥadd* punishment of forty stripes can be increased and more than forty stripes shall be considered as *ta'zīr.* The jurists further concur that the convict shall not be punished with *ḥadd* as long as he is intoxicated, ill or weak.

It is pertinent to mention here that non-Muslims shall refrain from drinking wine and other intoxicating liquors publicly and shall be punished on its violation. Further according to some jurists *ḥadd* shall be implemented on them like Muslims while others opine that they shall be punished with *ta'zīr* only. But the majority of the jurists are of the view that *ḥadd* of drinking wine shall not be implemented on non-Muslims if they are guilty of drinking wine or other intoxicating liquor, but they shall be punished with *ta'zīr* if they drink wine publicly or sell it or purchase it publicly. Some of the later jurists are in favour of implementing *ḥadd* punishment on non-Muslims like Muslims if they drink any intoxicating liquor publicly.[45]

If a person consumes wine or other intoxicating liquor by any means other than the mouth, he shall not be liable for *ḥadd* but shall be liable for *ta'zīr.*

If a person is ill and an authorised medical officer prescribes that his illness can only be cured by drinking wine or an intoxicating liquor, he is allowed to drink wine or that intoxicating liquor till he recovers from his illness and he shall not be punished for that either with *ḥadd* or *ta'zīr.*[46]

VI. Rebellion

Rebellion literally means speech or behaviour directed against the peace of a state and in terms of Islamic law it means to turn against a righteous Muslim ruler and disturb the peace of the community. A rebel is a person who works for toppling the established government or for overthrowing those in authority or one, who relying on his own power; refuses to obey the established government. Rebellion is an offence directed against the government or the ruler and not against the social order. It is a political offence.[47] Obedience to a righteous ruler has been made compulsory in Islam. The Qur'ān states:

يَا أَيُّهَا الَّذِينَ آمَنُواْ أَطِيعُواْ اللّهَ وَأَطِيعُواْ الرَّسُولَ وَأُوْلِي الأَمْرِ مِنكُمْ

O you who believe! Obey God and obey the Apostle and those of you who are in authority (power). (4:59)

Abdullah Yusuf 'Alī, while commenting on this verse, writes:

---

[45] 'Awdah, *al-Tashrī' al-Jinā'ī al-Islāmī,* vol.2, pp.496-500

[46] Al-Kāsanī, *Badā'i' al-Ṣanā'i',* vol.8, p.40

[47] Ibn 'Abidīn, *Radd al-Muḥār,* vol.3, p.426

> As Islam makes no sharp division between sacred and secular affairs, it expects ordinary government to be imbued with a righteous Imām, and we must respect and obey such authority; otherwise there will be no order or discipline. Where, in actual fact, there is a sharp division between law and morality, between secular and religious affairs, as is the case in most countries in the present day, Islam still expects secular authority to be exercised in righteousness and on that condition, enjoins obedience to such authority.[48]

The Holy Prophet said, "The best rulers are those whom you (people) love and who love you (people) and who pray for you and you pray for them" The Prophet said, "He who dislikes any act of the ruler, should be patient (and should not aggress). He who opposes the order of consensus (Ummah) even a hand-span, he shall die as one dies in the days of ignorance (Jahiliyyah)."[49] Allamah Taftazani writes, "One of the qualities of the rulers is that entire people shall follow them".[50] The jurists concur that to turn against a Muslim ruler is rebellion and is a punishable offence in Shariah.

One of the conditions of rebellion is that it aims at the deposition of a ruler and the dissolution of legislature or direct defiance of the competent authority of the state. But if the purpose of the offence is to bring about a change inconsistent with the provisions of Shariah or to pave the way for a system contrary to the injunctions of Islam, the offence in question will not be treated as rebellion or political offence. It will amount to *ḥarābah* or creation of chaos on earth and will be treated as a habitual offence.

Another condition of rebellion is that the rebels have to rationalise their position by advancing arguments in their favour, justify their position to the established authority and offer reasons and arguments that may seemingly warrant their demand, although the arguments and reasons they put forth may be absurd and untenable. If they fail to do so they will not be treated as rebels but

---

[48]Yusuf 'Alī, *Commentary*, p.198

[49] Al-Shawkānī, *Nayl al-Awṭār*, vol.7, pp.80-81

[50] Sa'd-ud-Dīn al-Taftāzanī, *Sharḥ al-Maqāṣid*, p.108

will be liable for the punishments prescribed for such offences. Moreover a rebel is one whose power and grandeur does not originate from his personal capacity, but owes itself to his followers and supporters. If it does not spring from the followers and supporters then he will not be treated as a rebel, whatever arguments he may advance to prove himself to the contrary.

An important condition of rebellion is that it takes place in a revolution or in a state of civil war brought about for the achievement of a goal. If no revolution or state of civil war exists when the offence is committed, it does not amount to rebellion, but will be treated as a habitual offence.

During the Caliphate of Ḥaḍrat 'Alī, Khawarij refused to obey him and raised the slogan "None but Allah's command is acceptable!" The Caliph said, "Verily this is an unquestionable percept, but it has been returned into a slogan for an evil purpose. You enjoy three rights which we must respect:

i) We will not prevent you from worshipping in mosques
ii) We will not be the first to start a war against you and
iii) So long as you remain with us and do not revolt against our authority, we will not deprive you of your sights.

Punishment of Rebellion

According to some jurists *hadd* punishment of rebellion is death when during the rebellion the rebels start using force. The Holy Qur'ān states:

وَإِن طَائِفَتَانِ مِنَ الْمُؤْمِنِينَ اقْتَتَلُوا فَأَصْلِحُوا بَيْنَهُمَا فَإِن بَغَتْ إِحْدَاهُمَا عَلَى الْأُخْرَى فَقَاتِلُوا الَّتِي تَبْغِي حَتَّى تَفِيءَ إِلَى أَمْرِ اللَّهِ فَإِن فَاءَتْ فَأَصْلِحُوا بَيْنَهُمَا بِالْعَدْلِ وَأَقْسِطُوا إِنَّ اللَّهَ يُحِبُّ الْمُقْسِطِينَ

> If two parties among the believers fall into a quarrel, make peace between them: but if one of them transgresses beyond bounds against the other, then fight all against the one that transgresses until it complies with the command of God. But if it complies, then make peace between them with justice and be fair; for God loves those who are fair (and just). (49:9)

If a party is determined to rise up against a righteous Muslim ruler by force of arms etc. and it does not accept the answers of that ruler to their objections and does not, at any cost, agree to any compromise, the whole force of the government and the community will be used against them and they shall be killed until they agree to finish their rebellion and become loyal to the state. The jurists agree that it is necessary for the rebellion not to be against a right and just cause and that the rebels must have first used force against the Islamic state and have disturbed the law and order situation. Mere resistance against the Islamic state for a cause, which is right and just in the light of the injunctions of Islam, shall not be a rebellion liable to the killing of the rebels. Moreover oral rebellion does not amount to killing until the rebels start using practical force against the state. According to some jurists the rebels must be organized and must have a leader to command them failing which their killing will not be permissible.[51]

The jurists further agree that when a group of people rebel against a Muslim ruler, the ruler first has to hold a dialogue with them and try his best to satisfy them in any possible way other than fighting with arms. And when all possible efforts fail to satisfy them and the rebels insist on continuing their rebellion and start attacking and destroying public and government property, by using force then it is lawful for the state to kill them. Fairness and justice should be strictly adopted in this serious matter.[52] In this connection Abdullah Yusuf Ali writes, "Individual quarrels are easier to compose than group quarrels or in the modern world, national quarrels. But the collective community of Islam should be supreme over groups or nations. It would be expected to act justly and try to compose the quarrel, for peace is better than fighting. But if a party is determined to be the aggressor, the whole force of the community is brought to bear on it. The essential condition of course is that there should be perfect fairness and justice and respect for the highest principles; for Islam takes account of every

[51] Ibn Qudāmah, *al-Mughnī,* vol.10, pp.48-49
[52] 'Awdah, *al-Tashrī' al-Jinā'ī al-Islāmī,* vol.2, pp.680-81

just and legitimate interest without separating spiritual from temporal matters".[53]

If the rebels fight against the Islamic state, their prisoners shall be imprisoned until they offer submission and accept loyalty to the state. However, their women, old persons and children shall not be imprisoned. The rebels shall remain the owners of their properties and their properties shall be returned to them after the end of the rebellion.

But according to some jurists the punishment of the rebels will vary with the circumstances. The offences they commit prior to starting force and war will be treated as habitual offences which entail punishments laid down for such crimes. But when they start using force against the government by destroying public properties, taking over the control of the government, killing government servants, attacking military positions and bases etc. it is permissible to kill them, repulse and subjugate them and seize their properties to the extent that it is deemed necessary. But when the state gets full control over the rebels and the latter lay down arms, the security of their lives and property shall be ensured and then the head of the state shall be under an obligation to pardon them.

VII.Apostasy (ارتداد)

Apostate means a Muslim who intentionally and voluntarily abandons his religion. Apostasy means any words uttered or any act done by a sane and adult Muslim intentionally and voluntarily which contradicts any fundamentals of Islam such as refusing an admitted belief or practice of Islam for example, refusing belief in next life, praying five times a day, fasting in Ramadan or degrading Islam and its injunctions or believing in the eternal existence of the universe and its being not created by a creator or bowing before idols the, sun or moon or throwing the Holy Qur'ān in filth or dirt. Before convicting a Muslim for apostasy, he must be given a chance to explain as to what he means by the words he uttered or the act he committed. A Muslim, however, does not become an apostate by refusing to accept any belief or practice

---

[53] Yusuf Alī, *Commentary*, p.1405

which is not fundamental according to the injunctions of Islam. Similarly a Muslim does not become an apostate by rejecting or not believing in a thing which is disputed among the Muslim scholars of different schools of thought.

Punishment of Apostasy

The *ḥadd* punishment for all apostate is death after giving him a reasonable opportunity to repent. The Holy Prophet said, "Kill the person (Muslim) who abandons his religion". According to Imām Mālik, Imām Shāfi'ī and Imām Aḥmad the punishment of death is common for all apostates whether male or female. But according to Imām Abū Ḥanīfah a woman apostate shall not be punished with death but shall be imprisoned till she repents or dies. He bases his opinion on the *ḥadīth* wherein the Holy Prophet has ordered not to kill the women of non-Muslims during battle with them.[54]

Opportunity of repentance

The jurists concur that an apostate shall not be punished with death until he is given sufficient opportunity and asked to repent and if he repents, he shall not be punished. According to some jurists the period of opportunity is three days. And according to other jurists including Imām Abū Ḥanīfah the period of opportunity is left to the discretion of the judge to fix according to the circumstances of a particular case. It has been preferred by the later jurists. This is based on the practice of Ḥaḍrat 'Umar when he was informed by some persons that they had killed an apostate without giving him opportunity to repent, he said, "Why didn't you give him opportunity for repentance so that he might have repented"?[55] Further Ḥaḍrat 'Alī practised it in the case of Khawarij and Mu'tazilah. Moreover such a person must be asked as to what he means by the words he utters because sometimes a word bears a different meaning and interpretation. Criminal liability requires the wrongful act to be done intentionally or with

---

[54] Ibn Qudāmah, *al-Mughnī*, vol.10, p.86

[55] Ibn Ḥazm, *al-Muḥallā*, vol.9, p.192

some other wrong purpose in mind. Intention is the purpose or design with which an act is done.

It is pertinent to mention here that the *ḥadīth* of the death punishment for apostasy is in the form of a general provision which requires specification. According to Allamah Shawkānī, the general purpose of this *ḥadīth* has been specified in the Holy Qur'ān (16:106) with regard to a person who changes his religion outwardly under duress but remains faithful otherwise. The Ḥanafīs have also specified this general *ḥadīth* in the case of a woman apostate who is not punished by death but by imprisonment. The *ḥadīth* in question may therefore be further specified and the death punishment therein may be reversed for apostasy which is accompanied by active hostility to the community and its leadership of a kind that amounts to high treason (*ḥarābah*).[56]

Many prominent scholars across the centuries have taken the view that apostasy is not an offence liable to *ḥadd*. Ibrahim al-Nakha'i (d.59H) and Sufyān Thawrī (d.162H) have held that the apostate shall be invited to Islam and shall never be condemned to death. The Mālikī jurist Ibn al-Walīd al-Baji (d.494H) and the Hanbali jurist Ibn Taymiyyah have held that apostasy is a crime which carries no *ḥadd* punishment and that a crime of this kind may be punished only under the discretionary punishment of *ta'zīr*.[57]

The late Shaikh of al-Azhar, Mahmood Shaltut, has analyzed the relevant sources and has drawn the conclusion that apostasy carries no temporal punishment because in reference to apostasy the Qur'ān only speaks of punishment in the Hereafter. Shaikh Shaltut also concurred with the analysis that the key factor in the *ḥadīth* which prescribed the death punishment for apostasy was 'aggression and hostility against the believers and the prevention of a possible sedition *(fitnah)* against the religion and state'.[58]

Allamah Mahmasani has also made a similar observation saying that 'the death punishment was not meant to apply to a

[56] Al-Shawkānī, *Nayl al-Awṭār*, vol.7, pp.218-19

[57] Ibn Taymiyyah, *al-Sarim al-Maslūl*, p.318, see also Abd al-Wahhab Sha'rani, Kitab al-Mizan, Vol. II, p.134

[58] Muhammad Shaltut, *al-Islam 'Aqidah wa Shariah*, pp.292-293

simple change of faith but to punish acts such as treason, joining forces with the enemy and sedition'.[59] This view is in line with the Qur'ānic verse "There is no compulsion in religion". (2:256)

Subsidiary punishment for apostasy is confiscation of property. However, the jurists differ on this question. According to Imām Mālik, Imām Shāfi'ī and Imām Aḥmad, the entire property of the apostate should be confiscated. But according to Imām Abū Ḥanīfah and some Mālikis that portion of the property of the apostate is to be confiscated which he may have acquired after becoming an apostate. Property acquired by him prior to renunciation of Islam belongs to the heirs of the apostate.[60] Moreover, the marriage of an apostate with his Muslim wife is dissolved as soon as turns apostate.

Contempt for the Prophets

One of the offences liable to *ḥadd* is the contempt for any Prophet. Contempt means to abuse or insult any person. Explaining the seriousness of the contempt for the Prophet, Qazi Ayaz writes, "Whoever curses the Holy Prophet or blames him or attributes imperfection to him in his person, his lineage, his religion or any of his qualities or alludes to that or its likes by any means whatsoever, whether in the form of a curse or insult or belittling him or detracting from him or finding fault with him or maligning him, is a contemner".[61] In this connection Ibn Taymiyyah writes, "Any person who curses the Prophet, invokes against him, desires to harm him, ascribes to him what does not behove with his position or uses any insulting, false and unreasonable words about him or imputes ignorance to him or blames him with any human weakness, he is a contemner".[62]

Punishment for Contempt of the Prophet

The jurists opine that the offence of the contempt of the Prophet is punishable by death as *ḥadd*. The Holy Prophet said, "Kill the

[59] Subhi Mahmas..i 'Arkan Huquq al-Insan fi'al-Islam, pp.123-24
[60] Ibn Qudāmah, *al-Mughnī*, vol.7, p.174
[61] Qazi Ayad, *al-Shifā*, vol.2, p.192
[62] Ibn Taymiyyah, *al-Sārim al-Maslūl*, p.526

person who abuses a Prophet and whip the one who abuses my companions".[63] But according to an opinion among Shafi'īs the offence of the contempt of the Holy Prophet is liable to *ta'zīr.*[64]

It has been related on the authority of Ḥaḍrat 'Alī that a Jewish woman used to abuse the Holy Prophet (pbuh) and thus a person killed her. The Holy Prophet (pbuh) declared the shedding of her blood as permissible.[65]

It has been related on the authority of Abu Bardah who said, "I was sitting with Caliph Abū Bakr when he became furious at a person". I said to him, "O! Caliph of the Prophet of Allah! Order me to kill him". On hearing this his anger subsided and he went inside and called me and said, "If I order you, you will kill him" I said, "Yes" He said, "No, I swear by Allah that no one other than the Holy Prophet (pbuh) is in the position that his contemner be killed".[66]

Intention of the contemner must be ascertained before his conviction. The mere fact that the words uttered are contemptuous of the Prophet is not an offence until it is based on malicious action or degradation. The meaning and import of words differ from place to place. Again context may also suggest a different meaning. It is, therefore, after the contemner's explanation that the court can decide whether the words used by him were intended to malign and were used contemptuously or were uttered innocently.

Further according to Imām Mālik and Imām Aḥmad the repentance of the contemner is not acceptable if he repents. But according to Imām Shāfi'ī and the preferred view among the Ḥanafīs is that repentance of the contemner is acceptable like that of the apostate and he shall not be punished after repentance. Moreover according to Imām Mālik, Imām Shāfi'ī and Imām Aḥmad the *ḥadd* punishment for contempt of the Prophet is applicable to both Muslims and non-Muslims. But according to Imām Abū Ḥanīfah non-Muslims shall not be punished with death if he or she commits contempt of the Prophet but shall be punished

---

[63] Qazi 'Iyaḍ, *al-Shifā,* vol.2, p.199
[64] 'Awdah, *al-Tashrī'al-Jina'ī al-Islāmī*, vol.2 p.725
[65] Abu Dawūd, *Sunan* vol.2, p.356
[66] Ibiḍ., vol.2, p.357

with *ta'zir.*[67] Moreover according to Imām Abū Ḥanīfah a woman shall not be punished with death if she commits contempt of the Prophet but shall be imprisoned until she repents or dies.

It is important to point out that all the Prophets of Allah are equal in status being Messengers of God and the Muslims have been ordered to believe in them and treat them equally. Many of the Prophets have been mentioned in the Holy Qur'ān such as Adam, Noah, Abraham, Ismā'īl, Isaac, Jacob, Moses, Jesus. The Holy Qur'ān states:

لاَ نُفَرِّقُ بَيْنَ أَحَدٍ مِّن رُّسُلِه

> We make no distinction between one and another of His Messengers. (2:285)

It means that it is not for the Muslims to make any distinction between one or the other of Allah's Messengers. The Muslims must honour them all equally, though Allah in His wisdom sent them with different kinds of mission and gave them different degrees of rank. Thus the same punishment of death shall apply in case any person commits contempt of any one of the Prophets of Allah.

---

[67] Ibn Taymiyyah, *al-Sārim al-Maslūl*, pp.286, 312, 314.

Chapter Seven

Crimes Liable to *Ta'zīr*

Ta'zīr literally means to prevent, to honour, to correct, to moderate, to avoid, to assist. It is said (he disciplined, chastised, corrected or punished him, meaning he did something to him that should prevent the criminal from returning to disobedience). Similarly it is said (he beat him moderately). But generally it signifies a punishment intended to prevent the culprit from relapsing, to purify him.[1]

In terms of Islamic criminal law *ta'zīr* signifies punishment for a crime for which punishment has not been fixed by the Qur'ān and the *Sunnah* of the Prophet Muhammad (pbuh) and has been left to the discretion of the ruler or the judge to fix it in accordance with the prevailing circumstances so as to reform the culprit and restrain him from recommitting the crime and to restrain others from committing the crime. The Qur'ān says: "Whoever works evil, will be requitted accordingly". (4:123) *Ta'zīr* varies according to the various circumstances with respect to the culprit, society and state. Al-Mawardi, a Shāfi'ī jurist, while defining *ta'zīr* writes, "*ta'zīr* means the punishment inflicted in cases of crime for which the law (*Sharī'ah*) has not enacted written penalties. The rules relating to it differ depending upon the circumstances in which it is inflicted and the circumstances with

[1] Lane, *Madd al-Qamus, Bk.I*, Pt.2, p.2034

respect to the culprit".[2] The jurists concur that *ta'zīr* also signifies a crime for which punishment has not been fixed by the Qur'ān and the *Sunnah* of the Prophet (PBUH).[3]

Unlike *ḥadd, ta'zīr* is an unfixed and alterable punishment for an offence. *Ta'zīr* is a whole code of penal measures ranging from warning to capital punishment. The judge may, at his discretion, order any of those corrective measures in view of the offender's conduct. The judge is empowered to award more than one punishment, commute a punishment or award a more severe one or suspend the execution of a sentence or remit the sentence if he deems it necessary for the correction of the offender.

The basic sources of Islamic criminal law, i.e. the Qur'ān and the *Sunnah*, do not contain express provisions for each and every *ta'zīr*. These sources, however, contain provisions relating to the crimes liable to *ta'zīr* which are perpetually detrimental to individuals, the community and general peace and tranquility. These sources rather empower the head of the state to declare any act unlawful, which he deems prejudicial to peace and tranquility under the prevailing circumstances keeping in view the fundamental Islamic principles. The head of the state is also empowered to frame rules and regulations for the maintenance of peace and tranquility and punish those who violate them.

The crimes for which punishments have not been fixed by the Qur'ān and the *Sunnah* of Prophet Muhammad (PBUH) are innumerable. However, they are of two kinds:

(i) The actions and omissions in which any Divine provision *(Shariah* text) or any principle thereof is violated. For instance, commission of theft, breach of trust, bribery, gambling etc.

(ii) The violation of the rules, regulations and orders of the rulers acting as sub-legislative authority.

But such rules and regulations must not be arbitrary and must be based on the larger interest of the society. Not only these rules

---

[2]Abū Ḥasan 'Alī ibn Muḥammad, al-Māwardī, *al-Aḥkām al-Sulṭāniyyah*, pp.236-37

[3]Abū Zahrah, *al-Jarīmah*, p.4

and regulations should not contravene any Divine provision but also they should develop and execute some Divine injunction. The legislative powers of the rulers are limited to this extent.[4] The Qur'ān says:

يَا أَيُّهَا الَّذِينَ آمَنُواْ أَطِيعُواْ اللّهَ وَأَطِيعُواْ الرَّسُولَ وَأُوْلِي الأَمْرِ مِنكُمْ

O you who believe! Obey God and obey the Apostle and those of you who are in authority (rulers). (4:59)

Abdullah Yusuf Ali, while commenting on this verse writes:

> As Islam makes no sharp division between sacred and secular affairs, it expects ordinary government to be imbued with righteousness and stand in the place of the righteous Imam, and we must respect and obey such authority; otherwise there will be no order or discipline.[5]

The Islamic state is authorised to prescribe punishments for crimes for which punishments have not been prescribed either by the Qur'ān or the *Sunnah* of the Prophet. For example the Holy Qur'ān has declared that to spread obscenity is a punishable crime but has not prescribed punishment for that. The Qur'ān says,

إِنَّ الَّذِينَ يُحِبُّونَ أَن تَشِيعَ الْفَاحِشَةُ فِي الَّذِينَ آمَنُوا لَهُمْ عَذَابٌ أَلِيمٌ فِي الدُّنْيَا وَالْآخِرَةِ

Those who love to spread obscenity among the believers, for them is painful punishment in this life and in hereinafter. (24:19)

The above verse authorises an Islamic state to prescribe punishment for those who spread obscenity in the Islamic society by any mean such as speech, physical display, publishing, advertising or transmission on radio or television. These punishments may vary according to the severity of the offence. The state should, in a compiled form, prescribe the minimum and maximum limits of such punishments with a short description of

---

4 'Awdah, *al-Tashrī' al-Jinā'ī al-Islāmī*, vol.1, p.81

5 Yusuf Alī, *Commentary*, p.198

other substantive elements of the respective crimes and leave it to the Court to grant either minimum or maximum punishment to the convict or within these limits in accordance with the circumstances of the case. These prescribed punishments should be changed from time to time according to the change in the circumstances relating to them.

As discussed in the previous chapters a specified kind and quantum of testimony have been prescribed for the proof of the crimes liable to *ḥudūd, qiṣāṣ* and *diyat.* For the proof of *zinā* and false accusation of *zinā* liable to *ḥadd* at least four eye-witnesses are required who have to testify in their testimony that they have seen the accused man and woman in the actual state of intercourse. Similarly for the proof of theft liable to *ḥadd* two eye-witnesses are required who have to testify in their testimony that they have seen the accused entering the place from where theft has been committed and coming out from it along with the stolen property. Similarly for the proof of the other crimes liable to *ḥudūd,* the testimony of two eye-witnesses is required. If the prescribed evidence is not available in such cases, these *ḥadd* punishments shall not be imposed. If lesser authentic evidence is available, the accused shall be punished with *ta'zīr* to be determined according to the circumstances of the case and evidence available. Moreover the Prophet (pbuh) said, "Remove *ḥudūd* with doubts". This means that if there is any doubt on any part of the commission of the crime, *ḥadd* punishment shall not be given to the accused. In addition to this, crimes liable to *ḥudūd* are also proved by the confession of the accused which must be with his free consent without coercion and must be explicit with respect to the crime. The jurists concur that the judge must instruct the confessor to retract his confession and if he retracts *ḥadd* punishment shall not be implemented on him. Retraction from confession is admissible at any stage before the execution of the punishment and even during the execution of the punishment whether expressly or impliedly and it nullifies the *ḥadd* punishment.

Contrary to the crimes liable to *ḥudūd, qiṣāṣ* and *diyat,* no specific kind and quantum of evidence have been prescribed for the proof of a crime liable to *ta'zīr.* Thus crime liable to *ta'zīr* can be proved by the testimony of one or more witnesses, secondary evidence, circumstantial evidence, opinion of an expert or any kind of evidence which, in the opinion of the court, is sufficient to prove the fact at issue.[6]

---

[6] Ibn Qudāmah, *al-Mughnī*, vol.3, p.189

Chapter Eight

Ta'zīr in Qur'ān and *Sunnah*

A large number of crimes and transgressions liable to *ta'zīr* have been mentioned in the texts of the Qur'ān and the *Sunnah* of the Prophet Muhammad (pbuh). These texts empower the legislators and judges to fix the punishments for these crimes and transgressions keeping in view the requirements of these texts and the prevailing circumstances. This also shows that legislators and judges have no absolute authority in fixing the punishments of *ta'zīr* for these crimes but they have to look into the relevant texts and their requirements while they have also to look into the requirements of the prevailing circumstances with respect to the culprit, society and state.[1] Some of these crimes are as under:

1. Prohibition of certain edibles

The Qur'ān says:

إِنَّمَا حَرَّمَ عَلَيْكُمُ الْمَيْتَةَ وَالدَّمَ وَلَحْمَ الْخِنزِيرِ وَمَا أُهِلَّ بِهِ لِغَيْرِ اللَّهِ

> He has forbidden you only carrion and blood and swine flesh and that which has been immolated to (the name of) any other than Allah. (2:173)

---

[1] 'Awdah, *al-Tashrī' al-Jinā'ī al-Islāmī*, vol.1, p.143

حُرِّمَتْ عَلَيْكُمُ الْمَيْتَةُ وَالْدَّمُ وَلَحْمُ الْخِنْزِيرِ وَمَا أُهِلَّ لِغَيْرِ اللّهِ بِهِ وَالْمُنْخَنِقَةُ وَالْمَوْقُوذَةُ وَالْمُتَرَدِّيَةُ وَالنَّطِيحَةُ وَمَا أَكَلَ السَّبُعُ إِلاَّ مَا ذَكَّيْتُمْ وَمَا ذُبِحَ عَلَى النُّصُبِ وَأَن تَسْتَقْسِمُواْ بِالأَزْلاَمِ ذَلِكُمْ فِسْقٌ

Forbidden to you (for food) are carrion and blood and swine flesh and that which is dedicated to any other than Allah, and the dead through beating and the strangled and the dead through falling from a height, and that which has been killed by (gorging of horns and the devoured of wild beasts, saving that which you make lawful (by the death-stroke), and that which has been immolated to idols. And (forbidden to you is) that you swear by the divining arrows. This is an abomination. (5:3)

وَيُحِلُّ لَهُمُ الطَّيِّبَاتِ وَيُحَرِّمُ عَلَيْهِمُ الْخَبَآئِثَ

And makes lawful to them pure things and makes unlawful to them impure things. (7:157)

It has been related on the authority of Jabir that they slaughtered horses, mules and donkeys during the battle of Hunain. The Prophet prohibited the eating of mules and donkeys but did not prohibit the eating of a horse. It has also been related on the authority of Ibn Abbas that the Prophet prohibited the eating of birds and animals of prey having talons or claws. Again, the Holy Prophet said, "The dog is unclean and its price is unclean.[2]

Thus eating any of these things or trade in them is an offence liable to *ta'zīr*.

2. Breach of trust

The Qur'ān says,

إِنَّ اللّهَ يَأْمُرُكُمْ أَن تُؤدُّواْ الأَمَانَاتِ إِلَى أَهْلِهَا وَإِذَا حَكَمْتُم بَيْنَ النَّاسِ أَن تَحْكُمُواْ بِالْعَدْلِ

---

[2] Ibid., p.139

Lo! Allah commands you that you restore trusts to whom they are due and when you judge between mankind, that you judge justly. (4:58)

يَا أَيُّهَا الَّذِينَ آمَنُواْ لاَ تَخُونُواْ اللَّهَ وَالرَّسُولَ وَتَخُونُواْ أَمَانَاتِكُمْ

O you who believe! Betray not Allah and His messenger, nor knowingly betray your trusts. (8:27)

وَآتُواْ الْيَتَامَى أَمْوَالَهُمْ وَلاَ تَتَبَدَّلُواْ الْخَبِيثَ بِالطَّيِّبِ وَلاَ تَأْكُلُواْ أَمْوَالَهُمْ إِلَى أَمْوَالِكُمْ

Give to orphans their wealth. Exchange not the good for the bad nor absorb their wealth into your own wealth" (4:2)

The Prophet said, "He who is guilty of breach of trust is not a complete believer". Again the Holy Prophet said, "A man having four qualities is a hypocrite. If he possesses one of the four qualities, he has then one quality of an imposter unless he shakes it off. The qualities are: he commits breach of trust whenever something is kept in his custody, whenever he tells something, it is a lie, whenever he enters into a contract, he is dishonest and whenever he picks up a quarrel, he abuses".[3]

Thus breach of trust is an offence punishable with *ta'zīr*.

3. Fraud in Weights and Measures

The Qur'ān says,

وَيْلٌ لِّلْمُطَفِّفِينَ الَّذِينَ إِذَا اكْتَالُواْ عَلَى النَّاسِ يَسْتَوْفُونَ وَإِذَا كَالُوهُمْ أَو وَّزَنُوهُمْ يُخْسِرُونَ

Woe to the defrauders; those who when they take the measure from mankind demand it full. But when they measure to them or weight for them, they cause them less. (83:1-3)

---

[3] Ibid., p.140

أَوْفُوا الْكَيْلَ وَلَا تَكُونُوا مِنَ الْمُخْسِرِينَ وَزِنُوا بِالْقِسْطَاسِ الْمُسْتَقِيمِ
وَلَا تَبْخَسُوا النَّاسَ أَشْيَاءَهُمْ وَلَا تَعْثَوْا فِي الْأَرْضِ مُفْسِدِينَ

Give full measure and be not of those who give less (than the due). And weight with true balance. Wrong not mankind in their goods, and do not do evil, making mischief in the earth. (26:181-183)

وَأَوْفُوا الْكَيْلَ إِذا كِلْتُمْ وَزِنُواْ بِالقِسْطَاسِ الْمُسْتَقِيمِ ذَلِكَ خَيْرٌ
وَأَحْسَنُ تَأْوِيلاً

Fill the measure when you measure and weight with a right balance; that is useful and better in the end. (17:35)

According to a *ḥadīth* related on the authority of 'Abdullah ibn 'Umar, those who bought provisions wholesale without measures or weights in order to sell them again with less measures or weights were punished by whipping in the time of the Prophet (pbuh).[4]

Thus using false weight and measure is an offence liable *ta'zīr*.

4. Charging and taking interest

The Qur'ān says:

الَّذِينَ يَأْكُلُونَ الرِّبَا لَا يَقُومُونَ إِلاَّ كَمَا يَقُومُ الَّذِي يَتَخَبَّطُهُ الشَّيْطَانُ
مِنَ الْمَسِّ ذَلِكَ بِأَنَّهُمْ قَالُواْ إِنَّمَا الْبَيْعُ مِثْلُ الرِّبَا وَأَحَلَّ اللَّهُ الْبَيْعَ
وَحَرَّمَ الرِّبَا

Those who swallow usury cannot rise up save as he arises whom the devil has prostrated by (his) touch. That is because they say: Trade is just like usury, whereas Allah has permitted Trade and prohibited usury". (2:275)

يَمْحَقُ اللَّهُ الْرِّبَا وَيُرْبِي الصَّدَقَاتِ

---

[4] Al- Bukhārī, *Ṣaḥīḥ*, p.192

Allah has blighted usury and made alms giving fruitful. (2:276)

يَا أَيُّهَا الَّذِينَ آمَنُواْ اتَّقُواْ اللّهَ وَذَرُواْ مَا بَقِيَ مِنَ الرِّبَا إِن كُنتُم مُّؤْمِنِينَ

O you who believe! Observe your duty to Allah and give up what remains (due to you) from usury, if you are true believers. (2:278)

The Holy Prophet (pbuh) cursed the receiver and the payer of interest, the one who records it and the one who is a witness to such transaction and said, "They are all alike (in guilt)".[5]

The Holy Prophet said at the occasion of his last pilgrimage, "The interest prevailing in pre-Islamic period is annulled. The first interest that I annul is the interest that accruing to Abbas bin Abdul Mutalib, it is cancelled completely.[6]

Thus taking and granting interest is an offence punishable with *ta'zīr*.

5. Concealment of evidence

The Qur'ān says,

وَلاَ تَكْتُمُواْ الشَّهَادَةَ وَمَن يَكْتُمْهَا فَإِنَّهُ آثِمٌ قَلْبُهُ

And conceal not testimony. He who conceals it, verily his heart is sinful". (2:283)

وَلاَ يَأْبَ الشُّهَدَاء إِذَا مَا دُعُواْ

And the witnesses must not refuse when they are summoned. (2:282)

يَا أَيُّهَا الَّذِينَ آمَنُواْ كُونُواْ قَوَّامِينَ بِالْقِسْطِ شُهَدَاء لِلّهِ وَلَوْ عَلَى أَنفُسِكُمْ أَوِ الْوَالِدَيْنِ وَالأَقْرَبِينَ إِن يَكُنْ غَنِيًّا أَوْ فَقَيرًا

---

[5] Muslim, *Ṣaḥīḥ*, vol.2, p.112

[6] Ibid., p.114

O you who believe! Be you staunch in justice, witnesses for Allah, even though it be against yourselves or your parents or your kindred whether (the case be of) a rich man or a poor man.(4:135)

Concealment of evidence in case when a witness is summoned by the court for giving evidence is an offence liable for *ta'zīr*.

6. False evidence

The Qur'ān says,

وَالَّذِينَ لَا يَشْهَدُونَ الزُّورَ

And those who witness no falsehood. (25:72)

فَاجْتَنِبُوا الرِّجْسَ مِنَ الْأَوْثَانِ وَاجْتَنِبُوا قَوْلَ الزُّورِ

So shun the filth of idols and shun false speeches. (22:30)

The Prophet (pbuh) in a *ḥadīth* has equated false testimony with partnership with God and the disobedience of the parents and declared it a grave sin.[7]

Thus giving false evidence is an offence punishable with *ta'zīr*.

7. Abuses, insults and defamations

The Qur'ān says,

وَلاَ تَسُبُّواْ الَّذِينَ يَدْعُونَ مِن دُونِ اللّهِ فَيَسُبُّواْ اللّهَ عَدْوًا بِغَيْرِ عِلْمٍ

Abuse not those to whom they pray beside Allah lest they wrongfully abuse Allah through ignorance. (6:108)

يَا أَيُّهَا الَّذِينَ آمَنُوا لَا يَسْخَرْ قَومٌ مِّن قَوْمٍ عَسَى أَن يَكُونُوا خَيْرًا مِّنْهُمْ وَلَا نِسَاء مِّن نِّسَاء عَسَى أَن يَكُنَّ خَيْرًا مِّنْهُنَّ وَلَا تَلْمِزُوا أَنفُسَكُمْ وَلَا تَنَابَزُوا بِالْأَلْقَابِ بِئْسَ الاِسْمُ الْفُسُوقُ بَعْدَ الْإِيمَانِ

---

[7] 'Awdah, *al-Tashrī' al-Jinā'ī al-Islāmī,* vol. 1, p.140

> O you who believe! Let not a folk deride a folk who may be better than they (are), nor let women deride women who may be better than they are; neither defame one another nor insult one another by nicknames. (49:11)

The Prophet (pbuh) said, "A Muslim is the brother of another Muslim and thus he will neither depress him nor deride him nor insult him". Prophet (pbuh) also said, "The blood, prestige and property of a Muslim are sacred for another Muslim". According to a tradition related by Abdullah ibn Abbas, the Prophet (pbuh) is said to have threatened with 20 lashes any man who insults another by calling him soft or effeminate.[8] Similarly any insult, scorning or defamation is an offence punishable with *ta'zīr*.

8. Bribery

The Qur'ān says,

وَلاَ تَأْكُلُواْ أَمْوَالَكُم بَيْنَكُم بِالْبَاطِلِ وَتُدْلُواْ بِهَا إِلَى الْحُكَّامِ لِتَأْكُلُواْ فَرِيقًا مِّنْ أَمْوَالِ النَّاسِ بِالإِثْمِ وَأَنتُمْ تَعْلَمُونَ

> And eat not up your property among yourselves in vanity, nor seek by it to gain the favour of the judges that you may knowingly devour a portion of the property of others wrongfully. (2:188)

سَمَّاعُونَ لِلْكَذِبِ أَكَّالُونَ لِلسُّحْتِ فَإِن جَآؤُوكَ فَاحْكُم بَيْنَهُم أَوْ أَعْرِضْ عَنْهُمْ

> Listeners for the sake of falsehood! Greedy for illicit gain! If then they have recourse to you judge between them or disclaim jurisdiction. (5:42)

The Prophet (pbuh) said, "The one who gives bribes and the one who is bribed will be in hell". The Prophet also said, "It is bribery to give a gift to an officer". The Prophet (pbuh) also said, "Allah curses the one who gives bribe, the one who receives the bribe and the one who settles this matter between them". Once the Prophet (pbuh) sent Ibn Al-Lutbiah to collect *zakat*. When he

---

[8] Al-Qazwini, Muhammad Ibn Yazid, *Ibn al-Majah*, p.168

came back he said, "This is *zakat* and this is what was given as a gift to me". The Prophet (pbuh) said, "What happened to the person whom we appointed for the collection of *zakat* and when he returned, he said, "This is *zakat* and this was a gift to me". Let him sit in his house and see as to who will give a gift to him".[9]

Bribery is, therefore, an offence punishable with *ta'zīr*.

9. Gambling

The Qur'ān says,

يَا أَيُّهَا الَّذِينَ آمَنُواْ إِنَّمَا الْخَمْرُ وَالْمَيْسِرُ وَالأَنصَابُ وَالأَزْلاَمُ رِجْسٌ مِّنْ عَمَلِ الشَّيْطَانِ فَاجْتَنِبُوهُ لَعَلَّكُمْ تُفْلِحُونَ إِنَّمَا يُرِيدُ الشَّيْطَانُ أَن يُوقِعَ بَيْنَكُمُ الْعَدَاوَةَ وَالْبَغْضَاء فِي الْخَمْرِ وَالْمَيْسِرِ وَيَصُدَّكُمْ عَن ذِكْرِ اللّهِ وَعَنِ الصَّلاَةِ فَهَلْ أَنتُم مُّنتَهُونَ

> O believers! Wine, gambling, sacrificial stones and divining arrows are an abomination wrought by Satan. Thus avoid it! Perhaps you may prosper. Satan just wants to cause hostility and hatred to occur among you in wine and gambling and to bar you from the remembrance of God and from prayer. Thus, would you not want to stop it. (5:90-91)

The Prophet (pbuh) said, "He who swears and doing so says by Al-lat and Al-Uzza! He should say, "There is no god but God". And he who says to his companion, "Let me gamble with you, he should make a contribution to charity".[10]

Gambling is thus an offence punishable with *ta'zīr*.

10. Spying and backbiting

The Qur'ān says,

يَا أَيُّهَا الَّذِينَ آمَنُوا اجْتَنِبُوا كَثِيرًا مِّنَ الظَّنِّ إِنَّ بَعْضَ الظَّنِّ إِثْمٌ وَلَا تَجَسَّسُوا وَلَا يَغْتَب بَّعْضُكُم بَعْضًا

---

[9] Ibn Taymiyyah, *al-Siyāsah al-Shar'iyyah*, p.19

[10] Al-Bukhārī, *Ṣaḥīḥ*, vol.2, p.82

O you who believe! Shun much suspicion, for lo! Some suspicion is a sin. And spy not neither backbite one another. (49:12)

يَا أَيُّهَا الَّذِينَ آمَنُوا لَا تَتَّخِذُوا عَدُوِّي وَعَدُوَّكُمْ أَوْلِيَاء تُلْقُونَ إِلَيْهِم بِالْمَوَدَّةِ وَقَدْ كَفَرُوا بِمَا جَاءكُم مِّنَ الْحَقِّ يُخْرِجُونَ الرَّسُولَ وَإِيَّاكُمْ أَن تُؤْمِنُوا بِاللَّهِ رَبِّكُمْ إِن كُنتُمْ خَرَجْتُمْ جِهَادًا فِي سَبِيلِي وَابْتِغَاء مَرْضَاتِي تُسِرُّونَ إِلَيْهِم بِالْمَوَدَّةِ وَأَنَا أَعْلَمُ بِمَا أَخْفَيْتُمْ وَمَا أَعْلَنتُمْ وَمَن يَفْعَلْهُ مِنكُمْ فَقَدْ ضَلَّ سَوَاء السَّبِيلِ

O believers choose not my enemy and your enemy as friends. Do you give them friendship when they disbelieve in the truth which has come to you, driving out the messenger and you because you believe in Allah, your Lord? If you have come forth to strive in My way and seeking My good pleasure, (show them not friendship). Do you show friendship to them in secret, when I am best aware of what you hide and what you proclaim? And who soever does it among you, he verily has strayed from the right way. (60:1)

Thus spying and backbiting is an offence punishable with *ta'zīr*.

11. Entering another person's house without permission

The Qur'ān says,

يَا أَيُّهَا الَّذِينَ آمَنُوا لَا تَدْخُلُوا بُيُوتًا غَيْرَ بُيُوتِكُمْ حَتَّى تَسْتَأْنِسُوا وَتُسَلِّمُوا عَلَى أَهْلِهَا ذَلِكُمْ خَيْرٌ لَّكُمْ لَعَلَّكُمْ تَذَكَّرُونَ

O you who believe! Enter not house other than your own without first announcing your presence and invoking peace upon the folk thereof. That is better for you, that you may be heedful. (24:27)

Thus entering the houses of others without permission and violating the privacy of others is an offence liable for *ta'zīr*.

12. Spreading of obscenity

The Qur'ān says,

إِنَّ الَّذِينَ يُحِبُّونَ أَن تَشِيعَ الْفَاحِشَةُ فِي الَّذِينَ آمَنُوا لَهُمْ عَذَابٌ أَلِيمٌ فِي الدُّنْيَا وَالْآخِرَةِ

Lo! Those who love that obscenity should be spread among the believers, for them will be a painful punishment in the world and the hereafter. (24:19)

وَلاَ تَقْرَبُواْ الزِّنَى إِنَّهُ كَانَ فَاحِشَةً وَسَاء سَبِيلاً

And come not near to adultery. Lo! It is an abomination and an evil way". (17:32)

ولاَ تَقْرَبُواْ الْفَوَاحِشَ مَا ظَهَرَ مِنْهَا وَمَا بَطَنَ

And that you draw not high to lewd things whether open or secret. (6:151)

قُلْ إِنَّمَا حَرَّمَ رَبِّيَ الْفَوَاحِشَ مَا ظَهَرَ مِنْهَا وَمَا بَطَنَ وَالإِثْمَ وَالْبَغْيَ بِغَيْرِ الْحَقِّ

So my Lord forbiddeth only indecencies, such of them as are apparent and such as are within and sin and wrongful aggression. (7:33)

Thus demonstration and spread of obscenity is an offence to be punished with *ta'zīr*.

13. Misuse of Orphan's Wealth

The Qur'ān says,

وَلاَ تَقْرَبُواْ مَالَ الْيَتِيمِ إِلاَّ بِالَّتِي هِيَ أَحْسَنُ حَتَّى يَبْلُغَ أَشُدَّهُ

And approach not the wealth of the orphan save with that which is better, till he reaches maturity". (6:152)

وَآتُواْ الْيَتَامَى أَمْوَالَهُمْ وَلاَ تَتَبَدَّلُواْ الْخَبِيثَ بِالطَّيِّبِ وَلاَ تَأْكُلُواْ أَمْوَالَهُمْ إِلَى أَمْوَالِكُمْ

Give to orphans their wealth. Exchange not the good for the bad nor absorb their wealth into your own wealth. (4:2)

إِنَّ الَّذِينَ يَأْكُلُونَ أَمْوَالَ الْيَتَامَى ظُلْمًا إِنَّمَا يَأْكُلُونَ فِي بُطُـــونِهِمْ نَارًا وَسَيَصْلَوْنَ سَعِيرًا

Lo! Those who devour the wealth of orphans wrongfully, they do but swallow fire into their bellies and they will be exposed to burning flame. (4:10)

Misuse of orphan's wealth is, therefore an offence punishable with *ta'zīr*.

14. To gain wealth by illegal means

The Qur'ān says,

يَا أَيُّهَا الَّذِينَ آمَنُواْ لاَ تَأْكُلُواْ أَمْوَالَكُمْ بَيْنَكُمْ بِالْبَاطِلِ إِلاَّ أَن تَكُـــونَ تِجَارَةً عَن تَرَاضٍ مِّنكُمْ

O you who believe! Eat not up the wealth of one another with illegal means except it be a trade by mutual consent. (4:29)

The Prophet (pbuh) said, "Whoever takes possession of any part of land without having a right to it, shall be as a punishment for it sunk down into the earth on the Day of resurrection to the depth of seven earths".[11]

The Holy Prophet said, "Your blood, your property and your prestige are sacred as this day (day of *Arafat*) and this city (Makkah).[12]

Thus gaining the property of another person by illegal means is an offence punishable with *ta'zīr*.

15. Breach of contract

The Qur'ān says,

يَا أَيُّهَا الَّذِينَ آمَنُواْ أَوْفُواْ بِالْعُقُودِ

---

[11] Al-Bukhārī, *Ṣaḥīḥ*, p.175

[12] Muslim, *Ṣaḥīḥ*, vol.2, p.114

O you who believe! Fulfill your undertakings. (5:1)

وَأَوْفُواْ بِالْعَهْدِ إِنَّ الْعَهْدَ كَانَ مَسْؤُولاً

And fulfill the contract. Lo! Of the contract it will be asked. (17:34)

The Prophet said, "The Muslims have to fulfill the conditions mutually agreed upon in a contract except the condition which prohibits what is permissible in *Shariah* or permits what is prohibited in *Shariah*".[13]

Breach of contract is thus an offence punishable with *ta'zīr*.

16. Slander

The Qur'ān says,

وَمَن يَكْسِبْ خَطِيئَةً أَوْ إِثْمًا ثُمَّ يَرْمِ بِهِ بَرِيئًا فَقَدِ احْتَمَلَ بُهْتَانًا وَإِثْمًا مُّبِينًا

And who so commits a delinquency or crime, then throws (the blame) thereof upon the innocent, has burdened himself with falsehood and a flagrant crime. (4:112)

Thus slander is an offence liable for *ta'zīr*.

17. Disobedience of a woman to her husband

The Qur'ān says,

وَاللاَّتِي تَخَافُونَ نُشُوزَهُنَّ فَعِظُوهُنَّ وَاهْجُرُوهُنَّ فِي الْمَضَاجِعِ وَاضْرِبُوهُنَّ

So those (women) from whom you fear disobedience, admonish them and banish them to beds apart and scourge them. (4:34)

Disobedience of a woman to her husband is thus an offence punishable with *ta'zīr*.

---

[13] Ibn Taymiyyah, *Majmū' al-Fatāwā*, Vol.28, p.232

18. *Aḥādīth* about *ta'zīr*

(i) The Prophet (pbuh) said, "No one will be punished with more than ten stripes of the whip except where the offence is one for which God has fixed punishment".[14]

(ii) The Prophet (pbuh) said, "He who punishes a convict with *ḥadd* punishment in a crime not liable to *ḥadd,* is a transgressor."[15]

Similarly a large number of omissions and commissions have been mentioned in the Holy Qur'ān and *ahādīth* of the Holy Prophet and their violations have been declared crimes but their punishments have not been prescribed. The jurists concur that violation of any order of the Holy Qur'ān or Holy Prophet whether in the form of commission or omission is punishable even if punishment has not been prescribed for that specially when such order relates to the rights of individuals, society or state. In the same way violation of any law enacted by a ruler being not repugnant to the injunctions of the Qur'ān and the *Sunnah* is a crime for which punishment may be prescribed by the ruler or his delegated authority. The field of *ta'zīr* is very vast and every *ta'zīr* changes with the change of time, place and other relevant circumstances.

---

[14] Ibn Qudāmah, *al-Mughnī*, vol.10, p.347
[15] Ibid.

Chapter Nine

Ta'zīr in Crimes Liable to *Qiṣāṣ* and *Ḥudūd*

Due to their severity, there are strict conditions for the implementation of *qiṣāṣ* and *ḥudūd* in Islamic criminal law, for example, the commission of the crime must be in a complete form being with the intention and consent of the accused and the prescribed authentic evidence must be available which proves the offence beyond any shadow of doubt. Thus if any of these conditions is not fulfilled, *qiṣāṣ* or *ḥudūd* shall not be imposed but *ta'zīr* shall be imposed in accordance with the circumstances of the case.[1]

Moreover, if there is any doubt in the commission of an offence liable to *ḥadd,* the accused shall not be punished with *ḥadd* and may be punished with *ta'zīr* if required in the circumstances of the case. It is based on the *ḥadīth* of the Prophet who said, "In cases of doubts, set aside *ḥudūd*". The majority of the jurists have adopted this view. Doubt means anything which appears to be like something proven although it is not really proven and as such it creates uncertainty in the proof of an offence. Doubt is sometimes involved on the part of the offender and sometimes it is involved with respect to the subject-matter of an offence or things connected thereto. In case of doubt the

---

[1] 'Āmir, *al-Ta'zīr*, pp.156-58.

accused may be released or may be punished with *ta'zīr* keeping in view the circumstances of the case. For instance if two witnesses testify that the accused has committed theft but later on they retract their evidence and there is no other evidence on the record against the accused, he shall be released. But if an accused confesses the offence voluntarily without any force or threat and later on he retracts his confession, he shall be punished with *ta'zīr*. The difference in these two cases is that no man as a rule would confess an offence which he has not committed while it is easy to accuse a man of an offence that he is not guilty of. It is thus up to the court to award *ta'zīr* in case of doubt if it seems fit in the circumstances of a particular case or it may acqnit the accused.

Although the *ḥadīth* is primarily concerned with the evidential process, court proceedings and proof, it is nevertheless not exclusively related nor confined to that context. Doubt (*shubhah*) in other context is defined as a mere resemblance to certainty of that which is not certain. It relates to situations where the perpetrator of a *ḥadd* offence acts under a mistaken perception, for example, liquor is drunk mistakenly for vinegar or medicine, or *zinā* is committed with a woman who is mistaken for one's wife, or theft is committed from the property that has been earmarked for charity. In all these cases, *ḥadd* punishment shall not be given to the perpetrator. There is, however, a difference of opinion among the jurists as to what exactly amounts to doubt (*shubhah*) and what does not. Whereas the Mālikīs and Ḥanbalīs do not classify doubt (*shubhah*) as such and tend to look at each doubt individually, the Ḥanafīs and Shāfi'īs have divided doubt (*shubhah*) into three kinds, namely, (i) doubt pertaining to acts whereby a person wrongly believes an unlawful act or conduct to be lawful owing to ignorance, such as sexual intercourse with one's estranged wife during her waiting period (*iddah*) following a final divorce on the wrong assumption that it is lawful (ii) doubt pertaining to ownership such as stealing from one's debtor or son (iii) contractual doubt which, according to Imām Abū Ḥanīfah, means to have sexual intercourse with a woman during a contract of marriage with her even though such a contract is not valid such as marriage with a close relative within the prohibited degree or during a marriage with a woman in her waiting period *(iddah)* from another man.

The Hanafis and Zaidi Shia maintain that the inability of the accused to reveal doubt (*shubhah*) is also doubt which removes *ḥadd* punishment such as in the case of a dumb person, who might have spoken about a possible doubt had he or she been able to speak. The other three Imāms have, however, disagreed and maintain that a dumb person may express himself by writing or even with gestures.[2]

If the principle of nullifying *ḥudūd* by doubt is applied in a total sense in the present society then the *ḥudūd* would automatically be reduced to *ta'zīr* which can include a variety of punishments, including corporal punishment, that the legislature and court might consider most suitable for purposes of reformation and deterrence.

It would be appropriate to mention some *ta'zīr* crimes in matters of *qiṣāṣ* and *ḥudūd.*

1. Murder

In Islamic criminal law if a person intends to murder another person and he neither makes any preparation for that nor takes any practical step towards that, he shall not be punished at all. But if a person intends to murder another person and makes some preparation for that, for example, he purchases a gun or any other instrument of murder, he shall not be punished for that. And if a person intends to murder another person and he attempts by going towards that person along with a gun or other instrument of murder but is arrested before attacking him he will be punished with *ta'zīr*. Similarly if a person is accused of murdering another person and there is only one witness to the commission of his offence or there is only circumstantial evidence for his offence which does not reach to the degree of certainty, he shall be punished with *ta'zīr*. Whenever the prescribed authentic evidence for *qiṣāṣ* (retaliation) in a murder case is not available and any lesser authentic evidence is available, the accused shall be

[2] 'Awdah, *al-Tashrī'al-Jinā'ī al-Islāmī*, vol. 1, pp.212-14

punished with *ta'zīr.* In the same way it a person causes death to another person by negligence, he shall be liable to *ta'zīr.*[3]

2. Hurts

If a person causes hurt to another person and the hurt of the victim is not liable for *qiṣāṣ* (retaliation) or *qiṣāṣ* (retaliation) cannot be executed, the offender shall be punished with *ta'zīr.* All hurts not liable to retaliation, *diyat* or *ursh* (prescribed compensation) are liable to *ta'zīr* which may either be compensation or imprisonment or both in accordance with the circumstances of the case.[4]

3. *Zinā*

Zinā in Islamic law means willful sexual intercourse of an adult man and an adult woman who are not validly married, and do not suspect to be married to each other. Thus if a man has sexual intercourse with a woman he suspects to be his wife and later on it appears that she is not his wife, both shall be punished with *ta'zīr.*[5] Similarly if a man commits *zinā* with his divorced wife thinking that it is permissible, both shall be punished with *ta'zīr.*[6] And if a man has sexual intercourse with a dead woman, he shall be punished with *ta'zīr* to be fixed according to the circumstances of the case. In the same way if a man commits sodomy with another man, both shall be punished with *ta'zīr.* Moreover if a man has carnal intercourse against the order of nature with any woman, both shall be punished with *ta'zīr.*[7] If a man has sexual intercourse with an animal, he shall be punished with *ta'zīr.* If a man makes sexual intercourse with a minor girl, he shall be punished with *ta'zīr.*[8] If a man kisses a woman with lust or lies with her on one bed for sexual purpose but does not have intercourse with her, both shall be punished with *ta'zīr* to be fixed according to the circumstances of the case.[9]

---

[3] Ibid., pp.168-70

[4] Ibid.

[5] Al-Kāsanī, *Badā'i' wa al-Ṣanā'i*, vol.7, pp.31-32

[6] Ibid., p.34

[7] Ibid., p.36

[8] Ibn Qudāmah, *al-Mughnī*, vol.10, p.152

[9] Ibid., pp.161-62

As regards the proof of the offence of *zinā,* if a man and a woman are accused of having committed *zinā* and there are less than four eye-witnesses but their evidence is otherwise authentic, the accused shall be punished with *ta'zīr*. Similarly if there is only circumstantial evidence any *zinā,* the accused shall be punished with *ta'zīr*. However, if the evidence is not authentic, the accused shall be released. If there is indirect evidence or delayed evidence in an adultery or fornication case, the accused shall be punished with *ta'zīr*. Similarly if the witnesses testify in a case of adultery that they have only seen the accused man and woman kissing one another for sexual purpose or lying naked on one bed or in suspicious circumstances, the accused shall be liable to *ta'zīr*.[10]

It is pertinent to mention here that Ḥaḍrat 'Umar gave *ta'zīr* punishment in two cases of adultery which are as under:

(i) Once a woman married a man while she was in *'iddat* and had sexual intercourse with him. Ḥaḍrat 'Umar whipped her but did not implement *ḥadd* on her.

(ii) Once a man was found with a woman in the dark in the period of Ḥaḍrat 'Umar in a suspicious state. Ḥaḍrat 'Umar whipped them but did not implement *ḥadd* on them.[11]

If any condition of the *ḥadd* of *zinā* is not fulfilled and other evidence is available on the record, the accused shall be liable to *ta'zīr*. Similarly if the offence is less than intercourse, the accused man and woman shall be liable for *ta'zīr*.

4. *Qazf* (False accusation of *zinā*)

If a person accuses another person of *zinā* and cannot produce four eyewitnesses in support of his allegation, he shall be liable to *ḥadd* of *qazf* i.e. eighty stripes provided his offence is proved either by his own confession or by the testimony of two adult, sane and reliable witnesses. But if the proof is less than that for example the accused does not confess to the offence and there are less than four eyewitnesses or there is only circumstantial evidence, the accused

[10] 'Awdah, *al-Tashrī' al-Jinā'ī al-Islāmī*, vol.2, pp.413-20

[11] Muḥammad Rawwās Qal'jī, *Mawsū'ah Fiqh 'Umar ibn al-Khaṭṭāb*, p.169

shall be liable to *ta'zīr*. Similarly if a person accuses another person of an act other than adultery for example of sodomy etc, the accused shall be liable to *ta'zīr*. If the accused, after confessing his offence, retracts his confession or a witness retracts his testimony before the execution of the punishment, the accused shall not be punished with *ḥadd* but shall be liable to *ta'zīr* if there is any evidence on the record. In the same way if a person accuses any of his descendents and is unable produce four witnesses, he shall not be liable to *ḥadd* but shall be liable to *ta'zīr*. Moreover if a person prints or engraves any matter with the intention to harm the reputation of another person he shall be liable to *ta'zīr*.[12]

All defamations other than that of *zinā* are liable to *ta'zīr* in Islamic criminal law.

5. Theft

Theft means to take away the property owned by another person surreptitiously from the custody of the owner. Its *ḥadd* punishment is amputation of the right hand from the joint of the wrist provided the stolen property is of the value of or more than a specific limit *(niṣāb)* to be fixed in accordance with the value of gold or silver in the market and that two witnesses give testimony that they had seen the accused entering the place from where the property was stolen and coming out from it along with the stolen property. Theft liable to *ḥadd* is also proved by the confession of the accused without coercion.

So if the stolen property is less than the prescribed limit, the accused shall be punished with *ta'zīr*. Moreover *ḥadd* shall not be imposed and *ta'zīr* shall be imposed in the following cases of theft, namely:

(a) When the offender and the victim of the theft are related to each other as:
- (i) Spouses;
- (ii) Ascendants, paternal or maternal;
- (iii) Descendants, paternal or maternal;
- (iv) Brothers or sisters of father or mother, or;
- (v) Brothers or sisters or their children

---

[12] 'Awdah, *al-Tashrī' al-Jinā'ī al-Islāmī*, vol.2, pp.475-77

(b) When a guest has committed theft from the house of his host;
(c) When a servant or employee has committed theft from the custody of his master or employer to which he is allowed access;
(d) When the stolen property is wild grass, fish, bird, dog, pig, intoxicant, perishable foodstuffs for the preservation of which provision does not exist;
(e) When the offender has a share in the stolen property the value of which, after deduction of his share, is less than *niṣāb;*
(f) When the offender has stolen public property;
(g) When a creditor steals his debtor's property the value of which, after deduction of the amount due to him, is less than the *niṣāb;*
(i) When the offender has committed theft under compulsion or dire necessity;
(j) When the offender, before his apprehension, has, on account of repentance, returned the stolen property to the victim and surrenders himself to the authority concerned;
(k) When the offender has stolen the property from a public place.[13]

Similarly if a person makes arrangements for the stealing of some property and he attempts by going towards that property and is arrested before stealing that property either out of the place of the property or inside that place before getting out the property from that place or if the eyewitnesses didn't mention in their testimony that they had seen the thief entering the place from where the property was stolen and coming out along with the stolen property or if there is only one eyewitness or there is only circumstantial evidence, the accused shall be punished with *ta'zīr.*[14] In the same way, *ta'zīr* shall be given to the accused when the theft is proved by his confession but he retracts his confession before the execution of the punishment or when theft is proved by testimony, but before the execution of the punishment, any witness retracts his testimony so as to reduce the number of witnesses to

---

[13] 'Āmir, *al-Ta'zīr*, pp.230-35.
[14] Al-Māwardī, *al-Aḥkām, al-Sulṭāniyyah*, pp.255-66

less than two. Moreover, if the witnesses are not credible or are suspected of being relatives, partners or close friends of the victim, the accused shall be punished with *ta'zīr.*[15]

6. Dacoity and Robbery

The crime of dacoity and robbery is punishable by *ḥadd* if it is proved either by the confession of the accused with his free consent or by the testimony of two adult, sane and reliable witnesses other than the victim. Thus if there is only one witness or there is only circumstantial evidence on any offence of dacoity and robbery or the witness or witnesses are not *adil* or are suspicious of being relatives, partners or close friends of the victim, the accused shall be punished with *ta'zīr.* If the confessor retracts his confession or any of the witnesses retracts his testimony before the execution of the punishment, the accused shall not be punished with *ḥadd* but shall be punished with *ta'zīr* if there is other evidence.[16]

It is pertinent to mention that taking away the property of other person by usurpation, seizure and plunder is liable for *ta'zīr.*

7. Drinking Wine (Intoxicating Liquor)

The crime of the drinking wine (intoxicating liquor) is punishable by *ḥadd* if it is proved either by the confession of the accused with his free consent without coercion or by the testimony of two adult, sane, Muslim and reliable witnesses. Thus if there is no confession of the accused or there is only one witness or there is delayed testimony or there is only medical report or other circumstantial evidence, the accused shall not be punished with *ḥadd* but shall be punished with *ta'zīr.* The consumption of any solid intoxicant is punishable by *ta'zīr.* If a non-Muslim is found guilty of drinking wine (intoxicating liquor) publicly, he shall be punished with *ta'zīr.* Selling, purchasing and serving of wine (intoxicating liquor) is liable to *ta'zīr.* If a person consumes wine (intoxicating liquor) not by mouth, he shall be punished with *ta'zīr.*[17]

---

[15] 'Awdah, *al-Tashrī' al-Jinā'ī al-Islāmī,* vol.2, pp.611-16

[16] Al-Kāsanī, *Baḍā'i' al-Ṣanā'i'* vol.7, pp.90-95

[17] 'Awdah, al-Tashrī' al-Jinā'ī al-Islāmī, vol.2, pp.510-12

Ta'zīr for public interest

Jurists are of the view that *ta'zīr* can be given to a person if it is required for public interest even if the person concerned has not committed any crime.

The jurists base this view on a case in the period of Ḥaḍrat 'Umar. Once 'Umar was on his usual reconnaissance duty in Madinah when he heard the voice of a young girl singing in her melodious voice an erotic poem, "Is there a way to wine so that I may drink it or a way to get access to Naṣr ibn Ḥajjāj?" Next morning 'Umar summoned Nasr ibn Hajjaj and found him extremely handsome and charming whom the ladies were attracted. 'Umar first ordered him to shave his head but this increased his charm. He then banished him to Basrah. Thus Nasr Ibn Hajjaj had not committed any crime but his attraction and physical charm were a source of mischief for the women in Madinah for which he was banished from Madinah. The order of banishment was based on public interest. The preventive detention laws are based on *ta'zīr* for public interest. If the government is informed through a reliable source that a person or a group of persons are going to do an act which is against the public interest, the person or persons concerned will be arrested and imprisoned or detained before the commission of that crime till the danger of their proposed crime is removed. However, *ta'zīr* for public interest should not be given arbitrarily. Before giving such *ta'zīr* the state or the judge must confirm that it really is in the public interest and prevents evil. Such a person has committed an act prejudicial to public interest and maintenance of law and order or he is found in a condition prejudicial to public interest and maintenance of law and order. It is also based on the tenets of Shariah which provide for eliminating general nuisance by causing particular nuisance and for the remedy of greater harm with lesser harm.[18]

Remission or alteration of *ta'zīr*

A legislator or a judge is authorized under Islamic law to remit *ta'zīr* or alter it if it relates to the rights of Allah and is so required

---

[18] Ibid., pp.510-12

in public interest. The jurists have based the permissibility of remission in the matter of *ta'zīr* on a *ḥadīth* wherein the Holy Prophet said, "Ignore the *ta'zīr* punishment of noble persons" and a *ḥadīth* wherein the Holy Prophet said, "Pardon the wrongs done by noble persons," and that the Holy Prophet said about *Anṣār*, "Accept their good deeds and ignore their wrongs". Moreover, it has been related that a person came to the Holy Prophet and confessed to have kissed a woman without having sexual intercourse. The Holy Prophet said to him, "Have you prayed with us"?. He said, "Yes". The Holy Prophet released him and read the verse: "Good deeds annul ill deeds". Once a person said to the Holy Prophet about his decision in a case in favour of Zubair. "This is because but he is the son of your aunt". The Holy Prophet became furious but did not give him *ta'zīr* punishment. In the same way a person said to the Holy Prophet on the occasion of dividing something. "This division is not in accordance with the orders of Allah". The Prophet did not give him any *ta'zīr* punishment. Thus, if a ruler deems it a public interest to pardon an offender in *ta'zīr,* he is empowered to do so. And if he does not deem it a public interest he should impose *ta'zīr* punishment.[19] However, such a pardon may be given in minor offences only.

Similarly a legislator or a judge is allowed to alter *ta'zīr* if he deems necessary in the interest of the public and which relates to the rights of Allah.

However, a legislator or a judge is not allowed to remit or alter any *ta'zīr* which relates to human rights. It can, however, be remitted or altered by the victim or with his consent.

Some important aspects of *ta'zīr*

(i) All crimes other than those which are liable to *ḥudūd* and *qiṣāṣ* such as criminal conspiracy, false evidence, contempt of lawful authority or religion, fraud, breach of contract, defamations, criminal intimidation, attempt to commit offence are liable to *ta'zīr* to be fixed according to the nature and severity of the offence.

---

[19] 'Āmir, *al-Ta'zīr,* p.510

(ii) The right of discretion of a legislator or a judge in *ta'zīr* is not absolute. It must be based on public interest. Moreover, the crime can be pardoned after it is committed and not before that. Similarly the punishment can be pardoned after it is awarded.

(iii) The crimes liable to *ta'zīr* and their punishments are changed from time to time according to the requirements of the circumstances.

Chapter Ten

Punishments for crimes liable to *ta'zīr*

Punishment is usually defined as the infliction of some pain, suffering, loss or social disability as a direct consequence of an action or omission by the person punished. The primary object of punishment is reformation of the culprit for the protection of society. Its kind and quantum vary according to various circumstances with respect to the culprit, society and state. Generally the punishments of imprisonment, whipping, fine, compensation, banishment, confiscation of wealth etc. have been given in *ta'zīr*. However, a ruler or a judge is fully authorized to prescribe any suitable punishment in whatever form it may be to serve the purpose. Similarly a legislator or a judge is authorized to give more than one kind of punishment to a culprit in the same offence if he deems it fit in the public interest. The jurists have discussed the following punishments which have been given in crimes liable to *ta'zīr* throughout Islamic history.[1]

1. Whipping stripes

The punishment of whipping has been recognized in Islamic law. It has been prescribed as *ḥadd* punishment for adultery, false accusation of adultery and drinking wine. It has also been given in many crimes liable to *ta'zīr* in the period of the Prophet (pbuh). The Prophet (pbuh) said, "Punishment of more than ten stripes of the whip will not be given except where the offence is one for

---

[1] 'Āmir, *al-Ta'zīr*, pp.302-305.

which Allah has fixed punishment".[2] The Prophet said, "He who punishes a criminal with *ḥadd* in a crime which is not liable to *ḥadd*, is a transgressor".[3] The Prophet said, "If theft is committed from the fruit trees, the offender will be whipped some stripes and will also be liable to pay the double price of the stolen property".[4]

Ḥaḍrat 'Umar in many cases of crimes liable to *ta'zīr* gave punishment of whipping. Some of these cases are as under:

(i) He gave the punishment of 100 stripes to Maan bin Zaidah who had faked the official seal of *Bayt al-Māl* (treasury) and had received money from the treasury through that seal.

(ii) He gave the punishment of 100 stripes to a man who drank wine in the month of Ramadan, 80 stripes as punishment for drinking wine and 20 stripes as punishment for the insult of the month of Ramadan.

(iii) He gave the punishment of 40 stripes to a man who gave false testimony in a case.

(iv) He gave the punishment of 30 stripes to a man who ill-treated Umm Al-Salamah in connection with a loan to her nephew who had died.[5]

The punishment of whipping has been given in crimes liable to *ta'zīr* in the period of the Prophet (pbuh), the period of right-guided caliphs and later periods.[6]

The jurists agree that if any of the conditions is lacking in the commission or proof of a crime liable to whipping as *ḥadd* like adultery and drinking wine, the accused may be punished with whipping wherein the number of the stripes should be less than that in the case of *ḥadd* and may also be punished with imprisonment or fine if considered fit in the circumstances of the case. Further according to Imām Abū Hanīfah and Imām Shāfi'ī the punishment of. whipping in *ta'zīr* should not be more than 39

---

[2] Ibn Qudāmah, *al-Mughnī*, vol.10, p.347

[3] Ibid., p.354

[4] Ibn Taymiyyah, *al-Siyāsāh al-Shar'īyyah*, p.47

[5] Qal'ajī, *Mawsu'ah 'Umar,* pp.170-71

[6] Ibn Qudāmah, *al-Mughnī,* vol.10, p.348

stripes. This is also the view of Imām Aḥmad Ibn Ḥanbal. But according to Imām Mālik the quantum of whipping in *ta'zīr* is at the discretion of the ruler or judge and if it is required, it can be increased to more than that for *ḥadd.* Islamic law has stressed on the punishment of whipping for general crimes liable to *ta'zīr* except when it is not required in a special case on a special ground.[7]

According to some jurists both *ḥadd* and *ta'zīr* punishments can be given to a criminal for the same offence while others opine that *ta'zīr* cannot be given with *ḥadd* in a case liable to *ḥadd.* However, if the criminal act of an offender amounts to different offences, he may be punished both with *ḥadd* and *ta'zīr* if it is so required.

Mode of the execution of the punishment of whipping

It is necessary to explain that the mode of the punishment of whipping in Islamic law is quite different from that in English law which is in practice in many Muslim and non-Muslim countries of the present world. The emphasis of English law in whipping is on the physical torture of the culprit and as such its mode of execution in this law is very harsh and sometimes fatal and inhumane. But in Islamic law the punishment of whipping is for the humiliation of the convict with some pain and is not for causing him physical injuries. Under the English law the lashes are required to be whipped on the bare buttocks of the convict from some distance with full force.

As far as the mode of the punishment of whipping is concerned, it is based on the following traditions:

(a) It has been related that once a person came to the Holy Prophet and said, "Oh Prophet! I have committed a crime (*ḥadd*) and thus implement its punishment on me". The Holy Prophet called for a fresh whip. So he was offered a fresh whip on which there was some fruit. The Holy Prophet said, "A whip less than this". Then he was offered a whip which was cut from one side. The Holy Prophet said, "A whip better than this". Then he was offered a moderate whip and thus he

---

[7] 'Āmir, *al-Ta'zīr*. pp.234-36

ordered the man to be whipped with it and that person was whipped."[8]

(b) It has been related that once a she-slave (of Ḥaḍrat Fāṭimah) committed *zinā* and the Holy Prophet ordered Ḥaḍrat 'Alī to whip her. When he went to whip her, he found her in a position that her blood of childbirth was still flowing and returned without whipping her. The Holy Prophet said, "Oh Ali! Did you whip her". Ḥaḍrat 'Alī said, "No, When I went there I found that her blood of childbirth was still flowing". The Holy Prophet said, "Wait till her bleeding is totally stopped and then implement *ḥadd* on her".[9]

(c) It has been related that Ḥaḍrat 'Umar said to an executioner, "Don't raise your hand above your head so that the whiteness of your armpit may not appear".[10]

(d) It has been related that Ḥaḍrat 'Alī ordered an executioner to whip a person, "Whip him and give every part of the body its share and don't whip the face and shames".[11]

(e) Ḥaḍrat 'Umar ordered a woman to be whipped and said to the executioner of the punishment, "Whip her but do not lacerate her skin".[12]

(f) It has been related that once a very thin and weak person who was ill committed adultery with a female slave and asked the Holy Prophet to implement *ḥadd* on him. The Holy Prophet ordered whipping with a branch of a tree in which hundred very small branches exist and ordered a single stroke.[13]

Allamah Shawkānī has related that the jurists have described that the width of the whip be equal one finger and its length be one yard.[14]

---

[8] 'Abd al-Razzāq, *al-Muṣannaf,* vol.7, p.329
[9] Abū Dawūd, *Sunan* vol.2, p.282
[10] Ibn Ḥajar, *al-Talkhīs al-Habīr*, vol.2, p.78
[11] Abdul Razzaq, *al-Muṣannaf*, vol.7, p.37
[12] Ibid., p.38
[13] Abū Dawūd, *Sunan* vol.2, p.280
[14] Al-Shawkānī, *Nayl al Awṭār*, vol.7, p.130

Based on the above traditions the jurists have derived that the main aim of the punishment of whipping is humiliation of the convict with reasonable pain to his body as well. Imām Al-Nawawi while describing the mode of the punishment of whipping in the offences of *zinā, qazf* and drinking wine, writes, "the lash should be moderate neither a very fresh branch nor entirely dry, the application of whipping should be normal not to cause severe pain, the lashes should be applied one after another, the executioner should not raise his hand over his head to the extent that the whiteness of his armpit does not appear otherwise it will be very painful to him, the lash should not remain on his body but be raised and applied with normal force, the lash should not be applied on the face, shames, head and delicate parts of the body of the convict, the convict should not be tied, the convict should not be naked but be in his normal dress provided his dress does not save him from the pain, the male should be whipped when he is standing and the female when she is sitting and is covered with her dress, the executioner should be a mature man, the application of whipping should be continuous and not after intervals"[15] According to the Shāfi'ī school the punishment of whipping in case of a *ta'zīr* offence should be less in quantity than that of a *ḥadd* offence. 'Allamah Sheikh Muḥammad Al-Sharbini Al-Khatīb while discussing the punishment of whipping in *ta'zīr* offence, writes, "If the punishment of whipping is in a *ta'zīr* offence it must be less than forty lashes and it is equally applicable to all offences of *ta'zīr*."[16]

The Ḥanafeites differentiate between the quality of whipping in *ta'zīr* offence and that of *ḥadd* offence and opine that the severity in *ta'zīr* should be more than in *ḥadd,* and after that the punishment of whipping in *zinā* must be more severe than for drinking wine and the punishment of whipping for drinking wine must be more severe than in *qazf.*[17] They base their view on the practice of Ḥaḍrat 'Umar in case of the person who misbehaved with Ḥaḍrat Ummi-Salmah as related above in which Ḥaḍrat 'Umar said, "Whip him 30 strokes in such a way as not to effect

---

[15] Al-Nawawī, *Rawḍat al-Ṭālibīn*, vol.X, p.172

[16] Ibn Qudāmah, *al-Mughnī,* vol.6, p.193

[17] Al-Jaṣṣāṣ, *Aḥkām al Qur'ān*, vol.3, pp.256-57

his skin his blood flow". Abū Bakr Jaṣṣāṣ has, however, asserted that it is at the discretion of a judge in case of *ta'zīr* to order for the severity of the punishment of whipping keeping in view the circumstances of the case.[18] According to one view of Imām Shāfi'ī, the force of a lash shall be equal both in *ḥadd* and *ta'zīr* and this view has been accepted by the later jurists throughout.[19]

The jurists, however, concur that a pregnant woman shall not be given the punishment of whipping until she gives birth to the child and recovers from the bleeding etc. of the childbirth. Similarly this punishment shall not be executed on a person who is ill and can't bear the severity of this punishment until he recovers from the illness. In the same way this punishment shall not be implemented in extreme cold or heat.[20]

It is thus obvious that the punishment of whipping in Islamic law is not severe and inhumane. It is more to awaken in the convict a realization of his wrong so that he may repent his misdeeds and become purified and become a responsible person in the society. A study of Islamic history shows that the life of a convict has never been threatened and the humane treatment meted out to him has turned the convict into a responsible citizen.

2. Imprisonment

The next punishment which has been given in crimes liable to *ta'zīr* throughout Islamic history is imprisonment. *Habs* (imprisonment) means to deprive a person of his liberty by restraining him from free movement and confining him in a house, mosque or any other place or by appointing another person to keep him in his custody and restrain him from free movement.[21] The punishment of imprisonment is very old and it was usually given to convicted criminals, suspicious persons and the accused persons remanded in custody and awaiting trial. According to verse 12:42 of the Holy Qur'ān Prophet Joseph remained in prison for some years which indicates that such institutions existed in Egypt before Prophet Jesus Christ and there were proper prisons for criminals,

---

[18] Ibid.

[19] Al-Qurṭūbī, *Jāmi' li Aḥkām al-Qur'ān*, vol.11, p.163

[20] 'Awdah, *al-Tashri' al-Jinā'ī al-Islāmī*, vol.2, pp.448-50

[21] Ibn Qayyim, *al-Ṭuruq al-Ḥukmiyyah,* pp.102-3

suspected persons and accused persons awaiting trial. Such punishment also existed in Pre-Islamic Arabia. Islam didn't prohibit this punishment and retained it. The Holy Qur'ān says about the adulteress women, "Confine them to the houses". (4:15) According to Imām Abū Ḥanīfah and Imām Mālik the punishment of banishment mentioned in verse (5:33) for dacoits and robbers means imprisonment.[22] Ḥaḍrat 'Umar used to give the punishment of imprisonment and not banishment in such cases.[23]

The punishment of imprisonment was in practice in the period of the Prophet (pbuh). Reference may be made to the following *aḥādīth:*

(a) It has been related on the authority of Bahz Ibn Ḥakīm who relates from his father and grandfather that the Prophet (pbuh) detained a man on account of some allegations against him.[24]

It has been related on the authority of Abū Hurairah that the Prophet (pbuh) imprisoned a man on account of some accusations against him.[25]

(b) According to another *ḥadīth* on the same authority, the Prophet (pbuh) detained a man suspected of murder for some hours of the day and then set him free.[26]

(c) According to another *ḥadīth* the Prophet (pbuh) imprisoned a person who was accused of committing theft from his co-traveller.[27]

(d) It has been related on the authority of Hirman Ibn Ḥabīb who relates from his father that he brought his debtor to the Prophet. The Prophet said, "Confine him". Afterward the Prophet said to him, "What about your prisoner". This is called *habs al-dayn* (imprisonment for default of payment of debt).[28]

---

[22] Al-Qurṭubī, *Jāmi'* vol.6, pp.152-53
[23] Ibid., p.153
[24] Abū Dawūd, *Sunan*, vol.2, p.122
[25] Ḥākim, *al-Mustadrak*, vol.4, p.104
[26] Al-Bayhaqī, *al-Sunan al-Kubrā*, vol.6, p.53
[27] Al-Tarābulusī, *Mu'īn al-Ḥukkām*, p.210
[28] Abū Dawūd, *Sunan*, vol.2, p.138

(e) It has been related on the authority of 'Abd Allāh Ibn 'Umar that the Prophet said about one who seizes a person and another who murders him, "Kill the murderer of that person and imprison the one who seizes him".[29]

(f) It has been related that there was a separate place where women were imprisoned in the period of the Prophet.[30]

In the period of the Prophet (pbuh) and Abū Bakr there was no proper building for prisoners. But when the territory and population of the Islamic state considerably expanded and the number of the offenders increased tremendously in the period of Ḥaḍrat 'Umar, he purchased a house from Safwan Ibn Umayyah for four thousand *dirhams* and made it a proper prison. The three right-guided caliphs and the later Muslim rulers had made proper prisons for the convicts, suspicious persons and accused persons awaiting trial and they used to give the punishment of imprisonment in certain crimes liable to *ta'zīr*.

The majority of the jurists opine that a legislator and a judge are authorized to give the punishment of imprisonment in certain crimes liable to *ta'zīr* and a Muslim ruler should make proper prisons for the convicted criminals, suspicious persons and accused persons awaiting trial. The punishment of imprisonment can be given exclusively and can also be given along with other punishment like fine or whipping if it is required in the circumstances of a case.[31] According to one opinion of Imām Shafi'ī the quantum of the punishment of imprisonment should not be extended to more than one year but according to other opinions among the Shāfi'ī school of thought there is no limit for the quantum of the punishment of imprisonment and it is at the discretion of the legislator or judge to prescribe any quantum which serves the purpose of reformation of the convict. According to Imām Abū Ḥanīfah, Imām Mālik and Imām Aḥmad the quantum of the punishment of imprisonment has been left to the discretion of the legislator or judge. The punishment of

---

[29] Ibn al-Tall'a, Muḥammad Ibn Fajr al-Mālikī al-Qurtubi, *Aqdiyat al-Rasūl,* pp.5-6

[30] Al-Kattānī, 'Abd. Al-Ḥayy, *Niẓām al-Hukūmah al-Nabawiyyah*, p.288

[31] Ibn Qudāmah, *al-Mughnī*, vol.10, p.348

imprisonment is given usually for a limited period, but in some heinous crimes it can be unlimited. Such offenders will ever remain in prisons and they will be released only when they repent and mend their conduct.[32]

It is important to mention here that contrary to the modern laws, the punishment of imprisonment in Islamic law is not a common punishment for crimes. In Islamic law this punishment is a secondary punishment and should only be given when it is needed and to the extent required in the circumstances of the case. The jurists have opposed long term imprisonment as well as giving the punishment of imprisonment in general crimes and transgressions.[33]

It is pertinent to mention here that nowadays the problem of jails and their inmates is very serious. The result of treating imprisonment as the basic punishment for all offences is unlimited increase of prisoners who have filled the jails beyond capacity. Besides, prisons have turned into centers of conspiracies and training for committing offences, not withstanding the main object of their establishment, which is to protect the society against offenders. When the prisoners are put together in a jail, they are provided with the opportunity of getting introduced to each other. Thus they are able to chalk out programs of criminal activities and benefit from one another's knowledge and experience. In other words, it has been practically proven that prisons have failed to teach a lesson to the offenders. In fact, simple offenders guilty of misdemeanors turn into habitual offenders capable of committing felonies.

Some people have made attempts to do away with the harmful effects of imprisonment. Methods have been devised to minimize such effects. But these methods have not served their purpose. They have rather brought in their own disadvantages. For instance, the inmates may live in isolation at night and live together in the daytime but should be totally disallowed to talk to one another. But this method involves a lot of additional expenditure. Besides, in order to prevent them from associating and talking with one another, they have been awarded painful

---

[32] 'Awdah, *al-Tashrī' al-Jinā'ī al-Islāmī,* vol.1, pp.694-95

[33] Ibid.

punishment. Another method is to keep every prisoner in strict isolation. This, too, involves heavy expenditure. Besides, solitary confinement often results in insanity. Some prisoners even go to the extent of committing suicide in isolation. There is another method involving gradual process. This has been devised in Ireland.

Under this arrangement the prisoner is initially kept in solitary confinement. After this initial phase extending to a certain length of time, he is allowed to mix up with other inmates but is disallowed to communicate with any of them. This has both the disadvantages that characterize the other two methods.

If prisoners are provided proper primary and higher education in jails, then people outside jails will prefer to commit offences and go to jails to avail the opportunity of higher education without any tough competition and expenses. This would encourage the offenders to commit offences which ultimately amounts to disturbance in society and non-protection of the blood and properties of the public. However, if all these defects are removed as far as possible, then the punishment of imprisonment is a useful punishment even in the modern world.

3. Banishment

One of the punishments to be given as *ta'zīr* in Islamic law is the banishment of the culprit from his city or village to another part of the country or abroad. According to Imām Shāfi'ī the banishment of the convict for one year is *ḥadd* in the crime of *zinā* committed by an unmarried person, but other Imāms do not consider it *ḥadd* in *zinā* committed by an unmarried person, but consider it *ta'zīr* and leave it to the discretion of the legislator or judge. Moreover according to Imām Mālik, Imām Shāfi'ī and Imām Aḥmad one of the *ḥadd* punishments mentioned in verse 5:33 of the Holy Qur'ān for dacoits and robbers is banishment.[34]

Ḥaḍrat 'Umar banished Naṣr Ibn Ḥajjāj from Madinah to Basrah because due to his physical beauty and charm, he was a source of mischief for the women of Madinah.[35]

---

[34] Al-Zayla'ī, *Tabyīn al-Ḥaqā'iq*, vol.3, p.174

[35] Al-Sarakhsī, *al-Mabsūt*, vol.9, p.45

According to the majority of the jurists the punishment of banishment can be given in a crime liable to *ta'zīr* to such a culprit in whose case punishment is more effective for his reformation and it should not be given in general crimes. The period of banishment has been left to the discretion of the legislator or judge.

Due to the change in the social, geographical and political structure of the world, the banishment of culprits from one country to another is very difficult because of immigration laws and security purposes. Moreover different parts and areas of a state do not accept the culprits of other areas. This is why some jurists are of the view that punishment of banishment should not be given nowadays and instead the punishment of imprisonment should be given in such cases. When Ḥaḍrat 'Umar, expelled Rabiah Ibn Umayyah and he (Rabiah) joined the Byzantines he said, "I shall never banish anyone again".[36]

4. Fine

Another punishment which has been given in crimes liable to *ta'zīr* is fine or a financial burden. The Prophet (pbuh) said, "If theft is committed from the property which is not in the custody of the owner, the offender shall be liable to pay double the price of the stolen property". In one case the Prophet (pbuh) ordered the destroying of pots used for making wine.[37]

Ḥaḍrat 'Umar and Ḥaḍrat 'Alī ordered to burn the buildings in which wine was sold and served secretly. They also fined those who refused to pay *zakat* in full. They also gave financial punishment in many other cases.[38]

The majority of the jurists like Imām Mālik, Imām Shāfi'ī in his old view, Imām Aḥmad and Imām Abū Yūsuf are of the opinion that a culprit in some crimes liable to *ta'zīr* can be punished with the confiscation or destruction of all or some of his wealth or with fine or with compensation or with any other financial burden. Financial punishment was given in the early and middle periods of Islam in many crimes liable to *ta'zīr* which

---

[36] Razi, Fakhruddin, *Mafatih,* vol.VI, p.217
[37] 'Āmir, *al-Ta'zīr* p.399
[38] Ibn Taymiyyah, *al-Hisbah*, pp.42-43

proved fruitful in the reformation of the culprits specially the culprits who belonged to the poor or middle classes. The quantum of financial punishment has been left to the discretion of the legislator or judge to fix it according to the prevailing circumstances with respect to the culprit, society and state. Moreover financial punishment can be given exclusively and can also be given along with some other punishment like imprisonment, whipping etc. at the discretion of the legislator or judge keeping in view the circumstances with respect to the crime, culprit, society and state.[39] However, financial punishment should not be given to rich persons unless such a punishment affects their position. They should, instead, be given other punishments which can be effective in reforming them and restraining them from the re-commission of the crimes.

5. Death punishment

Jurists differ as to whether death punishment can be given as *ta'zīr* or not. According to some Shafeis and Hanbalis death punishment cannot be given as *ta'zīr* because *ta'zīr* cannot be more than *ḥadd* and further its primary object is the reformation of the culprit which cannot be achieved if death punishment is given to the culprit. But according to Imām Abū Ḥanīfah and Imām Mālik the kind and quantum of *ta'zīr* have not been fixed and have been left to the discretion of the legislator or judge to fix them in accordance with the circumstances with respect to crime, culprit and society and as such if a legislator or a judge thinks fit, he can prescribe or give death punishment to the culprit as *ta'zīr* due to the gravity of the crime with respect to society or in the case of a professional offender who cannot be restrained from the commission of grave crimes by other punishments. But according to some Shāfi'īs and Ḥanbalīs death punishment can be given in *ta'zīr* to a culprit who commits a grave offence like a spy who leaks out the secrets of the state to its enemy.[40] Similarly the jurists opine that death punishment can be given to an offender who commits a crime which is dangerous for the lives of other human beings. However, death punishment has been discouraged by the

---

[39] 'Āmir, *al-Ta'zīr*, pp.54-55

[40] Ibn Taymiyyah, *al-Siyāsah al-Sha'riyyah*, pp.54-55

jurists in general crimes and has only been allowed when it is entirely needed in the circumstances of a specific case because the blood of a human being is sacred in Islam, Qur'ān says, "Whoever killed a human being for other than manslaughter or corruption in the earth, it shall be as if he killed all mankind". (5:32)

6. Other punishments

Jurists concur that there is no limit to the kinds of punishments to be given to the culprits who commit crimes liable to *ta'zīr* and any kind or form of punishment can be given which, in the opinion of a legislator or judge, is suitable for the reformation of the culprit. Ḥaḍrat 'Umar and Qaḍī Shurayḥ had given the punishment of publicizing the crime of the culprit in the society by informing the public that he had committed such and such crime and to be careful of him. They had also punished some culprits by taking them around on animals after blackening their faces and bringing them to public places so that they may be humiliated and may repent and not repeat the offence.[41]

The Prophet (pbuh) and the right-guided caliphs had also given *ta'zīr* to an offender who was a servant with dismissal from service in certain crimes like bribery, embezzlement, misuse of the official powers etc. Similarly an employee can be given *ta'zīr* by stopping one or more annual increments or salary for a reasonable period. Similarly an offender who is a servant can be given *ta'zīr* by transferring him to an unsuitable station.[42]

In addition to the above, the punishment of social boycott of the culprit had been given to the offenders as *ta'zīr*.

The Prophet (pbuh) had ordered the boycott of Ka'ab bin Malik, Murarah bin Rabiah and Hilal bin Umayyah who had not gone with the army of the Muslims in the battle of Tabuk and remained in their houses. The Qur'ān says about them,

وَعَلَى الثَّلاَثَةِ الَّذِينَ خُلِّفُواْ حَتَّى إِذَا ضَاقَتْ عَلَيْهِمُ الأَرْضُ بِمَا رَحُبَتْ وَضَاقَتْ عَلَيْهِمْ أَنفُسُهُمْ وَظَنُّواْ أَن لاَّ مَلْجَأَ مِنَ اللّهِ إِلاَّ إِلَيْهِ ثُمَّ تَابَ عَلَيْهِمْ لِيَتُوبُواْ إِنَّ اللّهَ هُوَ التَّوَّابُ الرَّحِيمُ

[41] Al-Sarakhsi, *al-Mabsūt*, vol.16, p.145

[42] Ibn Taymiyyah, *op.cit,* pp.51-54

> And to three who were left behind, when the earth, vast as it is, was straitened for them, and their own souls were straitened for them and they perceived that there is no refuge from Allah save toward him. Then he turned to them in mercy that they (too) might turn (repent to him). (9:118)

The social boycott of these three companions of the Prophet (pbuh) proved very fruitful in their reformation. Thus social boycott may be prescribed in a crime liable to *ta'zīr* where the purpose of reformation cannot be achieved by any other punishment.[43]

Similarly an offender can be given probation for some time by keeping him under the supervision of a probation officer so as to check the reformation of his conduct. Threat or warning by a responsible officer or judge can also serve the purpose of the reformation of an offender in some minor crimes. In the same way the license of an offender who is a license holder can be cancelled on the commission of an offence liable to *ta'zīr.*

Multiplicity of punishments

It is pertinent to mention that punishments multiply side by side with multiplication of crimes. Crimes multiply when the same offender commits several crimes and is not prosecuted for any of them. Multiplicity of crimes may be both formal and substantial. If an offender does the same act more than once, it is formal multiplicity and if the offender's acts are such that each of them may turn into a substantive crime then the commission of several criminal acts is substantial multiplicity. In case of multiplicity of crimes the offender involved should not be awarded punishments for all the offences he is guilty of although he exhibits a natural tendency towards crime. In the event of multiplication, the punishments of various crimes would overlap and only a single punishment would apply to all the offences on the whole. Usually a small punishment merges in with the bigger punishment, for example, if a person causes death to one person and causes hurt to two other persons, he shall be given the punishment of death only.

---

43 . Ibn Taymiyyah, op.cit, pp.51-54

But if the offences are numerous and of a different nature, all the punishments would interpenetrate and only a single punishment would be enough provided that the purpose of the punishments prescribed for the offences involved is one and the same. For instance, a person insults a government servant, combats and oppresses him, he shall be liable to a single punishment for all the three offences, for the purpose of the punishments is the same i.e. the protection of the government servant and government service. But if the offender commits various offences for which different punishments have been prescribed he may be punished with all such punishments as it is in the interest of the reformation of the offender and the larger interest of the public. The legislators and the judges have been given discretionary powers in such matters keeping in view the circumstances with respect to the offenders, state and society. They can give a single punishment for various offences, all the punishments for all the offences, substitute any punishment or punishments, various punishments for only one offence or remit the punishment or punishments for the offence committed.[44]

However, *ḥadd* punishment shall not be reduced, enhanced, altered, remitted or merged.

Remission of the punishment

The punishments of *ḥudūd* cannot be remitted, enhanced, reduced or substituted by anyone even by the head of the state. Whenever any *ḥadd* punishment is proved, it must be implemented accordingly and remission is ineffective in such a case whether remission is granted by the aggrieved party or the competent authority.

However, if the matter of *ḥudūd* is not reported to the court, the ruler or the victim may grant pardon. It has been related on the authority of 'Abdullah Ibn 'Umar that Holy Prophet said, "Forgive *ḥudūd* among yourselves but when a matter of *ḥadd* comes before me, it becomes compulsory".[45] It has further been related on the authority of Safwan bin Umayyah who said, "I was sleeping in the mosque and a woolen sheet costing about 30 dirhams was under

[44] 'Awdah, *al-Tashrī' al-Jinā'ī al-Islāmī*, vol.1, pp.734-38
[45] Abū Dawūd, *Sunan*, vol.4, p.362

my head. A person came and took it away from me while I was sleeping. When I got up I ran after the thief. After catching the thief I brought him before the Prophet. He confessed his guilt before the Prophet who ordered the amputation of his hand. On this Safwan said, "I did not intend this (amputation of his hand), I give him this sheet as a gift". The Prophet said, "This should have been done before bringing him to me".[46]

The aggrieved party is authorized to remit the punishment of *qiṣāṣ* and *diyat*. The head of the state or any other person has no power to remit the punishment of *qiṣāṣ* and *diyat*. The aggrieved party in case of *qiṣāṣ* or *diyat* is also authorized to compromise with the offender on anything agreed upon mutually.[47]

The jurists, however, concur that as far as *ta'zīr* offences and punishments are concerned, the head of the state or his delegated authority has the full power of remission. He may forgive the offence as well as the punishment thereof, and he may remit the entire punishment or any part thereof if it is required in the public interest. But the pardon by the head of the state will not, on any account, have a bearing on the rights of the victim. The aggrieved party in any case of *ta'zīr* is fully authorized to pardon the offence as well as the punishment thereof, and he may remit the entire punishment or any part thereof, or may come to a compromise with the offender. The jurists opine that the head of the state or any other person has no power to pardon any *ta'zīr* offence or punishment thereof if it relates to the rights of individuals except with the consent of the victim or his legal heirs.[48]

Lapse of time

Lapse of time means that a certain length of time lapses before the enforcement of punishment resulting in the suspension of the punishment. The jurists differ on the question of lapse of time as a cause of invalidation of punishment. According to Imām Mālik, Imām Shāfi'ī and Imām Aḥmad whatever length of time may elapse, without enforcement of punishment, punishment cannot be nullified and the offence does not cease to be an offence in cases

---

[46] Ibid., p.389

[47] Ibn al-Humām, *Fatḥ al-Qadīr*, vol.4, pp.212-13

[48] Al-Mawārdī, *al-Aḥkām al-Sulṭāniyyah*, p.207

of *ḥudūd* and *qiṣāṣ*. But in case of the punishments for offences liable to *ta'zīr,* the competent authority is authorized to invalidate such a punishment because the lapse of time if it deems it necessary in the public interest. But according to Imām Abū Ḥanīfah, in both cases of *ḥudūd* as well as *ta'zīr,* the punishment is nullified by the lapse of time except the offences involving *diyat* and *qazf.* Nevertheless, the Ḥanafeites who believe in the invalidation of punishment as a result of the lapse of time differentiate between the establishment of an offence liable to *ḥadd* by testimony and confession. If the offence is proved by the testimony of eyewitnesses, the prescribed punishment will be invalidated by the lapse of time, but if it is proved by the confession of the accused, the punishment will not be invalidated. However, they do not believe in such a difference in cases of *ta'zīr* and consider the punishment invalidated by the lapse of time.

Imām Abū Ḥanīfah does not fix such a time and leaves it to the discretion of the court or legislator because it varies according to various circumstances, times and places.[49]

Re-commission of a crime

Recommission of a crime means that an offender, after being punished for a crime, commits another crime. In other words, recommission of an offence is repetition of an offence by the same offender. Recommission of a crime by the same offender denotes that the offender persists in the recommission of the offence and the punishment for the previous offence has proved fruitless. It is thus necessary that harsher punishment should be awarded to a habitual offender. According to Islamic law an offender ought to be awarded punishment for the crime committed by him. If he commits it again, he should be given harsher punishment, if he develops the habit of committing crimes, he will either be given the punishment of death or indefinite imprisonment. Thus the community will be protected from the evil caused by him. The legislator or the court will choose either of the two punishments in view of the particulars of the offence and its potential impact on the society. The Islamic law conceives of repetition of crime in absolute terms and does not differentiate in this matter between

---

[49] Ibn Qudāmah, *al-Mughnī*, vol.9, p.362

general and special recommission of crime just as it does not distinguish between offences repeated consecutively and those repeated after the lapse of definite lengths of time. The rulers and legislators are empowered to frame rules for the control of the recommission of crimes as they deem fit in the public interest.[50]

[50] 'Awdah, *al-Tashrī' al-Jinā'ī al-Islāmī,* vol.1, pp.766-67

Bibliography

Abdul-Rahīm, *Principles of Islamic Jurisprudence.* Kitāb Bhawan, New Delhi, India, 1911 A.D.

'Abd al-Razzāq, *al-Muṣannaf*, Dār al-Fikr al-'Arabī, Cairo, 1978 A.D.

Abū Dāwūd al-Sijistani, Sulaymān ibn al-Asha'th, *al-Sunan*. Dār Ihyā al-Sunnah al-Nabawiyah, Cairo, 1975 A.D.

Abū Zahrah, Muḥammad. *Al-Jarimaḥ wa al-Uqubah*. Dār al-Kutub al-'Arabī, Cairo, 1975 A.D.

Afzal-ul-Raḥmān, *Encyclopedia of Seerah*. The Muslim Schools Trust, London, 1981 A.D.

Aḥmad ibn Ḥanbal. *al-Musnad*. Dār al-Kutub al-Islāmī, Beirut, 1978 A.D.

Al-'Aynī, Badr al-Dīn, *Umdat al-Qārī Sharḥ Ṣaḥīḥ al-Bukhārī*. Dār al-Kutub al-Islāmī, Beirut, 1976 A.D.

Al-Alusī, Sayyid Muḥammad, *Rūḥ al-Ma'ānī*. Dār al-Kutub al-Islāmī, Beirut, 1978 A.D.

'Āmir, 'Abd al-Azīz. *al-Ta'zīr fī al-Sharī'ah al-Islāmiyyah*. Dār al-Fikr al-'Arabī, Beirut, 1969 A.D.

Al Anṣārī, Jamāl al-Dīn Muḥammad ibn Mukarram ibn al-Manẓūr. *Lisān 'al-'Arab*. Dār al-Fikr al-'Arabī, Cairo, 1933 A.D.

Ibn Ḥajar al-Asqalānī, *al-Talkhīṣ al-Ḥabīr*. Dār al-Kutub al-Islāmī, Beirut, 1978 A.D.

'Awdah, 'Abd al-Qādir, *al-Tashrī' al-Jinā'ī al-Islāmī*. Dār al-Kutub al-'Arabī, Beirut, 1978 A.D.

Bahnasī, Aḥmad Fatḥī. *al-Jara'im fī al-Fiqh al-Islāmī and al-'Uqūbah fī al-Fiqh al-Islāmī*. Dār al-Shuruq, Cairo, 1983 A.D.

Al-Bayhaqī, Aḥmad ibn Husain. *al-Sunan al-Kubra*. Dār al-Fikr, Beirut, 1973 A.D.

Bassiouni, M. Cherif. *Islamic Criminal Justice System*. Oceana Publication Inc. New York, 1980 A.D.

Al-Bukhārī, Muḥammad ibn Ismā'īl. *Ṣaḥīḥ al-Bukhārī*. Kārkhānah Tijārah Kutub, Karachi, 1938 A.D.

Council of Islamic Ideology. *Draft Law of Qiṣāṣ and Diyat*. Islamabad, Pakistan, 1981 A.D.

Daryabadi, Abd al-Mājid. *English Translation and Commentary of the Holy Qur'ān*. Lahore, 1945 A.D.

Execution of the Punishment of Whipping Ordinance, 1979. Islamabad, Pakistan.

Al-Ḥattāb, Muḥammad ibn 'Abd al-Raḥmān, *Mawāhib al-Jalīl li Sharḥ Mukhtaṣar Khalīl*. Matba'ah Sa'adah, 1909 A.D.

Ibn 'Ābidīn, Muḥammad Amīn ibn 'Umar. *al-Durr al-Mukhtār al-Radd al-Muḥtār*. Dār al-Tabā'ah al-Miṣriyah. Cairo, 1851 A.D.

Ibn al-Athīr, Majd al-Dīn al-Jazrī. *Jāmi' al-Uṣūl fī Aḥādīth al-Rasūl*. Maktabah al-Halwani, Cairo, 1969 A.D.

Ibn Ḥazm, 'Alī ibn Aḥmad. *Al-Muhalla*. Al-Maktabah al-Jumhūriyyah al-'Arabiyyah, Cairo, 1968 A.D.

Ibn al-Humām, Kamāl al-Dīn. *Fatḥ al-Qadīr Sharḥ al-Hidāyah*. Al-Maktabah al-Tijāriyyah al-'Arabiyyah, Cairo, 1937 A.D.

Ibn Mājah, Muḥammad ibn Yazīd al-Qazwīnī. *al-Sunan*. Dīnī Kutub Khānah, Lahore, 1968 A.D.

Ibn Nujaym, Zayn al-Dīn. *al-Baḥr al-Rā'iq*. Dār al-Ma'arifah, Beirut, 1938 A.D.

Ibn Qayyim al-Jawziyyah, Muḥammad ibn Abū Bakr Shamsuddīn, *al-Ṭuruq al-Hukumiyah fī al-Siyāsah al-Shar'iyyah*. Matba'ah al-Muḥammadiyah, Cairo, 1973 A.D.

Ibn Qudāmah, Muwaffaq al-Dīn 'Abd Allāh ibn Aḥmad ibn Muḥammad. *al-Mughnī*. Dār al-Kutub al-'Arabī, Beirut, 1972 A.D.

Ibn Rushd al-Hafid Abū al-Walīd, *Bidāyat al-Mujtahid wa Nihāyat al-Muqtaṣid*. Dār al-Kutub al-'Arabiah al-Kubrā, Cairo, 1907 A.D.

Ibn Aḥmad ibn 'Abd al-Halīm. *Siyāsah al-Shar'iyyah fī Islāḥ al-Rāi wa al-Raiyyah*. al-Matba'ah al-Khairiyyah, Cairo, 1904 A.D.

Ibn al-Talla, Muḥammad ibn Fajr al-Mālikī al-Qurṭubī, *Aqdiyat al-Rasūl*. Dār al-Kutub al-Lebonani, Beirut, 1982 A.D.

Al-Jazīrī, 'Abd al-Raḥmān, *Kitāb al-Fiqh 'alā al-Madhshib al-'Arba'ah*. al-Maktabah al-Tijāriyyah al-Kubrā, Cairo 1392 A.D.

Al-Jaṣṣāṣ, Aḥmad ibn Ali, *Aḥkām al-Qur'ān*. Al-Matba'ah al-Bahiyyah al-Miṣriyyah, Cairo, 1928 A.D.

Al-Kattānī, 'Aḅd al-Ḥay. *Niẓām al-Ḥukumah al-Nabawiyyah*. Matba'ah Muṣṭafā al-Bābī al-Ḥalbī, Cairo, 1958 A.D.

Al-Kasānī, 'Alā al-Dīn Abū Bakr ibn Mas'ūd, *Badā'i' al-Ṣanā'i'a fī Tartīb al-Sharā'i'*. H.M. Saeed Company, Karaçhi, 1980 A.D.

Lane, Edward William. *Madd al-Qamūs*. Arabic-English Lexicon, Islamia Book Center, Lahore, 1978 A.D.

Al-Maghribī, Muḥammad ibn Sulaymān, *Jāmi' Fawā'id*. Dār al-Fikr, Beirut, 1937 A.D.

Majallat al-Aḥkām al-'Adliyyah. Nūr Muḥammad Kārkhanah Tijārah Kutub, Karachi, 1968 A.D.

Al-Marghīnanī, Burhān al-Dīn 'Alī ibn Abū Bakr. *Al-Hidayah*. (English translation by Charles Hamilton), Premier Book House, Lahore, 1975 A.D.

Al-Mawardī, 'Alī ibn Muḥammad. *Al-Aḥkām al-Sulṭāniyyah*. Matba'ah al-Watan, Cairo, 1880 A.D.

Muslim, Ibn al-Ḥajjāj al-Qushayrī. *Saḥīḥ Muslim*. Kārkhanah Tijārah Kutub, Karachi, 1930 A.D.

Al-Nawawī, Abū Bakr Yaḥyā ibn Sharaf al-Dīn. *Rawdat al-Tālibīn wa 'Umdat al-Muftiyyīn*. Al-Maktabah al-Islāmī, Beirut, 1985 A.D.

Qal'ajī, Muḥammad al-Rawwas. *Mawsū'ah Fiqh 'Umar ibn Khaṭṭāb*. Dār al-Naf'ais, Beirut, 1985 A.D.

Al-Qurṭūbī, Muḥammad ibn Aḥmad. *Al-Jami' li Aḥkām al-Qur'ān*. Matba'at al-Sa'adah, Cairo, 1912 A.D.

Saḥnūn. *Al-Mudawwanah al-Kubrā*. Maktabah al-Muthanna, Baghdad.

Shiblī Nu'manī, *al-Farooq*. (English translation by Zafar Ali Khan), Shaikh Muḥammad Ashraf, Lahore, 1939 A.D.

Al-San'ānī, Muḥammad ibn Ismā'īl. *Subul al-Salām Sharḥ Bulugh al-Marām*. Dār al-Fikr, Beirut, 1938 A.D.

Al-Sarakhsī, Muḥammad ibn Aḥmad. *Al-Mabsūṭ*. Matba'at al-Sa'adah, Cairo, 1324 A.D.

Al-Shāfi'ī, Muḥammad ibn Idrīs. *al-Umm* (Abū Muḥammad al-Rabī' al-Murād version), al-Matba'ah al-'Amiriyyah, Cairo, 1901 A.D.

Al-Shawkānī, Muḥammad ibn 'Alī. *Nayl al-Awṭār Sharḥ Muntaqā al-Akhbār*. Matba'at Muṣṭafā al-Ḥalbi, Cairo, 1982 A.D.

Al-Shīrāzī, Ibrahīm 'Alī ibn Yūsuf. *Al-Muhadhdhab fī al-Fiqh al-Shāfi'ī*. Dār al-Kutub al-'Arabiah, Cairo, 1913 A.D.

Al-Sayyid Sābiq. *Fiqh al-Sunnah*. Dār al-Fikr, Beirut, 1982 A.D.

Al-Tirmidhī, Muḥammad ibn 'Isā. *Sunan al-Tirmidhī.* Shaikh Muḥammad Ashraf, Lahore, 1978 A.D.

Yusuf 'Alī, Abdullah, *English translation and commentary of Holy Qur'ān.* Qatar, 1946 A.D.

Al-Zayla'ī, 'Uthmān ibn Alī. *Tabyīn al-Ḥaqā'iq Sharḥ Kanz al-Daqā'iq.* Al-Matba'ah al-Kubrā al-Amiriyyah, Cairo, 1893 A.D.

Al-Zuhaylī, Wahbah. *al-Fiqh al-Islāmī wa Adillatuhū.* Dār al-Fikr, Damascus, 1997 A.D.

Index